ADVANCE PRAISE FOR *Passionaries*

"Each one of these powerful profiles is a home run and a chance for us to look at a significant winning plan in the game of life."
—Dick Enberg, CBS Sports

"Barbara Metzler has tapped into what makes people great and has made their greatness available to the rest of us."
—Dr. Tony Campolo, Campolo School of Social Change at Eastern University, St. Davids, PA

"*Passionaries* will soon be included in every dictionary and on the *must read* list of everyone seriously concerned with improving the health and well-being of humankind."
—Dr. Warren Bennis, distinguished professor of business at the University of Southern California and author of *On Becoming a Leader*

"Barbara Metzler's book chronicles American generosity at its best—highlighting people who give of both their time and money to help people here and abroad. Her book is essential reading for all, especially those who want to better understand the amazing stories of America's leading and most effective philanthropists."
— Dr. Carol Adelman, director, Center for Global Prosperity, Hudson Institute

"One person *can* make a difference in our world. Barbara Metzler inspires us all with these powerful stories about individuals who demonstrate that we can translate visions of hope into programs of healing. May the tribe of passionaries increase!"
—Dr. Richard J. Mouw, president of Fuller Theological Seminary

"Barbara Metzler's *Passionaries*, like her life, is an inspiration. Not only has she assembled the stories of 'can-do' people who have transformed their convictions into constructive, life-changing actions, but she provides us the links to do likewise."
—Linda LeSourd Lader, co-founder, Renaissance Weekends

"If you are questioning whether God still works through people, you'll stop wondering after reading about these miraculous lives. Life has handed each of these inspiring individuals challenges that they have faced with courage. Courage isn't a gift, but a decision."
—Dr. Robert Schuller, pastor of the Crystal Cathedral

"It's one thing to be simply motivated and another thing to become deeply inspired. In this collection of real life stories, Barbara Metzler enables you to be inspired and lifted up to make a difference with your life. You come away believing you too can be a 'passionary' and help change your world and leave a lasting, positive legacy. Don't miss this chance to help change your world!"
—Dr. Ron Jenson, international speaker and author;
chairman, Future Achievement International

"*Passionaries* provides proof that one person can still make an everlasting difference in our world. In this book there are many blueprints that allow one to take their success and turn it into significance for the world they live in!"
—Stan Curtis, founder and chairman of USA Harvest

"These heroes are all compassionately committed to a 'magnificent obsession,' turning their visions into reality."
—Dr. Art Ulene

"*Passionaries* is a fascinating testimony to one of life's most profound questions: What can I do to make a difference? In writing *Passionaries*, the author herself makes a huge difference. Her compelling and readable testimony on a wide range of projects, created by so many people from such diverse backgrounds, makes the case that we all have the potential to truly change the world . . . and in so doing Barbara Metzler fits perfectly her definition of the term passionary."
—Matthew P. Caulfield, major general, U.S. Marine Corps (retired), president of Helmets to Hardhats

"If you are seeking meaning in life, become a 'passionary.' This book will show you how and lead you down the path to knowing a genuine happiness, one that is real and lasting."
—Dr. Bettie B. Youngs, author of *Woman to Woman Wisdom*

Passionaries™

Definition of *passionary*: \'pa-shen-er-ē\ *n* (ca. 2005) 1. one inspired passionately through vision and compassion to change the world for the better: visionary in action on a mission. 2. society's agent of change: pioneer of benevolent innovation giving forward and causing positive ripples. 3. a social entrepreneur emboldened to make a difference, volunteering above and beyond responsibilities to family and work: inspirational difference-maker.

Passionaries™

TURNING COMPASSION INTO ACTION

Barbara R. Metzler

TEMPLETON FOUNDATION PRESS
PHILADELPHIA & LONDON

Templeton Foundation Press
300 Conshohocken State Road, Suite 670
West Conshohocken, PA 19428
www.templetonpress.org

Templeton Foundation Press helps intellectual leaders and others learn about science research on aspects of realities, invisible and intangible. Spiritual realities include unlimited love, accelerating creativity, worship, and the benefits of purpose in persons and in the cosmos.

Most of *Passionaries'* profiles have involved personal telephone interviews with information updated through each nonprofit's Web site listed at the end of each profile. Stories included in this book were collected over a period of four years. Reasonable care has been taken to trace original ownership and, when necessary, to obtain permission to reprint. If the author has overlooked giving proper credit to anyone, please contact the publisher at the address above.

Designed and typeset by Gopa & Ted2, Inc.

Library of Congress Cataloging-in-Publication Data

Metzler, Barbara R.
  Passionaries : turning compassion into action / Barbara R. Metzler.
     p. cm.
  Includes index.
  ISBN-13: 978-1-59947-105-1 (pbk. : alk. paper)
  ISBN-10: 1-59947-105-1 (pbk. : alk. paper) 1. Compassion—Case studies.
  2. Conduct of life—Case studies. I. Title. II. Title: Turning compassion into action.
  BJ1475.M48 2006
  361.7092'273—dc22
                                                          2006014146

Printed in the United States of America

06 07 08 09 10 11   10 9 8 7 6 5 4 3 2 1

PASSIONARIES™ is a trademark and service mark of Barbara Metzler.

Contents

Preface

H AVE YOU EVER WANTED to make a difference in the world and didn't know the means or avenues to pursue? Perhaps you have looked at a major social problem that tugs at your heart and thought to yourself—"what difference can I make? I am just one person." After reading all 35 chapters in this book, you'll never wonder again. But beware— in reading this book, your heart may be touched and changed forever and new questions and passions may arise.

For a long time, I have been captivated by social entrepreneurs and how the organizations they started significantly impact our world, most just in the past 30 years. These individuals are making waves and they create "ripples" emanating positive forces that also move the world forward. Since there was no word to accurately describe these present-day heroes, I created the term *passionaries* to describe "passionate visionaries who take positive actions and significantly change the lives of others." My intent in writing this book is to give a voice to these "good news makers" of all ages whose stories often go unheard.

After observing the unified, altruistic actions of Americans following the September 11 attacks and Hurricane Katrina, I have learned that we *can* come together to make a difference in our world. It is my hope that *Passionaries* will be a vehicle to inspire you to action. I have collected the stories of Americans who, through their passion for a single cause, have made a significant impact on hundreds, thousands, or millions of people's lives. As you read about these magnificent individuals, their organizations, and their 20 million like-minded volunteers, consider how you might also get involved.

What are you going to do with the information within these profiles? *It is your life and your choice.* Pass on the power of these stories of goodness that surround us to friends and family. You have no idea what fervor you may spark or how many lives your spark may reach. Find your own passion. Start, build, or join any of the organizations that touch your heart. Like these passionaries and their ripples, you too hold the power to change our world in the palm of your hands.

"I am only one, but I am one. I can't do everything, but I can do something. The something I ought to do, I can do. And by the grace of God, I will."
—Edward Everett Hale

Acknowledgments ⌒

I'D LIKE TO THANK the many people who were such a big part of my life during the creation of this book. First to the 35 passionaries and their organizations' volunteers profiled herein: Your incredible visions have inspired me and will always remain in my heart. Your commitment is a legacy to the world and a blessing to us all.

My immense gratitude is also given to amazing personal heroes of mine who have written the introductions to each part. Tom Sullivan, Bettie Youngs, Art Ulene, and Robert Schuller—each of you continues to make indelible, irreversible marks on the world with your presence, passion, and positive action.

I am especially grateful for the "Earth Angels" I'm so fortunate to have in my life who have been there for me in oh-so-many ways: First to my family: Denny, Erin, Douglas, Kersten, and David; and then to friends who have supported this passionary movement: Matt, Barbara, Ron, Mary, Katherine, Bettie, Chris, Paula, Shelby, Mickey, Ellen, Arlene, Alexia, Tom, Linda, Phil, Gary, Lorraine, and Jack. A most heartfelt thanks to my editor, Amy, whose love and "eyes" gave wings to my creativity. And of course, there are countless others. You know who you are!

Thank you so much Templeton Foundation Press, my publisher, especially Laura Barrett and Joanna Hill for sharing the vision and helping me grow. And bless you, Jack Templeton, for the wonderful acccomplishments you have bestowed on America, including your complete support for this heart-filled project.

Finally, this book is dedicated to my Lord and God, with all my love and thanks for your help and gentle nudging. You've bequeathed us with a world of possibilities and have touched the heart of many passionaries, as well as their millions of volunteers. Thank you for giving us a country that is free, where giving forward is both our legacy and our promise. May you continue to bless and watch over America.

PASSIONARIES™

Introduction

"America is great because she is good. When America ceases to be good, she will cease to be great." — attributed to Alexis de Tocqueville

JUST HOW GREAT and how good are the American people? Check out these facts and you will find America is filled with people of vast generosity and magnificent giving. The waves and ripples from unprecedented donations circle the globe from sea to shining sea—and way beyond all of our borders.

GIVING IN THE UNITED STATES

"It's wonderful . . . it's marvelous," as Cole Porter once crooned. The scope of our "giving forward" with both time and money is amazingly more than you'd ever imagine. The numbers and statistics on giving in the United States are in the billions every year, both in time and in resources. Most of us gloss over the magnitude of how much a *billion* really is or confuse the terms *millions* and *billions*. For perspective, think about this: One millionth is the equivalent of 1 second every 11 1/5 weeks; 1 billionth is the equivalent of 1 second every 32 years.

Giving Money

Charitable donations in the United States alone far surpass the entire economies of many countries, and the amounts are growing off the charts. Americans gave approximately $248.5 billion in 2004. It was only in 1990 that we first celebrated giving away $100 billion in a year. But who's actually doing the giving? Is this just tax write-offs for corporations? Surprisingly, more than 83 percent of this giving comes from individuals and their bequests.[1] After the disaster of September 11, 2001, when Americans seemed to give instinctually from hearts of compassion, most individual gifts were $100 or less, and an estimated total of $2.3 billion[2] was given toward the relief and recovery effort.

America's image as "the greed capital of the world" clearly does not hold water. Consider that in 2003 there were 825,000 charities registered in the United States valued at $1.76 trillion and 66,000 private foundations controlling $476 billion[3]—hardly a group of people who are "in it for the money." Above and beyond work and family responsibilities, we take care of those in need, both here and abroad. Putting it in a global perspective, in 2004 Americans privately sent more than $70 billion to aid people in developing countries, which is more than three times as much as the United States provides in overseas aid. According to a study by the Hudson Institute, that is far more than the aid distributed by any other country and is just $10 billion less than the nearly $80 billion donated by all the governments of the world.[4]

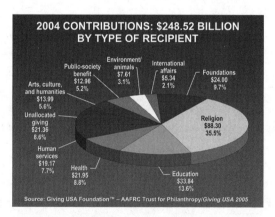

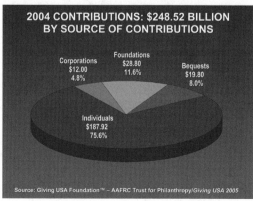

Who is doing the giving, and *where* are charitable donations being directed? The charts above illustrate an astronomical amount of giving from beautifully average Americans, and that giving is directed toward religious groups that care for others.

Giving Time

Our cynical sides think, "Money's one thing. But time? Now that's something people wouldn't offer quite so easily." Wrong. It's estimated that 109 million or 57 percent of American adults volunteered 19.9 billion hours in 1998, each averaging 3.5 hours a week.[5] That means people are volunteering time in astounding amounts. The Points of Light Foundation puts it another way: "The volunteer workforce represents the equivalent of over nine million full-time employees; their combined efforts were worth $225 billion."

This giving of time is not done grudgingly, either. Eighty-six percent of volunteers surveyed said they volunteer because they feel compassion for people in need or feel they can fill a need that is not being met.[6] It takes countless volunteers to make our churches, schools, libraries, parks, hospitals, civic groups, museums, and community centers run smoothly. People making a difference through volunteering are all around us. To name just a few:

- As of June 2002, there were 7,662 Rotary Clubs with 399,179 members.
- Since 1961, 165,000 people have served in the Peace Corps in 185 countries.
- Created in 1993, AmeriCorps engages more than two million Americans a year.
- Nearly 1.4 million Lions tackle tough problems in 190 countries.
- Three million U.S. businesspeople belong to Chambers of Commerce.
- The National PTA has 6.5 million members.
- Meals on Wheels volunteers serve one million meals daily to U.S. shut-ins.
- Shriners is an international fraternity of about 500,000 who support their hospitals and give free care to children in need.
- Through Junior League, 193,000 women volunteer within their communities.

And it's not just the grown-ups who understand their responsibility to society. Children and students volunteer as well, making a huge difference. A 1995 survey (the latest statistics available) showed that 59 percent or 13 million American teens volunteered for community service. In 2001, it was reported that 63 percent of all college-age Americans have volunteered at a local school, hospital, or neighborhood center; 38 percent have served as tutors or mentors; and 27 percent have raised funds locally. Our youth are giving their time and energy to improve the lives of others. The power of our youth is awesome.

Millions of Americans are ignoring the negative news heard daily and living the possible. Usually silent, many of these purposeful people seek to serve God by serving others. They speak to the reality of American hearts, and the world depends on these giving individuals who commit to doing the extraordinary.

≈≈*Starfish Make Ripples*

AS AN OLD MAN WALKED ALONG a deserted beach at sunset, he saw a young girl in the distance. Drawing closer, he noticed the girl kept bending down, picking up something, and throwing it into the water. She did this time and time again.

As the man approached, he was able to see the girl was picking up starfish that had washed up all over the beach. One at a time, she was throwing them back into the water. As she threw each starfish, the splash made ripples in the ocean.

The man asked the girl what she was doing. The girl replied, "I am throwing these starfish back into the ocean so they will live." "But," said the man, "you can't possibly save them all. There are thousands here, and this must be happening on hundreds of beaches along the coast. You can't possibly make a difference." She smiled, bent down, and picked up another starfish. As she threw it back into the sea, she replied: "It made a difference to that one. Would you like to help?" He did. Together they saved twice as many, and the ripples multiplied.[7]

—adapted from Loren Eiseley's *The Star Thrower*

Part 1

Passionaries for Humanity

INTRODUCTION BY TOM SULLIVAN

Tom Sullivan is known to many as an actor, singer, entertainer, author, and producer. As a special correspondent for ABC's Good Morning America, *Tom became a regular morning fixture in millions of American homes. He runs marathons, mountain climbs, snow skis, and is an excellent golfer. And he has been blind since birth.*

Tom's best selling autobiography, If You Could See What I Hear, *has been made into a motion picture. His latest must-read book is* Seeing Lessons: 14 Life Secrets I've Learned Along the Way.

W E ARE A NATION largely bereft of leadership. We seem to lack direction and focus as a people. Many of us, specifically young Americans under the age of 25, are more concerned about our rights and entitlements than our responsibilities. We are loud in our protests but short in our willingness to get actively involved in causes that extend beyond ourselves.

Why is that? What has been lost in our system of values? My friend, Barbara Metzler, has figured it out in the pages of this book. The nation needs to mount an army of those whom she has dubbed "passionaries." In every walk of life, from politics to education, from Fortune 500 corporations to nonprofit foundations, we must identify and celebrate those people willing to take their passions and apply them to universal goals much larger than themselves.

These leaders, these passionaries, are just like us. However, unlike us, they have stepped beyond personal gain and selfish motives to become missionaries of their passionate commitments. We all admire them. When we meet them, we know that they are special. But in this book, they teach us that any of us can become difference-makers. We, too, can become passionaries if we are willing to follow their example and expand our horizons to encompass the hopes and dreams of others.

I believe when you read this section entitled "Passionaries for Humanity," like me, you will be excited to become one of them.

1: Stan Curtis
USA Harvest

Harvesting the USA

STAN CURTIS' CHILDHOOD HOME was so dysfunctional that he and his four siblings spent most of their adolescent years in a Kentucky orphanage, which wasn't all bad. With guts and determination, he counted himself blessed for the opportunities that gave him a step up along the way—odd jobs, a couple of college classes, and several years as a professional tennis player—before becoming a hard-working investment broker. However, this was hardly the background you would expect from a man who would turn a simple event during a family dinner into a worldwide movement that would change the face of hunger for millions—and all without ever hiring a single employee.

The year was 1986, and the city was Louisville, Kentucky. Stan Curtis was living the life of the perfect American capitalist with all the outward signs of success: money, nice cars, a beautiful young wife, and a successful career as a stockbroker. Long gone were the days of his childhood nightmares and despair. Now 37, he had found the keys to success: hard work and a positive attitude.

Standing in line at his favorite local cafeteria one December night, Stan eyed a pan of green beans up ahead behind the glass partition. Just as he reached for them, a young man came out and replaced the pan with a heaping, hot new one, and then disappeared behind a door with the old. Stan turned to his wife and said, "Gee, one minute those were my green beans, and the next minute, they're gone. I wonder where they went."

After dinner, curiosity got the better of him, and he decided to find out what happens to the perfectly suitable green beans. He tracked down the manager and got a very consumer-oriented answer about how they like to keep the pans hot and full. Noticing the manager hadn't mentioned anything about edibility or nutrition, Stan inquired further. He was told that health department law says that once food has been removed from a steam table, it can't be put back. The beans were no longer of use to the restaurant, so by law they were thrown away. Stan was upset by the waste.

Three days later, Louisville made national headlines as one of America's leading cities in the growth of their homeless population—and the homeless weren't flying to Louisville because the weather is so wonderful in December. As he read the story, the idea occurred to Stan: the homeless could use a few green beans.

Nineteen years later, that passing thought about "a few green beans" has multiplied into 11.5 billion pounds of food, not only changing the direction of Stan's life, but also birthing a bountiful harvest across America for those in need. But it started small.

✦ *"Regardless of how old you are or who you are or where you're from, you can stand for something. Most people would like to stand for something."*

Stan had been working for two years with a group of young people putting together a little orchestra support group. He went to them with his original green bean idea and recruited their help. In January 1987, they began to meet weekly to brainstorm about setting up a nonprofit organization to get the beans where they were needed. They created bylaws and set up a structure for their dream organization. They had a very unusual but simple premise: take no money, take food. Stan's vision was to ask simply for food or time. "If you want to help us, you can either donate food or pick it up." Volunteers would pick up surplus food from restaurants, hospitals, hotels, and food suppliers and then deliver it to missions, soup kitchens, and food pantries.

Just six months later, Stan announced the formation of Kentucky Harvest—with a great deal of media hype—to a large group of people in a Louisville rescue mission. That day alone, he got more than 100 phone calls: 80 were from people who saw the story and wanted to volunteer precisely because Stan had said not to send money—that it would only be sent back; 20 calls were from people who wanted to give food; and 6 calls were from people who needed food.

The collecting began with immediate success. In the first year alone,

Kentucky Harvest brought in more than 750,000 pounds of food. The group was stunned. Restaurants, hotels, caterers, bakeries, and grocery stores donated all kinds of food collected by volunteers who began showing up wherever food was being thrown away in Louisville.

In October 1988, one year and four months after they'd announced their formation, Stan got a call from his friend Gary Bowman, asking, "Hey, did you read Ann Landers today?" Stan laughed having never read Ann Landers' column in his life. But the "Dear Ann" letter that day was from a guy staying in a hotel in Miami, griping about all the food he witnessed being thrown away. Gary decided to write to Ann and tell her about what they were doing with Kentucky Harvest.

On Thanksgiving Day, as luck would have it, Ann Landers personally called 589-FOOD in Louisville and asked for Stan. She broke the news that she was going to print Gary's letter in her national column. Sure enough, on New Year's Day 1989, the letter appeared in newspapers all across America with a headline that read, "Louisville Feeds Its Own." From January through March, Kentucky Harvest got more than 5,000 calls from around the world. People were simply asking if they could do this in their towns, too. With no paid staff, answering the calls was a challenge Stan and friends somehow managed.

Stan has kept his day job as an investment broker for Hilliard Lyons while also managing to keep his volunteer commitment to what is now called USA Harvest. With Kentucky Harvest as its model, USA Harvest quickly grew to become the largest all-volunteer food distribution organization in America. Amazingly, the organization has no staff. USA Harvest continues to be food-raisers, not fund-raisers. The program currently operates 123 chapters in 43 American states and 7 foreign countries. The American chapters alone serve over 417 communities with many chapters serving multiple cities in their regions. About 117,000 USA Harvest volunteers have distributed more than 11.5 billion pounds of food (375 million pounds of food every year), serving more than 5,200 agencies nationwide. They serve more than two million meals a day to those who would otherwise go hungry.

"A lot of food in this country goes to waste," Stan observes, having seen it firsthand. "Food that is prepared is not served. Someone might have baked 100 potatoes and only served 2 of them because the weather gets bad. What do you do with the other 98? Most restaurants will not use those 98 baked potatoes. They will just prepare another 100 the next day. The biggest sin for any restaurant in America is to run out of a certain food.

"People turn to 'Harvest pickup' to put their overproduction to great use. Instead of turning left to the trashcan, they go right to the chiller. Now they use this as a means to examine how well they're doing their jobs in terms of food that's being thrown away," Stan explained. "We've created a society where, if you see three cartons of milk in a store, you will take the one with the furthest expiration date. Well, milk shelf life is actually good for six days after the expiration date. It doesn't have anything to do with nutrition or edibility; it is just a legal expiration date. Our contributing stores are happy to donate these cartons, and the homeless have milk."

Stan Curtis explains the simple premise of his totally unique nonprofit USA Harvest in this way:

1. We are not a fund-raiser; we are a food-raiser.

2. We don't store food; we take it from where it is to where it is not. We take it from people who have it and don't want it, and give it to people who want it but don't have it.

3. We are blessed there are laws protecting the donation of food to nonprofit organizations like ours against civil and criminal penalties.

4. We don't charge for it. People give food for free, and you better believe we are going to distribute it free of charge.

Volunteers in each individual USA Harvest chapter are responsible for collection and distribution of food. Stan says, "A Harvest chapter in a very small town called Seymour got six of their local churches to claim two months each year during which they would be responsible for food pickup and deliveries. The large Tampa Harvest chapter in Florida—which delivers a remarkable seven and a half million pounds of food a year—plugged into their local diversification programs, drawing on the aid of people who have been sentenced to community-service hours. The judicial system has a fondness for our program, again specifically because we're not fundraisers. We don't sit behind desks, stuff envelopes, and lick stamps. So a lot of these community-service offenders are assigned to our programs. They even use their own vehicles to pick up and deliver food."

Stan continues, "Giving money is too cheap. Time is the most valuable commodity that we have. People are very gratified delivering food and looking into the eyes of someone who'll be able to eat. Frankly, it is not hard to empower volunteers. Regardless of how old you are or who you are or where you come from, you can stand for something. Most people would like to stand for something. So when we ask people to volunteer for Harvest, we're not asking them to fundraise, but to simply ask others if they will give food to people who are hungry.

"I get up every day, and I thank God for all he has given me. But I am bent on making even more of a difference and standing up for these people—so many of whom are kids. We have 6,000 homeless children factored into our school system in Louisville. I understand the feeling of going to a high school as an orphan—I have been there. You feel 'orphan' is tattooed across your forehead. It's definitely a slap to your self-esteem, and you start out already behind. Many kids are not getting the right nutrition, or much of anything to eat at all. Changing this would allow them at least a chance to learn. I can certainly relate to that. I take the tools I've been given and play the cards I've been dealt. I used them to get here, to help those whose places I understand, and I go forward."

≈≈*Ripples*

DAVID LEVITT'S FOOD FOR THOUGHT

IN 1989, 11-year-old David Levitt was preparing for his bar mitzvah in Tampa Bay, Florida. As part of the Jewish tradition, he was required to show responsibility by doing a community-service project. One Sunday while reading *Parade* magazine, David came across an article written by Stan Curtis who had just founded the Kentucky Harvest project. David knew he'd found what he was looking for.

"When I heard Mr. Curtis had gotten some schools involved, I thought it would be a great idea for me to try at my school, St. Pete's," David recalls. "Little did I know what I was getting myself into." He signed up to volunteer at the local Tampa Bay Harvest chapter. Taking it a step further, he also approached the principal of his middle school to ask if cafeteria leftovers could be donated to homeless shelters. Red tape prevented the principal from doing anything to help.

When the idealistic sixth-grader's mother suggested trying his luck with the school board, David immediately drafted a letter. "I didn't know what a school board was," he shared. To his surprise, the board invited him to speak at their next meeting—which also happened to be David's twelfth birthday. Not only was David's hunger project idea approved for his school—but for 100 others across the county. Dubbed "Operation Food for Thought" by Stan Curtis himself, the program was simple and efficient: schools packaged up leftovers and stored them in a freezer, while the Tampa Bay Harvest took care of all the logistics—including weekly pickups, deliveries, and distribution to the shelters.

From the first delivery, David became the project spokesperson. "Once, when I was doing an interview with a local radio station, I was asked: 'Why can't you go statewide?' I said, 'Maybe I'll do that,'" David shared. So he sought out his local state representative, Dennis Jones, who was instantly impressed with the idea. Representative Jones wrote up a resolution, which passed unanimously. From there, the project caught the attention of Florida State Senator Charlie Crist, who offered to rewrite the bill and get it through. "It was insane," David shared. "I love that man. Charlie Crist is one of my favorite people."

In May 1998, David's law passed requiring food suppliers in Florida to make "every effort possible" to donate all leftover food to charity. Governor Lawton Chiles surprised him with a call to express the state of Florida's gratitude. David ended up assisting in the governor's office and later interned under Governor Jeb Bush. When Governor Bush wrote a book entitled *Profiles in Character*, David Levitt was included as its youngest subject. A further honor came when the governor told David's story as part of his second gubernatorial debate. "It's amazing when you're young," remarked David. "Young people should never take their age for granted—you can make the world a better place."

➤In 1989, Stan Curtis founded Kentucky Harvest in Louisville, Kentucky. His organization morphed into USA Harvest as it expanded nationally through the efforts of more than 117,000 volunteers. Its chapters are in over 124 cities, and they serve more than 5,200 agencies nationwide serving 2 million meals a day (375 million pounds of food every year) to these deserving organizations. Uniquely, they don't solicit or accept any money from our government. They keep their primary focus on "foodraising," not "fundraising." Volunteers pick up surplus food from restaurants, hospitals, and food suppliers, and they deliver it to missions, soup kitchens, and food banks.

Glean greatness: It's all about the food! Contact:

USA HARVEST
Phone: (800) USA-4-FOOD
Web site: www.usaharvest.com

2: Dr. Mimi Silbert
Delancey Street Foundation

We Can Change the World

"WE TAKE ONLY THE WORST." And by "worst," Mimi Silbert, cofounder and president of the San Francisco-based residential program Delancey Street Foundation, means just that: ex-felons, prostitutes, substance abusers—just about anyone who has hit rock bottom. Residents apply for admittance, just like they would to a university. But unlike Harvard or Stanford, Delancey Street only accepts the neediest of the applicants, essentially the bottom of the class.

For the past 35 years, Delancey Street has provided its residents with academic, vocational, and social skills. This includes the discipline, values, and attitudes needed to legitimately succeed in society. Currently, 2,000 men and women are served through their centers around the country. More than 14,000 of its successful graduates are fully integrated back into society as taxpaying citizens leading successful lives. They are now lawyers, realtors, truck drivers, sales people, mechanics, and medical professionals in various fields.

Clients pay nothing, nor does the bill go to the taxpayers like so many other community rehabilitation organizations. Amazingly, this program is entirely self-sustaining through enterprise revenue and private donations. Naysayers believe criminals cannot be rehabilitated and therefore should not be let back into society. They ignore the fact that United States recidivism rates show that 67.5 percent of released criminals are re-arrested within three years. Delancey Street is proof that change is possible and that miracles can and do happen.

Credit all of this to the almost five-feet tall, diminutive dynamo, Dr. Mimi Silbert. She's a modern-day female David determined to slay her Goliath, and dislikes society's belief that criminals deserve what they get and should simply rot in prison. Mimi's battle plan was to implement the principle of helping others help themselves. Armed with doctorate degrees in psychology and criminology, she has worked as a prison psychologist, police trainer, and college professor to accomplish her mission.

Born in Boston, Mimi grew up in a neighborhood she describes as a ghetto, much like the famous down-and-out Delancey Street in New York City where immigrants lived with extended families. "We were the classic immigrant family. I grew up with an underdog mentality. Everybody looked out for everybody else as we struggled upward." This model is the rock she used to create her foundation, even naming it after Delancey Street. "These family groups pooled their resources and worked hard to help one another move up in society. It's what happens here now, every day. Together, we rise or fall. That feeling of camaraderie is how I was brought up."

Mimi Silbert put the values and idealism that stemmed from her youth into action in 1971 when she met and befriended former prisoner John Maher. Together, they decided to start a small residential program for ex-cons and drug addicts. They started with a $1,000 loan and four residents. "Imprisoning criminals," she says, "at someone else's expense, providing all their food and lodging and letting them just sit there with no responsibility is absurd. If you care about people, you hold them accountable." They began to house these ex-criminals and help them by providing counseling, teaching trade skills, instilling accountability, and putting them to work. When Maher died of a heart attack in 1988, Mimi carried on with the mission, and the program grew exponentially.

Today Delancey Street Foundation functions in precisely the way Mimi and John originally mapped it out, but on a much larger scale. Mimi personally designed the residence buildings that cover a huge square block of prime real estate in San Francisco. Ex-con residents with construction trade skills instructed and trained 300 formerly unemployed drug addicts, homeless people, and ex-felons. Together with union support, they built their very own four-story, massive complex. "If they didn't get a wall straight," she says, "we took it down and did it over." Built right on the Embarcadero, along the breathtaking bay waterfront, it was built at about half the cost of normal construction.

In 1990, the headquarters of Delancey Street moved into the new

400,000-square-foot facility built entirely by the hands of its formerly unemployable residents. This is a testimony to what can be accomplished when the disadvantaged of society are afforded opportunity. The building became home to 500 residents, including Mimi, who has a small, one-bedroom apartment there.

Delancey Street is self-supporting, running more than a dozen various training schools for its residents. These training schools provide vocational skills and the opportunities to put them to use, generating income and pooling the monies earned. Each resident plays an integral role. The foundation evolved and now runs a moving company, a popular gourmet restaurant and catering service, an event planning company, limousine and paratransit driving services, a special events decorating company, a bookstore, a café and art gallery, an automotive service center, a printing company, and a Christmas tree sales lot.

Mimi believes in and demands excellence in each of these diverse Delancey Street training schools, guaranteeing a high level of quality in their products and services. For example, diners entering the brick-front Delancey Street Restaurant delight in superb cuisine and friendly ambiance, often without realizing that every single person working in the restaurant, from the waiters to the chef, are residents of Delancey—all of them ex-felons and former drug addicts. Their culinary arts training program is so respected that those who graduate are in great demand by restaurants in the area.

Over the past 30 years, the residents, ranging in age from 18 to 68, have built and/or remodeled with sweat equity more than 1,500 units of very low-income housing, training over 800 people in construction trades. The ventures together earned about $12 million in 2002. Its residents run the entire organization. There is no paid staff. Even Mimi herself does not take a salary.

About 70 percent of residents enter Delancey Street as an alternative to prison or a condition of parole or probation; the rest arrive straight off the streets. The average resident has been jailed four times, has been a drug addict for 12 years, and is illiterate. "Approximately one-fourth are women, one-third African American, one-third Hispanic, and one-third Caucasian," explains Silbert.

The minimum stay at Delancey Street is two years; the average stay is four years. During their stay, those without a high school diploma must earn a GED in classes taught by other residents. They are also trained in three different marketable job skills before graduating—one manual, one clerical, and one dealing with public service. Upon graduation, they are placed in outside jobs. More than 90 percent of the residents successfully complete the program and go on to lead law-abiding lives.

Mimi tells her residents, "We teach you absolutely everything you need to know to make your life work *without* drugs or crime and to be successful at every level." She challenges any ex-prisoners who show signs of slacking: "You want to quit? That's what you have always done, given up when it got difficult. If you're too angry and hopeless to fight for yourself, then do it for the next guy." High expectations of small social-skill details positively influence residents, like dressing for dinner and attending opera and symphony performances. Says Mimi, "We are helping people become middle class in their values and attitudes."

Delancey Street to date has moved more than 10,000 violent gang members into active nonviolence. More than 5,000 Delancey residents have mentored others, teaching nonviolence and inter-racial mediation. The payoff is huge, even affecting their own homefront. "Despite the violent and criminal backgrounds of our residents, there has never been one arrest in the 25 years we've operated. Gang members once sworn to kill one another are now living in integrated dorms and working together cooperatively and peacefullly."

Sometimes Mimi has even fought to get California laws changed to benefit her graduates. "We got the first ex-felon admitted to the bar in California. We also had the first to get a real-estate license and the first to become a deputy sheriff. We even worked to get ex-felons the right to vote."

Mimi uses her criminal justice background to affect the world of society's castaways even beyond the borders of Delancey Street. She recently designed and implemented new juvenile justice programs for San Francisco, developing a one-stop Community Assessment Center for arrested youths, a girl's residential program, and two after-school "Safe Havens," a program to develop the strengths of at-risk youths. Additionally, she continues to design and provide training to more than 50 police, sheriff, and probation departments. She is driven to make a difference.

As a single mother, Mimi raised twin boys with help from her extended Delancey family. Son David, now 33 and a San Francisco lawyer, jokes, "I thought everyone had former pimps and prostitutes picking them up at school."

Now in her sixties, Mimi shows no signs of slowing down. "For 32 years, I've seen the lower 10 percent of society come through our door and walk out a few years later as strong, decent human beings. If a bunch of ex-cons, prostitutes, and drug addicts can bounce back against the odds, just imagine what you and I might accomplish through helping others help themselves." Dr. Mimi Silbert can sum up her entire philosophy in these words: "It does not matter how many mistakes you make, it only matters that you fix them."

≈≈*Ripples*

SHIRLEY LAMARR

"THERE IS NO WAY I'd go back to my old life. I went through the whole siege of drugs and prostitution, guns drawn on me, getting raped, and overdosing on pills . . . you name it. I've robbed people, all kinds of stuff, and each year I'd feel more disgusted. I lived on the street with my own space on the sidewalk," shared Shirley. "When I was arrested, I sent a letter to Delancey Street. I was at the bottom with a choice of coming here or going back out to die."

Shirley Lamarr was a second-generation prostitute, criminal, and drug addict with a daughter who followed her lead into drugs and prostitution. Shirley entered Delancey Street in 1990 at 40 years old. It was her last hope. Three years later, she graduated and married a man who was a fellow graduate. Together they went on to direct their own rehabilitation program, also in Northern California, modeled on the principles they had learned.

Shirley helped her daughter escape from a prison of drugs and pimps and later she poured the same devotion into helping her rebellious granddaughter, who graduated high school in 2002 and went on to become a college student. After three generations of self-destruction and crime, the cycle had finally been broken and replaced with a legacy of new life and hope.

➤Delancey Street, founded by Mimi Silbert and John Maher in 1971, is considered the nation's leading self-help residential education center for former substance abusers and ex-convicts. More than 14,000 of society's former misfits and castaways have graduated from Delancey. More than 90 percent of them successfully complete the program and go on to lead law-abiding lives.

During their stay, residents learn academic and vocational skills, as well as responsibility, self-reliance, social survival, interpersonal skills, and positive values and attitudes. These skills are all necessary to live drug free in the mainstream of society, successful and legitimate. Delancey Street currently has residents located in five facilities in: New Mexico, New York, North Carolina, Los Angeles, and its headquarters in San Francisco.

If the best of us care for and believe in the least of us, hope reigns—as on Delancey Street.

DELANCEY STREET FOUNDATION
600 Embarcadero, San Francisco, CA 94107
Phone: (415) 957-9800 I Fax: (415) 512-5186
Web site: www.eisenhowerfoundation.org/grassroots/delancey

3: Susan Corrigan
Gifts In Kind International

A CLOSED DOOR WAS OPPORTUNITY KNOCKING

SUSAN CORRIGAN is the proud mother of three: a daughter, a son, and the third largest charity in the United States in 2004. You may have never heard of Gifts In Kind International, but as a nonprofit receiving donations it is ranked just behind the American Red Cross and is the most extensive distributor of new donated products in the world. You may have never heard of Susan Corrigan, either, but this dynamic lady created Gifts In Kind and has steered its destiny for most of the past 23 years.

As assistant to the president of United Way of America in 1983, Susan found herself in an unusual situation when a corporation called 3M made a donation of $12 million in office supplies. Although more accustomed to receiving and distributing cash, the United Way leadership gratefully accepted the gift and then turned to Susan to manage the process of distributing it. Undaunted by the task, Susan soon had the entire donation on its way to 600 enthusiastic local communities who had expressed a need for such items.

While the United Way leadership was interested in the concept of accepting donated products, they determined that it did not fit in with their overall direction. Susan realized the opportunity to encourage product giving from corporations had landed in her lap, and she took a chance on what seemed to be impossible.

In 1984, Susan left United Way and, with a grant from the Lilly Endowment, gave birth to Gifts In Kind. She also received support from William Ellinghaus, former president of AT&T. Susan and William recruited board members from some of the largest companies in the world, including Digital Equipment Corporation, Hewlett Packard, IBM, JC Penney, Prudential, RCA, 3M Company, Westinghouse Electric Company, and Xerox Corporation.

Since its inception, her charity has generated more than $6.8 billion in manufactured product donations distributed through a network of more than 200,000 charities and schools around the world. Providing assistance to millions of people, Gifts In Kind International's average annual growth rate for the past ten years has been a heady 35 percent a year, making it the fastest-growing nonprofit with the lowest overhead in the United States. Gifts In Kind International is ranked as one of the most cost-efficient charities in the world by *Forbes* magazine.

✦ *"You not only have to have a dream, you have to have a plan as well."*

Susan Corrigan has always worked hard and doesn't know any other way. At an early stage of her working life, she was putting together a television commercial and found herself working until 3 a.m. to beat a looming deadline. After that, she decided that if she was going to put this much energy into her work, she would make sure the product was something that would really make a difference in the lives of others. She made the bold step of changing careers.

"It's difficult to always know if you're on the path that you're going to be on for the rest of your life," Susan shared. "Sometimes it's hard to find that path. I worked at many jobs before Gifts In Kind, and I had great careers. I learned something at every job I've ever had and always strove for excellence. Young people should not assume that their first job is going to be exactly what they will do for life. There's a great deal of work involved in being successful at what you do."

It was Susan's strong need to help other people get through their tough times that led her to work for United Way in Chicago. She has spent the last 23 years feeling very fortunate to have been able to dedicate her life to serving others.

The nickname of Susan's baby is "Product Philanthropy." And, like raising any child, it took the help of many to shape, plan, feed, encourage, and mentor her brainchild from its infancy. Gifts In Kind supporters now include many of the Fortune 500 corporations, as well as thousands of other smaller companies. In 2004, these companies generously donated nearly $850 million in products.

"We don't want the organization to become an expensive roadblock between the donor company and the recipient charity," Susan notes. "So we operate on a budget of no more than 1 percent of the total value of what we distribute. Many good nonprofits have an operating budget of 15 percent to 25 percent. And we are not only supporting a staff of 28 with our 1 percent, but also shipping donations all over the world. Fortunately, we have great partners—corporations that work with us, such as transportation companies that provide free shipping. I believe success is a matter of involving as many people and organizations as possible in the grand idea of what it is that you are trying to achieve."

Today's top manufacturers and retailers rely on Gifts In Kind International as a conduit for the donation of products, goods, and services from the private corporations to the charitable sector, partnering with hundreds of major nonprofit agencies.

"Companies feel really good about contributing," says Susan, noting that many manufacturers have "hiccups" in their marketing and distribution process, creating volumes of perfectly good inventory appropriate for donation. Companies look for worthy causes where their products can be put to good use in exchange for community goodwill, logistics, costs savings, and tax breaks. Rather than having to find the charities, discuss the details, and deliver the goods themselves, companies turn to Gifts In Kind to handle it all free of charge, anytime of the year. Susan says, "It's always a good time to give."

Susan sees corporate executives not as the inhabitants of gray buildings on far-off hills, but as next-door neighbors. "They care just as much as anyone does about what's going on in their community, and they're looking for ways where they can be engaged and really make an impact. Gifts In Kind would not exist if it weren't for the overwhelming generosity of companies."

Susan Corrigan has a *big* dream: that all corporations making or selling a product will include in their community involvement strategy a means for giving away products on an ongoing basis. "And if those products," she says, "are given to the nonprofit sector so that charitable organizations providing vital community services are able to function at their highest level, it's a way to better the world."

But, she explains, "You not only have to have a dream, you have to have a plan as well. We have a 10-year strategic plan that we monitor on a daily basis. And everybody at Gifts In Kind understands their part in achieving those goals."

Meanwhile, Susan Corrigan is still looking to the future. "Many people look back on their lives and say they've accomplished certain things. But I look ahead and say I haven't done this yet, and I haven't done that, and there is so much more that needs to be done." In 2005, Susan helped orchestrate a seamless transition and stepped down as president. And Susan now cheers on the new leaders from the sidelines. She shared proudly, "The organization will continue to flourish and do great work. And then I will feel successful."

≈≈*Ripples*

RED NATION CELEBRATION

GIFTS IN KIND INTERNATIONAL, the world's leading charity in product philanthropy, in partnership with Toys "R" Us and the Red Nation Celebration 2002, recently facilitated the distribution of more than 400 toys to children on the Rose Bud Native American Reservation in South Dakota. The toys were distributed as part of the 2002 Red Nation Celebration, an annual concert series that presents contemporary and traditional Native American music and dance to both Native American and non–Native American audiences.

"Through this donation," Susan Corrigan stated, "Gifts In Kind International is not only helping provide toys to underprivileged kids on the Rose Bud Reservation, but is also helping support promising Native American artists through our partnership with the Red Nation Celebration."

Speaking on behalf of the Red Nation Celebration, event founder Joanelle Romero said, "Hopefully this can become an annual donation. The children are our future and need to be cared for and honored. This is one way in which we can be of service to the future generations."

Also speaking on behalf of Red Nation was 16-year-old Sage Galesi, a Native American performer and the voice of youth on the Red Nation Board of Directors. "As a young person and a member of the Board, I want to reinforce how important it is for corporate America to support the future of our youth. Organizations like Gifts In Kind International and Toys "R" Us really make that happen, and I am proud to be part of this process."

➤Gifts In Kind International (GIKI), founded in 1983 by Susan Corrigan, was the third largest nonprofit organization in the United States in 2004. It is the world's leading organization in "product philanthropy." Through 2005, it has distributed $6.8 billion worth of quality products and services ($850 million in 2005) to 26 countries—with a paid staff of just 28. Ranked as one of the most cost-efficient charities in the world, GIKI operates at less than 1 percent of the value of products, goods, and services contributed annually. Today's top manufacturers and retailers, including many of the Fortune 500 companies, rely on this nonprofit to design and manage the donation process. In May 2005, Ms. Corrigan retired from the board after serving as founder and CEO for 22 years.

Gifts In Kind International is a network of more than 445 locally affiliated partnerships in 26 countries around the world serving 200,000 various nonprofits. Nearly half of the Fortune 500 manufacturer and retail corporations and thousands of other smaller companies contribute annually. Every one of their affiliates is looking for volunteers. It is a major factor in continuing its 1 percent cost of operation.

To be an in-kind superhero or super-corporate hero bearing incredible gifts, contact:

GIFTS IN KIND INTERNATIONAL
333 N. Fairfax Street, Alexandria, VA 22314
Phone: (703) 836-2121 Fax: (703) 549-1481
E-mail: registration@giftsinkind.org | Web site: www.giftsinkind.org

4: Paul Newman

Newman's Own/
The Hole in the Wall Gang

WHAT STARTED AS A JOKE

*"As an actor, I've often been asked to describe the process of
creating a character. Acting is a question of absorbing other people's
personalities and adding some of your own experience. If I had
to describe philanthropy, I'd say the process is just the reverse.
You start with your own experiences, and from there you grow
to embrace the needs of others."* —Paul Newman, 1999

S HAMELESS EXPLOITATION in pursuit of the common good is an odd
slogan for a company. "It started as a joke that got out of control,"
admits actor Paul Newman. The "it" refers to his homespun business that
started in his basement and ran amuck. Now known as Newman's Own,
it has grown into a substantial and unusual enterprise, famous for its line
of salad dressings, spaghetti sauces, salsa, microwave popcorn, steak sauce,
fruit juices, "virgin" lemonade—and for the good it has done. Every after-
tax dollar of profit goes directly to thousands of charitable causes.

Most people associate Academy Award–winning Newman with the
leading characters he has played, such as Butch Cassidy or Cool Hand
Luke, during his Hollywood career spanning more than 60 films. Many
also relate Newman with race-car driving; he won the Sports Car Club of
America's national championship four times and, at the age of 70, was the
oldest driver to win a professionally sanctioned race—24 Hours of Daytona. He also wears the hats of director/writer/producer of stage and
screen, and is married to his "co-star" of 48 years, Oscar-winning actress
Joanne Woodward.

But how many know of Paul Newman's reputation as the ultimate high-maintenance dinner guest? For many years, it was true. Newman often visited some of the swankiest restaurants in New York City and ordered olive oil, vinegar, and herbs so that he could blend his own salad dressing right at his table. This is not farfetched for a man who drinks Chateau Lafite with hamburgers.

✦ "There is a responsibility in a democracy to hold your hand out to the less fortunate."

One day in 1982, he mixed up some dressing for his neighbor, friend, and dinner guest, writer A. E. Hotchner. "This is good stuff," Hotchner said. "Let's share it with the world." The next thing the writer knew, he was in Newman's basement filling wine bottles with salad dressing. Newman reluctantly spent $20,000 for labels and formed a home-based company, expecting to lose every cent he invested in the project. (He couldn't have known how prescient he was at the time. He never would make a cent from his product, but surprisingly great things would come from losing it all.) However, they had inadvertently stumbled on a product idea that was unique: Newman's Own Original Salad Dressing was the only all-natural, bottled dressing available. Word about it poured out swiftly.

Stew Leonard, head of a regional grocery chain, stocked Newman's salad dressing on a trial run. "The stuff started to fly out of the store," Leonard recalls. "Within a few weeks, we had sold 10,000 bottles." First-year profits for this homemade enterprise soared. Stunned by the success, Newman told his friend Hotchner, "I'm an actor; you're a writer. We can't make money out of the food business—let's give it away." That first year alone, they gave almost a million dollars to charity. It was every cent of their profit.

In the same year that Newman launched his salad dressing venture, he was nominated for his sixth Oscar (for *The Verdict*) and went into high gear with his auto-racing team. He leveraged his acting and racing fame, putting his celebrity name and likeness on the products, and gave the Newman's Own brand instant visibility. It was now an enterprise committed to making a difference for charity and education.

By 2002, business was booming with a whole line of new products and revenues totaling more than $150 million and counting. Today, Newman's Own may be the largest and perhaps the only major corporation in the world where 100 percent of all after-tax profits go straight to charity.

Newman says, "The Ancient Greeks followed a profession to a given point and then worked for the common good. We can learn from them. There is a responsibility in a democracy to hold your hand out to the less fortunate."

The worldwide headquarters for Newman's Own remains a small building in Westport, Connecticut, where this down-to-earth company retains its small "folksy" feel. The boardroom has a ping-pong table where the winner of matches gets to sign the minutes of the meeting. Newman is serious about using his infectious sense of humor to have fun while creating profit and making a difference. He is also dead serious about keeping the highest quality of his ever-expanding product line that bears his image. From popcorn to pasta—only the best will do.

"How long," Paul wonders, "can any corporation last when it gives everything away? I don't know, but it's going to be an interesting experiment." Newman insists that giving away the profits at year's end is what makes the work worthwhile. "When we no longer have fun," he says, "we'll close the business."

Over the years, Paul's philanthropy has tended to focus on those who don't have a strong voice in society: the elderly, the children, and the disabled. But dearest to his heart is his Hole in the Wall Gang Camp, which he founded in 1988 as a nonprofit residential summer camp for children with cancer and serious blood diseases. Designed and equipped as a "Wild West hideout" in northeastern Connecticut, the camp now provides year-round activities for more than 1,000 children from ages 7 to 15. Campers travel free of charge from across the United States and overseas. New campers are greeted at the gate by a blue and purple sign, made by other campers, declaring, "Yippee, you're here!"

Tree-lined dirt roads wind their way amidst stables, barns, fields, totem poles, teepees, and wigwams, finally reaching the main complex. The camp has 15 log cabins, a swimming pool, an infirmary disguised as the "OK Corral," and a Shaker barn that doubles as a dining hall and recreation center. "Here," says Paul, "the children find camaraderie, joy, and a renewed sense of being a kid. They also get to do things no one knew they were capable of doing." Their philosophy is that every camper will become an adult and needs a good childhood to get there. Paul and his wife, Joanne, often drop by unexpectedly and join the kids in performing skits. "Whenever I'm in the dumps," he says, "I come up here, and it reaffirms everything that's really good and generous about this country."

Newman says the idea of creating camps for sick children had been on his mind for many years. He had lost a couple of young adult friends and family members to cancer. When Paul first considered the concept, he wanted to build a place where sick children could come and wouldn't be any different than the other kids who were there. At some of the similar camps he'd visited, he couldn't tell the difference between the camp and the hospital. "I wanted to create something instead with a sense of romance, fun, and imagination for the kids. The concept, The Hole in the Wall Gang, comes from *Butch Cassidy and the Sundance Kid*—an adventure movie," he points out.

According to Newman, the staff gets back as much as they give, and the children are giving more than they get. "To have some kid who's been in the hospital for six months out of the year come up and say, 'To come back here is what I live for'—that's pretty potent stuff," Newman says.

Newman fondly recalls the time actress Julia Roberts volunteered at the camp as a counselor. He says a child called home and said, "Mommy, guess who I've got in my cabin? Tinker Bell!"

Since its launch in Connecticut in 1988, more than 13,000 children have attended the camp. Originally intended as a summer camp, the Hole in the Wall Gang has evolved into a year-round activities compound that now includes children, siblings, parents, and health professionals. Newman's camp model now has duplicates in several states, from Florida to New York to California, where the Painted Turtle Camp opened in 2004. In North Carolina, the families of famed NASCAR racers Richard and Kyle Petty funded the creation of their Victory Junction Gang Camp, which opened in 2004 and was dedicated to honor Kyle's late son, Adam. Now international, Newman's children's camps have been set up in France, England, and Ireland. In Africa, eight tiny safari camps have opened in Botswana. All of the camps operate as a cooperating network under The Hole in the Wall Gang banner.

Wanting to expand the idea of corporate philanthropy even further,

Newman founded the Committee to Encourage Corporate Philanthropy in 1999, where he currently serves as co-chair. This impressive group of 110 CEOs is responsible for 40 percent of all corporate giving in America. Other recent Newman's Own contributions include a partnership with Ford Motor Company that provided 14 trucks for rural food banks; Bread of Life Mission, a transitional housing facility for the homeless in Seattle; Hope Rural School, a school for migrant children in Florida; and Youth at Risk, a program that supports troubled teenagers.

Paul Newman's penchant for his homemade salad dressing—"the joke that got out of control"—has led to a massive outpouring of contributions for the hundreds of charities that apply annually for aid. Newman and his founding friend Hotchner personally choose most of the winning grants. Newman is sole owner of Newman's Own, and donates all his profits and royalties after taxes for educational and charitable purposes, having given more than $150 million to thousands of charities since 1982. This includes creating and funding his children's camps, where more than 13,000 sick children attend and are loved. In addition, Newman's foundation annually funds $100,000 in grants to be divided among the ten winners of Make A Difference Day Awards. In his "spare-time," Newman continues to encourage corporate America to find other ways to reach out.

With a twinkle in his world-famous blue eyes, Paul Newman says that the only downside to the food business is that his spaghetti sauce makes more money than his Hollywood films did. This fast-driving superstar summed up his philanthropy when he quipped, "From salad dressing, all blessings flow." And the gift goes on . . .

≈≈*Ripples*

COSTCO AND NEWMAN'S OWN

THE IDEA TO CO-BRAND NEWMAN'S OWN grape juice initially came as a shock to Tim Rose, Costco's senior vice-president of foods and sundries—but it was an offer he couldn't refuse. With the creation of Kirkland Signature–Newman's Own Grape Juice, a new model for corporate philanthropy was born. Newman's Own and Costco split the profits from their joint venture, with Costco donating 100 percent of its gross profits to the Children's Miracle Network, and Newman's Own funneling its revenue to any of the 30 charities it supports.

About two years ago, as his teenage son was fighting cancer, Tim saw the video about Newman's Hole in the Wall Gang Camps for children stricken with serious illnesses. He was inspired to bring a similar camp to the Pacific Northwest.

Camp Korey is named after Tim's son, 18-year-old Korey, whose active life was cut short in 2004 by osteo sarcoma, a bone cancer. Located in Redmond, Washington, it will be a special spot where seriously ill children can safely forget about the limitations of their ailments. Camp Korey, scheduled to open in 2008, will be an affiliate of the Hole in the Wall Gang Camps, founded by actor Paul Newman in 1988. Currently, 10 such camps exist worldwide, serving thousands of kids a year. All children who attend the camps, no matter their illness or capacity, can fully participate in each activity, because of the subtle, yet liberating, access components built right into the camp facilities. All campers attend free of charge, thanks to generous contributions from individuals, corporations, and foundations.

At Tim's suggestion, Costco again partnered with Newman's Own to create a breakfast cereal, Newman's Own Hole in the Wall Cereal, which is sold exclusively in Costco warehouses, with 100 percent of the profits from the sale of the cereal donated to Hole in the Wall Camps and children's hospitals. This innovative concept lets everyone win, especially the kids who need it most.

"Nothing makes us happier than sending checks out to children's hospitals," says Rose. "It just tickles us pink."

Whether they're pink or purple, Costco and Newman's Own are forming rainbows of corporate love to kids who need them most.

≈≈*Ripples*

MAKE A DIFFERENCE DAY

USA Weekend magazine had a brilliant idea in 1992. It created "Make A Difference Day" to be held once a year on the fourth Saturday in October, with a huge ideal: give every person the chance to be significantly involved in making a real difference in the lives of others—at least for one Saturday a year. Supported by its more than 600 carrier newspapers, the idea flourished and by 2004, over three million people volunteered in myriad activities countrywide. Make A Difference Day is held in partnership with the Points of Light Foundation.

Paul Newman decided to support the Make A Difference Day idea by annually recognizing 10 outstanding Make a Difference Day volunteers with $10,000 donations to the charities of their choice. Here is a sampling of the 2004–2005 Make A Difference Day award recipients:

- As art teacher James Coley viewed his Hurricane Ivan–ravaged school and community in Pensacola, Florida, he gathered his Village Hope youth mentoring team of kids and dug in to clean up the hazardous heaps of dangerous debris. As a ton of nail-laced and glass-strewn trash was removed, Make A Difference Day turned into four Difference Days. The kids learned the power of being a part of something big and responding to a need.

- Hooray for Carpet One, in Manchester, New Hampshire, which sponsored a makeover contest for school libraries. At 85 schools in 33 states, 1,000 people volunteered and laid 80,000 square feet of flooring as their Difference Day project.

- Tony and Nikki Berti mustered a soul-filled brilliant plan to make a difference for youngsters in need through their Las Vegas Boys and Girls Clubs. They organized a "Goodie Two Shoes Giveaway," making sure that 500 kids in their community got the new shoes they needed and desired.

- Because of her Navajo mother's heritage, 29-year-old Tonya Jocelyn and her friend Lynn Ellis from Hurricane, Utah, longed to collect food, blankets, and clothing that she could share with the Navajo Nation, America's largest reservation. With posters hung, she canvassed local hotels and filled her yard with needed items. The two women crammed a rented U-Haul with 80 boxes of clothing, 100 hotel blankets, baby formula, and food and drove the 370 miles to Window Rock, Arizona. Meeting with an especially needy family of eight living in a two-room plywood shed with a dirt floor, no running water, and no electricity, Ellis's young son grabbed his favorite Hot Wheels monster truck and handed it to the Navajo boy. "That was when we knew the kids got it," Jocelyn says.

➤Newman's Own warns on its Web site: "We haven't quite mastered all facets of electronic communication, so we can't guarantee an answer if you write via e-mail. If you write the old-fashioned way, with stamp and envelope, you're pretty sure to hear from us." Since its founding in 1982, Newman's Own has generated $150 million in profits—all of which go directly to thousands of charities including its six Hole in the Wall Gang Camps. Over 13,000 sick children have been welcomed since the first Connecticut camp opened in 1988.

Keep the twinkles in Paul's eyes sparkling and join the gang—it's for the kids! Contact:

NEWMAN'S OWN
246 Post Road East, Westport, CT 06880
Whether you would like to contribute a recipe, apply for a grant, or give a compliment, you can contact Newman's Own Web site: www.newmansown.com.

For information about the Committee to Encourage Corporate Philanthropy, visit their Web site at: www.corphilanthropy.org

For more information about The Hole in the Wall Gang Camp, go to their Web site at: www.holeinthewallgang.org.

On the fourth Saturday of October in 2005, over three million people volunteered to help in a myriad of charitable activities for Make A Difference Day sponsored by *USA Weekend* magazine and Points of Light Foundation. Newman's Own awarded $10,000 donations to the charities of 10 outstanding volunteers who have created magic and miracles for the good of others.

Note to myself: Sign up for next October and I, too, can make a difference! Check out the Make A Difference Day Web site: www.usaweekend.com/diffday.

5: *Millie Webb*
Mothers Against Drunk Driving

Leading the MADD Charge

For Millie Webb, life as she knew it ended in a car crash, and that's also where it began. In 1971, on a quiet Tennessee road, the Webbs were on their way home. Seven months pregnant, Millie was just dozing off in the passenger seat when she was startled by the sound of screeching brakes. Out of nowhere, a driver with a blood alcohol content (BAC) level of .08 percent slammed into their family car. Inside were her husband, Roy, their 4-year-old daughter, Lori, and their 19-month-old nephew, Mitchell.

Millie was pulled from the mangled car with a broken neck and burns over 73 percent of her body. Roy suffered severe burns. Their nephew, Mitchell, and daughter, Lori, did not survive their injuries. Mitchell lived for just six hours, and little Lori endured two weeks in the hospital before dying from the burns covering 75 percent of her body. As a result of the crash, Kara, the Webbs' baby, was born premature and legally blind. "In just a matter of seconds," Millie declared, "our lives were forever changed." Unbelievably, the drunk driver responsible for the Webb family's devastating crash was convicted only of manslaughter and received just two years of probation under the lenient 1971 Tennessee laws.

Nine years after Millie's accident, another woman, Candy Lightner, lost her 12-year-old daughter Cari to an inebriated driver. Candy transformed her personal suffering into Mothers Against Drunk Driving (MADD), a movement that has changed laws, roused awareness about the dangers of drinking and driving, and saved untold thousands of lives. MADD coined the term *designated driver*—unheard of before 1980—and made it a national mantra.

That is when the stories of Candy and Millie and those of so many like them began to merge. "Candy declared war on drunk driving, and I joined in the fight," Millie shared about the inception of MADD.

It was then, through becoming involved with MADD, that Millie Webb truly began to triumph over tragedy. She learned to take her physical and emotional scars and turn them into stars lighting the path for victims, preventing other families from experiencing the pain and loss she faced due to one person's decision to drink and drive. "I was there in 1982 when Tennessee passed its first drunk-driving law," said Millie proudly.

✦ Together we strive to turn pain into purpose and make a difference."

On May 14, 1988, Millie was part of a Crisis Response Team following a Kentucky school bus crash. Considered the deadliest drunk-driving crash in U.S. history, the blazing collision killed 27 passengers, most of them children. Millie was selected to be part of the team based on her experience as a bereaved parent and burn survivor.

In 2000, the 20th anniversary of MADD's inception was heralded with the swearing-in of a new president. Working her way up the organizational ranks, long-time activist Millie Webb took over the reins of MADD.

During her tenure, Millie worked tirelessly, making changes long overdue to safeguard against the tragedies of drinking and driving. It was her own personal experience that served as a reminder of the urgency to establish a national .08 BAC level cut-off for drivers. Finally, on October 23, 2000, she witnessed the signing of the higher federal standard as law. Thanks to MADD's unwavering efforts to make America's roadways safer, this standard is now accepted in every state. This law drastically reduced alcohol-related traffic incidents and marked the biggest step toward toughened drunk-driving legislation since the passing of a minimum drinking age law in 1984.

Millie beams, "Thanks to MADD, not only do victims have a place to turn, but drunk driving is finally considered a violent crime." The combined efforts of the organization have accomplished greater enforcement and penalties for repeat and high-risk drunk-driving offenders. MADD is currently striving to pass a "victims' rights" constitutional amendment.

Frequently, Millie was asked to present workshops at MADD's National Victim Institutes. Speaking as a certified victim advocate, Millie raised public awareness about their services. She would tell audiences, "We have so many people helping in so many ways. Today MADD has two million volunteers and supporters and 600 affiliates, and that's not counting the folks who donate."

Despite all of MADD's accomplishments, alcohol use is still America's number one youth drug problem, killing 6.5 times more young people than all other illicit drugs combined. Currently, more than 10 million drinkers are between the ages of 12 and 20, and 20 percent of these young drinkers engage in binge drinking. Six percent are heavy drinkers. This is a problem that touches all families.

MADD's influence has been pervasive, both in law and social attitude. Millie shares, "I remember the first time I heard someone say, 'Why aren't you drinking?' and the response was, 'Somebody's got to drive these drunks home.' I wanted to hug that stranger!" Her tenure as president for two-and-a-half years capped her activism.

Millie still credits her husband, family, friends, and God with getting her through the worst. Five years after that tragic night, Roy and Millie were blessed with another child, Ashlea. Today, Millie, Roy, and Ashlea Webb live in Franklin, Tennessee. Their daughter Kara and her husband Dave Hensel live close by. Millie enjoys being a grandmother to grandsons Collin and Caston.

It's been more than three decades since the fiery crash that changed Millie's life and so many others, at a time when rampant drinking and driving bore little or no attachment to the thought of endangering lives. "I'm still recovering. I've had 20 surgeries from the crash. It took my husband 10 years to pay off my medical expenses. And someday, when I see Lori in heaven, I hope she'll say, 'I know you couldn't help what happened to me, Mom. And I know you've done everything in your power to keep it from happening to somebody else.' I think it's in the heart of MADD people everywhere to try to make a difference. Life will never be the same," she tells other victims, "but it can be good again."

Millie still works in her local MADD chapter made up entirely of volunteers like so many others across the country. "In the beginning, we were just a handful of mothers and victims. It's such a privilege to have seen the growth of MADD into mothers and others, men and women, victims and non-victims, working side by side. Together we strive to turn pain into purpose and make a difference."

≈*Ripples*

From Millie

"While I was speaking recently at my local chapter, a man stood up and shared, 'I heard you give a lecture 13 years ago, Millie. That night, a woman in the audience told of her child who had been injured by a mechanic who was driving drunk. That was me. I did it. I was an alcoholic. After hearing you share your story, I knew I could make it, and I stopped drinking. And now I know the pain firsthand. A drunk driver killed my son last February.'"

Death of an Innocent

I went to a party, and remembered what you said.
You told me not to drink, Mom, so I had a Sprite instead.
I felt proud of myself, the way you said I would,
That I didn't drink and drive, though some friends said I should.
I made a healthy choice, and your advice to me was right.
The party finally ended, and the kids drove out of sight.
I got into my car, sure to get home in one piece.
I never knew what was coming, Mom, something I expected least.
Now I'm lying on the pavement, and I hear the policeman say,
The kid that caused this wreck was drunk, Mom. His voice
  seems far away.
My own blood's all around me, as I try hard not to cry.
I can hear the paramedic say, this girl is going to die.
I'm sure the guy had no idea, while he was flying high,
Because he chose to drink and drive, now I would have to die.
So why do people do it, Mom, knowing that it ruins lives?
And now the pain is cutting me, like a hundred stabbing knives.
Tell Sister not to be afraid, Mom, tell Daddy to be brave,
And when I go to heaven, put "Daddy's Girl" on my grave.

Someone should have taught him that it's wrong to drink
  and drive.
Maybe if his parents had, I'd still be alive.
My breath is getting shorter, Mom. I'm getting really scared.
These are my final moments, and I'm so unprepared.
I wish that you could hold me, Mom, as I lie here and die.
I wish that I could say, "I love you, Mom!" so I love you
  and good-bye.

—Author Unknown

➤Alcohol-related traffic deaths are on the rise, and underage drinking levels continue to peak. MADD was founded in 1980 by Candy Lightner. Under the presidency of long-time activist Millie Webb, it celebrated its 20th anniversary in 2003 by successfully lobbying to create a law standardizing the federal BAC level to .08. MADD needs your help keeping our roadways safe and supporting victims of this violent crime. Join the two million MADD volunteers and supporters in over 600 chapters around the country. Stay sober and always have a designated driver.

Whether MADD, sad, or scared, get active. Contact:

MADD NATIONAL OFFICE
511 E. John Carpenter Freeway, Suite 700, Irving, TX 75062
Phone: (800) GET-MADD (438-6233) I Fax: (972) 869-2206/07
E-mail: volunteer@madd.org I Web site: www.madd.org

6: *Michael Spencer*
American Red Cross

YOUNG HANDS, BIG HEART

FOR MICHAEL SPENCER, it all began when a tornado struck his hometown of Van Buren, Arkansas, in 1996. "The tornado took a right turn about a quarter of a mile before it reached my house. I could hardly believe the devastation it caused. I remember seeing boards driven through brick walls and the faces of victims as they cleaned up and salvaged what they could." Even though he was just 14, Michael was asked by the local Red Cross director to help. He was needed, so he gladly volunteered and made a difference in resolving Van Buren's emergency.

Michael learned firsthand that when a disaster threatens or strikes, the American Red Cross is there, providing immediate shelter, food, or medical and mental-health services to thousands of victims. Impressed with their tornado relief efforts, Michael signed up as a local volunteer. He became hooked on helping. While still in high school, he taught water-safety classes in Fort Smith, Arkansas. He later became a CPR and first-aid instructor and, eventually, a lifeguard trainer. "I remained with the Red Cross because I believe so strongly in what they do every day across our country and around the world."

Values and community involvement were a deep part of Michael's upbringing. "Both of my parents frequently give of either time or treasure to charitable organizations," he said. "So in high school, I enjoyed organizing blood drives and raising money for the Salvation Army at Christmastime, as well as being a local volunteer for Emergency Preparedness for the Red Cross."

All of his Red Cross training was good preparation for when he would later face the horror of "the big one"— the 9/11 terrorist attacks. At both the Pentagon and in New York, 18-year-old Michael served on the front-lines with the Red Cross's Disaster Public Affairs (DPA) unit. Their role is to ensure that people needing help know where to go and how the Red Cross can be of service. On 9/11, thousands upon thousands poured into the Red Cross center to volunteer. Michael's job was to find the perfect match between their skills and appropriate emergency service needs.

To Michael, the most lasting impression of the 9/11 disaster was that of the country pulling together in the face of terror. "I was so proud of my country. While traveling to my hotel in D.C. from Dulles Airport, I saw thousands of people holding candles and singing with the still-smoking Pentagon in the background. Those people served as inspiration for many long days to come."

The scene was much the same when Michael went to help in New York. People lined the street to cheer for the flow of firemen and police who passed by on their way to and from Ground Zero. Every fire truck and nearly every car bore an American flag, and most people wore something red, white, and blue.

For Michael, there was joy and pride in serving as part of the Red Cross. To be stopped on the street by total strangers and thanked was a humbling experience for such a young man. "I am not sure I will ever be the same person—actually, I hope I am not ever the same person. Being there was a privilege."

While a sophomore at the University of Arkansas in Fayetteville, he spent all of his vacation time, including each summer, volunteering full-time at the national Red Cross headquarters in Washington, D.C. In 2002, Michael Spencer was nominated for the Woodrow Wilson Exemplary Youth Services Award. In accepting the award he stated, "The American Red Cross is important to me because of the opportunities it offers young people to make a real difference, not only in their own community, but around the world. The Red Cross will always be a major part of me."

Michael currently serves the Red Cross as its National Coordinator of Youth Volunteers for Disaster Relief and is responsible for increasing youth involvement in disaster services. "When I get to help people who've lost everything they own in a disaster, I get to see firsthand how volunteers can make a difference in people's lives. I'm incredibly grateful for that opportunity."

Clara Barton founded the American Red Cross in Washington, D.C., in 1881 and continued to direct its lofty mission for 23 years. During that time, the Red Cross conducted its first domestic and overseas disaster relief efforts, aided by the United States military during the Spanish-American War. In 1905, the year after Barton resigned, the Red Cross was given its congressional charter. Its official mission remains to this day: to give relief to and serve as a medium of communication between members of the American armed forces and their families and to provide national and international disaster relief and mitigation. A hot cup of coffee, a safe place to sleep, regular meals, a bottle of water, a jacket on a cold night— the services financed by the Red Cross Disaster Relief Fund may seem small, but for people impacted by a disaster, they make a big difference.

Red Cross volunteers live life to serve humanity and make the world a better place. Each year, over 175,000 American Red Cross volunteers respond immediately to more than 60,000 disasters and emergencies such as house or apartment fires (the majority of disaster responses), hurricanes, floods, earthquakes, tornadoes, hazardous materials spills, transportation accidents, explosions, and other natural and man-made disasters. Of these volunteers, 34 percent are under the age of 25, just like Michael Spencer.

Another 24,000 volunteers serve as chairs or members of advisory and directors' boards. Last year, more than 230,000 people donated their time to teach first aid, CPR, swimming, and other health and safety skills to over 15 million Americans. Operating on a $4.1 billion budget, all Red Cross disaster assistance is provided at no cost and made possible by voluntary donations of time and money from American people. These donations are a prime example of people power.

And the American Red Cross is international—working to ease human suffering on a global scale. Whether it is an earthquake in Iran, hurricanes in Honduras, or a tsunami leveling parts of India, Indonesia, and Thailand, the American Red Cross sends experts, volunteers, and whatever aid is needed. Within five weeks of the "Christmas Tsunami" of December 2004, the Red Cross had received donations totaling $249 million of the total $1 billion that everyday Americans had contributed to aid with the disaster. The 125-year-old charity was by far the biggest organization in responding to Hurrican Katrina, raising $2 billion, mobilizing 135,000 volunteers, and helping hundreds of thousands of displaced people.

"The Red Cross touches so many lives," Michael says. "It gives ordinary people like myself extraordinary opportunities to make a difference." Michael plans to continue with the Red Cross for the rest of his life, either as a volunteer or as an employee. "There are so many people who need help around the world—I wish I had dozens of lifetimes to help them all. The joy of being part of the American Red Cross is indescribable. Now I understand the value of life, and I try to make the most of it every day."

≈≈*Ripples*

THE WOOLVERTONS

ON SEPTEMBER 11, 2001, Karolyn Woolverton found herself in the midst of a nightmare. Her four-year-old daughter, Kate, was at home with a babysitter in their apartment, just blocks from the World Trade Center attacks. By the time Karolyn located her daughter, it was 9:00 p.m. It wasn't until the following day that they were reunited with Karolyn's husband, Frederick. He was stunned when he saw the terror on his daughter's face.

"I didn't recognize Kate at all," he said. "I have never seen an expression like that on Kate's—or anyone's—face before. Even her words and mannerisms were different, and she was terrified to be alone." With an apartment severely damaged by wreckage, no clothes, and a daughter who needed medical attention, Frederick took his family to the one place he knew they could turn—the American Red Cross.

Red Cross caseworkers quickly started paperwork for temporary housing, financial assistance, clothing, and even arrangements for Kate's enrollment in a new school. By October, Kate was back in a classroom, but was still traumatized by the attacks. In February 2002, both parents realized that their daughter needed emotional help. Through the Red Cross, the Woolvertons found therapy for Kate, who was diagnosed with chronic fatigue and post-traumatic stress disorder.

Kate is doing better today in the sense that she is finally talking about "the bad day" as she calls it. In April 2003, with the help of the Red Cross, the family moved back into their now environmentally safe apartment. To give back, Frederick is now in training to become an American Red Cross mental-health volunteer for disasters.

On 9/11, as in all other emergencies, the Red Cross was there for the Woolvertons and countless other traumatized and displaced families who needed their help. As usual, those who received help find it impossible not to want to give back—or give forward. In any emergency, the Red Cross and its band of awesome volunteers can be counted on to be ready on the front line.

➤"A hot cup of coffee, a safe place to sleep, regular meals, a bottle of water, a jacket on a cold night—the services financed by the American Red Cross Disaster Relief Fund may seem small, but for people impacted by a disaster, they make a big difference." Today, more than 1.2 million people volunteer with the Red Cross nationwide, and 40,000 nurses assist in all lines of service. One in every 200 Americans is a Red Cross volunteer. Over 34 percent of volunteers are people under 25, like Michael Spencer, and young adults are the fastest growing segment of volunteers.

Operating with an amazing $4.1 billion budget, the American Red Cross is made up of 990 chapters and annually mobilizes relief to more than 60,000 disasters nationwide. Ninety-seven percent of Red Cross staff members are volunteers.

When Clara Barton founded the American Red Cross in 1881, she was already world-renowned. Her service to the troops during the Civil War, her many philanthropic activities at home and abroad, and her lengthy campaign for American ratification of the 1864 Geneva Convention for the protection of the war-injured had made her a genuine American heroine. Since its start, the American Red Cross promise has remained: "We'll be there." And they are, with your help. They need our financial and volunteer support—now more than ever!

Don't just cross your fingers in an emergency. "HELP NOW." Support the Red Cross and/or volunteer:

AMERICAN RED CROSS
National Headquarters: (202) 303-4498
Make a donation: (800) HELP-NOW
Disaster Assistance Information: (866) GET-INFO
Call your local chapter or visit www.redcross.org

7: Senior Corps

Senior Corps is a network of programs that taps the experience, skills, and talents of older citizens to meet community challenges. Through its three programs—Foster Grandparents, Senior Companions, and RSVP (Retired and Senior Volunteer Program)—more than half a million "senior" Americans, ages 55 and over, assist local nonprofits, public agencies, and faith-based organizations in carrying out their missions.

More than 525,000 Senior Corps volunteers were proactive in 2001. The Corporation of National and Community Service administers and oversees Senior Corps, USA Freedom Corps, AmeriCorps, and Learn and Serve America. Together these programs engage more than 23 million Americans of all ages and backgrounds in volunteer service each year. For senior corps volunteers, they are discovering their pot of gold at the end of their rainbow.

The stories of John McConnell (RSVP) and Louise Jackson (Foster Grandparents) are just two of those thousands whose power and passion exemplify the ability of seniors to make a difference.

Don't Retire ⅲ➡ Refire!

John McConnell, RSVP

Mentoring the Love of Science

Seventy-five-year-old John McConnell has a message for high-school students: math and science are cool! He's been so brilliant at proving it that his award-winning protégé plans to thank John with a new red Chevrolet Corvette.

A physicist living in Grand Junction, Colorado, McConnell retired in 1990 from the Los Alamos National Laboratories in New Mexico. Instead of staying home to sit on his laurels, John joined RSVP and has since devoted his life to mentoring youth, both in large groups and one-on-one. Each year, he provides hands-on science demonstrations to more than 8,000 children.

RSVP engages volunteers in a diverse range of activities, such as organizing neighborhood watch programs, tutoring children, renovating homes, teaching English to immigrants, assisting victims of natural disasters, and serving their communities in a myriad of other ways. In fiscal year 2001, approximately 480,000 senior volunteers served an average of 4 hours a week. An estimated 65,000 local organizations are served through 766 different RSVP projects, just like John McConell's.

For John, retirement was just the beginning of a new quest to make the exciting world of science come alive for children. He recalls, "In 1991, a local principal asked if I might help with science in a fifth-grade class. Wow, I was hooked! As I began to get involved, I found that kids were thrilled to have the chance to be engaged with interactive science. Their excitement was infectious."

Traveling from school to school, McConnell conducted his demonstrations like a magician, pulling experiments from a chest full of scientific goodies—magnets, sound, electricity, and bubbles. "I was seeing up to 5,000 kids a year working out of the trunk of my car when the school district gave me 1,000 square feet of space to develop a Sci-Tech Exploratorium. It was phenomenally successful, drawing the children in droves."

In the spring of 1999, using his own retirement savings, a few grants from local contributors, and space provided by the school district, McConnell opened the Western Colorado Math and Science Center. This 6,000-square-foot center consists of 160 hands-on interactive learning stations dealing with scientific and mathematic concepts, complete with Braille capability. Each month it attracts more than 1,000 students from all over the state. Available to special groups even at night and over the weekend, it provides a stimulating experience for children *and* their parents. "To see and feel the excitement of kids of all ages having fun while learning is one of the great satisfactions in life," says John, who calls this special brand of learning SITHOK—Science In The Hands Of Kids.

John McConnell's dream has turned out just as he envisioned it—a place for kids of all ages to explore science and math, and to "touch, turn, look, listen, feel, pull, adjust, try out, and question." The center welcomes school classes, organized groups, and the general public. It is staffed entirely by volunteers who interact with visitors in order to enhance their appreciation of scientific principles.

McConnell also provides staff-development workshops to train teachers in strategies to make the Math and Science Center's concepts clear, teach-*able*, exciting, and reproducible beyond the center's walls. He also helped establish the Senior Corps RSVP Scholar Project to connect senior volunteers with local students.

One of his greatest joys now is the production of "Kits for Kids"— portable science in a toolbox. Teachers are invited to come into the center, check out a kit, use it to teach their students, and then return it for refurbishing. "We are starting with 70 kits of five science applications complete with our own videos, overhead projector materials, and everything the teacher needs," says John. "The Grand Junction Lions Club got the project started with $5,000. This is just the beginning. Once you've infected a teacher with a true love of science, you spread that out over a lifetime of teaching." Infecting a student with that same science-spark can change the world, or at least his understanding of the world.

In 1998, the U.S. Department of Education awarded John McConnell with its "Education Hero Award." At the age of 72, he was also selected to carry the Olympic torch through Grand Junction on its way to the Salt Lake City Winter Games. In 2000, he was named a national "Point of Light."

For John McConnell, all the tributes are nice, but "there is no greater joy than helping a young person gain their own wings, to get them flying and soaring to new heights. What a great satisfaction it is to see the young achieve their dreams. It's a huge thrill to be a part of it."

Long ago, John and his wife, Audrey, agreed that wherever they retired, they wanted to give something back to the community. "I grew up on a farm near Humboldt, Nebraska, where neighbors always helped one another," John says. "That attitude has stayed with me for 75 years. For us, this is payback time."

≈ *Ripples*

RYAN PATTERSON

JOHN'S GENUINE PASSION for mentoring youth in science comes shining through when he talks about one young man in particular. "In 1992," he fondly recalls, "I was asked to mentor a third-grade boy who was bursting with questions that his regular teacher couldn't answer. I was so impressed with his enthusiasm and focus on electronics that I just had to help this boy reach his dreams." Thus, he began a mentoring relationship that lasted more than 10 years. Every Saturday, until Ryan Patterson graduated from high school, John was at his side working and nurturing his love of science.

Ryan recently won first place in an Intel-sponsored scholarship competition for an unusual invention—the prize was $100,000. The inspiration for his invention struck while still in high school as he watched a deaf woman trying to order food at a Burger King. He felt there had to be a more effective and economical way of improving independence for the deaf in a hearing world. Why not create a device that translates sign language into text?

With less than $200, a leather golf glove, and John's considerable encouragement, Ryan built a prototype of his translation device and applied for a patent. The specially modified glove senses hand movements and translates them into words that appear on a tiny handheld monitor the size of a cell phone. Ryan's easy-to-use invention allows the deaf and hearing to communicate effortlessly. The idea also won Ryan top prize at the Siemens-Westinghouse Science and Technology Competition.

Mentoring one-on-one and seeing the passion for learning come alive in a child will always be John McConnell's ultimate achievement. Ryan Patterson's gratitude shows in the close friendship the two share. As soon as his business is profitable, Ryan has promised to buy John a red Chevrolet Corvette as a "thank you" for all those years of devoted mentoring. John jokingly encourages the young man: "Hurry up! I want to be able to drive it myself."

Louise Jackson, Foster Grandparents

Foster Grandparent, Anyone?

"A grandmother is the greatest thing these children ever had." —Louise Jackson

Eighty-nine-year-old Louise Jackson of Washington, D.C., touches lives in amazing one-on-one ways. She is one of the many "miracle grandmothers" in the Foster Grandparents program. The story of Louise illustrates the difference a senior can make.

The Foster Grandparents Program provides a way for those aged 60 and over—even if they have limited incomes—to serve as extended family members to children and youth with special needs. They serve 20 hours a week in schools, hospitals, correctional institutions, daycare facilities, and Head Start centers. The volunteers help children who have been abused or neglected, mentor troubled teenagers and young mothers, and care for premature infants or children with physical disabilities. In 2001, more than 30,000 foster grandparents tended to the needs of 275,000 young children and teenagers.

Louise was born in Alexandria, Virginia, where her grandmother was a mid-wife. "My great-grandmother raised me. She provided her home as one of the slaves' stations for the Underground Railroad. From the age of eight, I used to help her deliver babies. She delivered babies for people who couldn't afford a doctor. In those days, most poor people didn't have electricity, so I'd often hold a lamp for my grandma during the birthings. Sometimes, I'd have to put the lamp down and help her by holding the lady's hand while she'd push. I've been dealing with children since I was a very small child. I'd help grandma cooking and cleaning and taking care of the other children while the mother was having her baby.

"When I was the age of eight or nine, my grandmother told me, 'You're a great person. You wear your heart on your sleeve, Louise. People are going to take advantage of you. But just trust in the Lord and do good, and you'll live to be a ripe old age.'"

Fast forward to Louise as an adult who always worked and managed to scrape by; her children never missed a meal. In 1974, while in her late 50s, arthritis set in and she had to quit her job. Her knees became so painful that her doctor gave her a cane to help her walk. But when she became involved with Foster Grandparents, she found her days becoming so busy serving others that she forgot about her knees.

So just what is it that she does for the children through Foster Grandparents? "First, I let them know someone loves them. Most of these children need a hug, and some of them never get it. Then, I go into their homes and make sure the mothers don't beat the children and that they clean the house and are caring for them. I mostly just give these children love," she says.

"I work with children one-on-one at times. I can take them places they wouldn't ordinarily be able to go. More importantly, I counsel them. So many come from homes with five or six siblings, dealing with parents who are drug addicts or abusive. The parents go to court for these offenses, but the judges most often give the kids back to their parents. That's when I come into the home to counsel everyone together. Oh, some of the things I've seen! My heart breaks for these children."

At the age of 70, Louise was matched with twins Philip and Phyllis, abused and neglected crack babies. Their father was incarcerated and their mother a drug addict. No regular foster home would take both twins and keep them together, and Louise didn't think it possible to raise them herself—but she was falling in love. Fully understanding the challenges she would face, "Mama" Jackson courageously asked for custody of the twins, which she received, on a temporary basis. This gives new definition to the term "miracle babies."

"I just stepped up to the mark that the Lord had made for me," Louise said. Four years later, the judge gave Mrs. Jackson permanent custody of the two children she then renamed Charles and Louise who now, many years later, are prospering and still living with Louise.

Remember those bad knees from over three decades ago when she was in her 50s? One day, Louise lost her cane and never bothered getting another one. Today, at the age of 89, Louise Jackson still puts in full days teaching troubled parents how to parent their children. She has helped raise 30 non-related children, her own biological children and grandchildren, and has loved many more great-grandchildren. As a volunteer, she has worked for the juvenile courts as a mentor for youths who were locked up and also worked with youth in child-abuse cases with the responsibility of trying to keep the family unit together. Often, that meant finding food, clothing, and shelter and meeting their basic needs.

✦ *"Step-up, get-up, show-up, listen-up, and grow-up."*

Louise Jackson says the Senior Corps and Foster Grandparent Program is the best thing that's out there to help children. "This program creates a one-to-one relationship matching kids in need with an adult who cares. It's even more than just a volunteer thing. I encourage people to make a difference through the love they have for children."

Her volunteer experience does not end with kids. Three nights a week, Jackson volunteers with SOME (So Others Might Eat). She and her brood pick up donations of fresh food and blankets and distribute them to the homeless and needy in the district where she lives. One homeless person in the city said, "If you're looking for Mrs. Jackson, don't worry. She'll be around soon. She'll be the lady with the big smile and an old car with loaves of bread piled high in the back. She's coming. She always does."

Mrs. Jackson, who challenges everyone to "step-up, get-up, show-up, listen-up, and grow-up," says she learned her unselfish approach to life from her great-grandmothers and her grandmother, both of whom were slaves. They instilled in her a belief that "life is only good if you can give of yourself to others." Jackson notes, "It's the small things that really matter to a person in need."

And those bad knees? "I don't think about my knees anymore," she says. "If people would just get up out of their house and do something for other people, they'd feel better about themselves." Louise learned the legacy of love at the knees of her slave elders. Now as a grandmother (both foster and biological), she passes on this wisdom to new generations that follow in her footsteps.

►Senior Corps is a network of programs that taps the experience, skills, and talents of older citizens to meet community challenges. Through its three programs—Foster Grandparents, Senior Companions, and RSVP—more than half a million "senior" Americans, ages 55 and over, assist local nonprofits, public agencies, and faith-based organizations in carrying out their missions.

RSVP, one offshoot of Senior Corps, is a network of national service programs that provides older Americans with the opportunity to apply their life experiences to meeting community needs. In 2001, approximately 480,000 RSVP volunteers like John McConnell served in a diverse range of nonprofit organizations, public agencies, and faith-based groups. Among other activities, they mentor at-risk youth, organize neighborhood watch programs, teach English to immigrants, and lend their business skills to community groups that provide critical social services. Annually, senior volunteers served an average of 4 hours a week, benefiting over 65,000 local organizations.

Foster Grandparents like Louise Jackson provide older Americans the opportunity to put their life experiences to work for local communities. They serve at least 20 hours a week as mentors, tutors, and caregivers for at-risk children and youth with special needs through a variety of community organizations, including schools, hospitals, drug treatment facilities, correctional institutions, Head Start, and day-care centers. In 2001, more than 30,000 Foster Grandparents tended to the needs of 275,000 young children and teenagers.

Seniors are really making a difference! Make retirement rock! Call today:

CORPORATION FOR NATIONAL AND COMMUNITY SERVICE
1201 New York Avenue NW, Washington, DC 20525
Web site: www.seniorcorps.org
Phone: (202) 606-5000

RSVP
Phone: (800) 424-8867 or (800) 833-3722

John McConnell's science for kids project in Colorado has a *way cool* Web site at:
www.sithok.org
Phone: (970) 254-1626

8: Trevor Ferrell
Trevor's Campaign

SHELTER FROM THE COLD

IN THE WINTER OF 1983, Trevor Ferrell was watching television at his Philadelphia home with his parents when he first heard about the homeless. At just 11 years old, he couldn't believe people actually lived and slept outside in the cold.

Trevor deluged his parents with non-stop questions: "Don't they have any place to sleep? Where do they eat? How can they survive without beds and blankets? Won't they freeze?" His parents didn't know the answers to most of these questions, but he persisted. Later that night, he asked them just one more question: "Can you take me downtown to help them?"

Frank and his wife, Janet, found themselves in a quandary. They had raised their son to care about others, but were comfortable in their suburban house. Neither had a desire to go out into the cold searching for derelicts in dangerous parts of the city. They said no—at least for the first few nights. Trevor didn't give up. Finally, Frank and Janet Ferrell saw a chance to let him really help others. Little did they know that the short trip they took downtown with Trevor would change their lives.

"There!" Trevor yelled, spotting a pile of rags and cardboard bundled up on the sidewalk grate. On that first visit, he got out of the car and offered a shoeless man a yellow blanket and his own special pillow. The man's smile made such a deep impression that Trevor asked his parents to take him back a few nights later. This time, the sight of a sad-looking woman trembling with cold touched him. He wrapped her with an old warm coat his mother no longer used.

As Christmas approached, the Ferrells started making regular trips to see other homeless people. With continued prodding from Trevor, they brought sweaters, coats, blankets, and warm food. As he gave each person some gifts, he took time to talk with them. Because of their derelict appearance, street people usually receive no more than a sidelong glance. Trevor's friendship and caring meant as much to them as his gifts. He became their "Little Buddy," and they looked for him nightly.

Neighbors, friends, and others heard about Trevor's mission, and started dropping off warm clothing, blankets, and food to pass along to his homeless buddies. Eventually, the 11-year-old's endeavors caught the attention of the nightly news, and Trevor appeared on a local television show. As word spread, the Ferrells organized a compassionate group of dedicated volunteers and called it Trevor's Campaign. That first winter, every night 70 families took turns feeding more than 100 homeless people from a donated van. The following year, the campaign received a dilapidated hotel that was remodeled into Trevor's Place, a home for the homeless—but that was just the beginning.

Trevor's Campaign proliferated and took over the Ferrell household. "For the first few years, it was awful, just awful," Janet admits. "We went from the traditional suburban home with the station wagon, dog, and kids to Frank giving up his profitable electronics store to work full-time on our campaign. The family and house suffered." As he spent more and more time helping the homeless, the dyslexic Trevor also fell behind in school and had to repeat the sixth grade.

Still, Trevor's passion for the homeless grew, and word continued to spread—all the way to 1600 Pennsylvania Avenue. President Ronald Reagan invited him to the White House on three separate occasions, and once to his ranch in California. In his 1986 State of the Union speech, President Reagan introduced Trevor and told the story of how in just two years, the young boy's nightly campaign for the homeless had grown to 250 volunteers. A television movie of Trevor's dream entitled *Christmas on Division Street,* starring Fred Savage, was made.

More and more Americans became conscious of and involved in helping the homeless because of Trevor's commitment. Homelessness throughout the country was treated more seriously. As the campaign grew to 27 chapters, the boy with a dream grew into a man. Due to his learning disabilities, Trevor continued to have difficulties in school and completed one year of college before becoming a carpenter. In 1994, both Trevor and Frank left their organization after disagreeing with the nonprofit board they had founded.

Today, the Ferrells have a different vision of a full-time, live-in farm for kids. They dream that Trevor's Youth Farm School will provide 40 at-risk kids with a safe haven far from the distractions of the city. The Ferrells know firsthand the power of persistent passion, as well as the discouragement that comes when some dreams don't get realized. Trevor works with his family that now includes his wife and two young daughters. They all run a thrift shop in Philadelphia.

Only time will tell if they can raise the money for their farm. Frank had a brain tumor a few years back and passed away in 2004 and they continue to struggle financially. Yet the family holds the conviction that they will make a difference for needy kids.

Back in 1985, Trevor was left with a vivid recollection after meeting Mother Teresa for the second time in two years. "What you do may be just a drop in an ocean of need," she said to him, "but without that drop, you'd be missed." So many homeless men and women's lives continue to be touched by the "drops in the ocean" left by an 11-year-old boy who brought his buddies help, hope, warmth of friendship—and the attention of their nation.

≈≈*Ripples*

CONSTANCE LINDSAY

It was divine providence that Constance Lindsay went to work for Trevor's Campaign in 1992. Growing up in Philadelphia, she lost her mother at a very young age and turned to drugs for solace. After a 20-year addiction, she found the love of God in prison through Prison Fellowship and wanted to make a difference in the lives of others. Constance had heard vague stories about a boy who gave blankets and love to the homeless, but never understood his mission until she got a job helping the destitute at Trevor's Campaign. She has worked her way up to director of facilities and operations, and every day she touches the hearts of the mothers and children who live and learn in this sprawling home full of hope.

Constance, a round-the-clock staff of 12, and more than 2,000 volunteers are all involved in numerous outreaches to displaced families in this impoverished North Philadelphia neighborhood. After-school programs with computers donated by Verizon teach neighborhood children year-round. Churches throughout Philadelphia collect new toys for Trevor's Campaign. Mothers are taught life and employment skills, and receive mental and physical health treatment before they and their children move out to independent living.

"When people are hurting and afraid, I can share with them one-on-one my story, share my faith and strength, and give them a model for hope," says Constance. After 14 years, Constance is touched to see people who were once residents now volunteering at Trevor's Campaign. Others visit after work or while attaining graduate degrees. So many of the formerly homeless and hopeless now give back to others, sharing their knowledge of life's possibilities.

➤ Since its founding in 1983 by 11-year-old Trevor Ferrell, Trevor's Campaign has housed 2,300, helped 1,800 secure permanent housing, and served 2 million meals to homeless individuals. Aided by hundreds of volunteers, they have raised national consciousness for the plight of homeless people. It is their goal to help them secure permanent housing, find gainful employment, obtain GED or high school diplomas, and assist children. According to the U.S. Department of Health and Human Services, up to 600,000 men, women, and children go homeless each night. In American cities, families comprise 40 percent of the homeless population.

To find a place where the heart beats for the homeless, contact:

TREVOR'S CAMPAIGN
3415 West Chester Pike, Suite 201, Newtown Square, PA 19073
Phone: (610) 325-0640 or (800) TREVORS I Fax: (610) 325-0645
Web site:www.trevorscampaign.org

NATIONAL COALITION FOR THE HOMELESS
1012 Fourteenth Street NW, #600, Washington, DC 20005-3471
Phone: (202) 737-6444 I Fax: (202) 737-6445

9: Tom Harken
ProLiteracy Worldwide

THE MILLIONAIRE'S SECRET

TAKE ONE LOOK at fun-loving Texas millionaire Tom Harken, and it's tough to believe he's ever had any agonizing secrets. This Air Force soldier turned vacuum-cleaner salesman turned chairman of the board appears to have sailed through life with a smile on his face and a beautiful, compassionate wife on his arm. His is a blend of Michigan ease and Texan charm.

But life wasn't always easy for Tom. As a child, he fought for survival against polio and tuberculosis, spending almost his entire eleventh year isolated in an iron lung. He missed so much school that when he finally did get back into the classroom, Tom felt humiliated about being so far behind. So after only two weeks in the seventh grade, he dropped out and went straight to work as a stock-boy in his father's small store. "Dad always said I'd make it because I was a hard worker," Tom said. "If God had made eight-day weeks, I'd work eight days." And figuratively, he did.

At 17, Tom joined the Air Force. After basic training, he sold shoes and vacuum cleaners to augment his meager military pay. Still poor, he became rich with love when he met a "little girl from Oklahoma who didn't know what a hamburger or cheeseburger was." To this day he still calls his wife and soulmate "Miss Melba."

Finishing his stint in the Air Force, Tom found himself so successful at selling Kirby vacuums door-to-door that he was eventually offered his own distributorship in Beaumont, Texas. While building his life as a father and active community member, his business ventures multiplied. Expanding from vacuum cleaners to recreational vehicles, Tom later sold this business and opened a chain of 13 Mexican restaurants. "I felt as though I had conquered the world after all," he said.

As respected as he was, Tom Harken was a millionaire living with a secret: despite all he had "conquered" and accomplished, amazingly he could neither read nor write. It was the only shadow haunting his life. From presentations to contracts, he memorized everything. "I taught myself to fake it very convincingly," he remembers. "I could recognize enough basic terminology to feel my way through a contract, but I was also becoming known around town. It was increasingly difficult to continue keeping my secret from the world."

For many years Tom and his wife managed to conceal his illiteracy from virtually everyone they knew, from friends to entire corporate and community boards on which he sat. They even kept it from their two sons who grew up believing their father never wanted to read them bedtime stories. "I had been successful without coming to terms with it, persuading myself that not being able to read wasn't a problem anymore," Tom said.

All the hiding came to an end one night when Harken found himself lost in Dallas—or so he thought. He couldn't read the signs. A highway patrolman gently informed him he was in fact not in Dallas, but Fort Worth, and helped him find his way. "That night, I was ashamed that I was a grown man and couldn't even find my way home," said Tom. "This burden was getting in the way of my doing all the things I wanted to do. It was the one remaining shadow in my life and I knew I would have to shine the light on it at last."

At the age of 53, the self-made millionaire finally began working in earnest with Miss Melba, who had been trying for years to encourage him to start learning to read and write. The long process was frustrating for both of them. Every night, they worked together for hours, Melba helping her husband move from one-syllable sounds to two-syllable words, slowly progressing to reading complete sentences. "Really and truly, this story should be about my wife," he says. "Most people who can't read or write don't find a true partner like Miss Melba."

Eventually, Tom learned to read, spell, and write. He no longer memorized board presentations or needed help deciphering street signs. And after missing the years of reading bedtime stories to his children, he fully embraced the gift of being able to read them to his grandchildren.

Those lost years, however, had left their mark. The scars from spending most of his life harboring a secret lingered and Tom still didn't want anyone to know about his late-learning experience. Over time, he realized that he wasn't the only adult to suffer from illiteracy. He felt compelled to help others find the world that opened up through being able to read.

When a letter arrived in 1991 saying Tom had been chosen as a recipient of the prestigious Horatio Alger Award—an honor he would share with such luminaries as former Secretary of State Henry Kissinger, Supreme Court Justice Clarence Thomas, and author/poet Maya Angelou—he decided it was time to tell the world about his lifelong battle with illiteracy.

✦ *"Everyone can be great,*
because everyone can serve."
—*Dr. Martin Luther King Jr.*

The Horatio Alger Award is given to people who have overcome adversity to achieve success. Even more fittingly, Tom had overcome adversities his audience didn't know he'd faced. To Tom it was "the Oscar, the Emmy, and the Tony of *real* life," and he chose to go public with his secret in his acceptance speech. Gripping the podium with white knuckles, he shared his story. As his last words filled the room, 1,000 people stood in unison, many with tears. "I don't know if I was laughing or crying," Tom remembers, "but as I gazed at Miss Melba and our boys, I knew this was the most moving moment of my life." Many, including the future Secretary of State Colin Powell, stood in line that night to shake Tom's hand.

Now that the secret was out, Tom could focus on other things like instigating change and inspiring others to learn to read. "If I could bring myself to confess that I had become a multimillionaire despite varying degrees of reading deficiency, I might be able to inspire millions like myself—and those with even more crippling handicaps—to rise above their liabilities, too," he said. "Now, *that* would make me feel ten feet tall."

For over a decade, Tom has traveled throughout the nation telling his story, promoting literacy, and letting people who are struggling to read and write know that they are not alone. "If I can do it, what's your excuse?" he asks with a grin. Tom also works with illiterate prisoners who struggle to read and has been responsible for helping several inmates earn their high school diplomas from behind bars. He recalls a distinguished, young

African-American man crying and trembling after one of his speeches. When Tom walked over to him, the shaken man said, "You know what, Mr. Harken? Before hearing your story, I thought only black people couldn't read." Tom replied, "I know, I know. I'd always thought I was the only person in the world who couldn't read."

When Harken's autobiography, *The Millionaire's Secret,* was published in the late 1990s, about 40 million Americans could neither read nor write. Some are functionally illiterate, meaning they get by, as Tom did, with very low-level skills. They do just fine at their manual jobs but, primarily hide in the darkness of shame. They often resist promotions to positions that would require them to be literate.

No longer part of the statistic, Tom has dedicated his life to helping as many illiterate people as possible. "If my words reach just one struggling person," Harken said, "I want that person to be certain there's a little guy in Beaumont, Texas who knows how he feels and that help is within reach."

≈≈*Ripples*

Casey's Story by Tom Harken

Years ago, I was having problems, and the source of all of them came back to the fact that I couldn't read. A friend and mentor named Casey Southern removed a wrinkled, yellowed little poem from his wallet and asked me to read it. Casey told me his mother had given it to him many years ago, saying, "Every time you get down and out, go away to a quiet place and read this 'God's Minute.'" When he handed it to me, he said, "I don't know what the heck your problem is but I want to give you this because you need it. I don't know why, but I know you're worth saving." And he says, "Read this to me." And, of course, what he didn't know is I couldn't read. He didn't know my secret. "It would mean more if you would read it to me," I told him. That was 35 years ago, and this little verse has helped me many times. I hope it will help you, too.

GOD'S MINUTE

I have only just a minute,
only sixty seconds in it,
forced upon me—can't refuse it,
Didn't seek it, didn't choose it,
but it's up to me to use it,
I must suffer if I lose it,
give account if I abuse it,
Just a tiny little minute . . .
. . . but eternity is in it.

—Anonymous

Fast-forward to 9/11, when a young Iranian by the name of Sam was working at his new job at Goldman Sachs when the Towers were hit. He found himself running for his life just as the first tower started to collapse. Disoriented and panicked, he ran until he reached the water. He couldn't swim but believed his best chance was to jump into the river, 40 feet below. He could hardly see but he knew the water was there. Before climbing the rail, he reached into his wallet and pulled out a yellowed copy of "God's Minute," which he'd gotten from me some years ago when I gave a speech in New York. Just before he jumped, he paused to read it one last time when a friend found him and led him to safety—saving his life. He called me the next day to tell me about the miracle, and I realized that it does matter. One person can really make a difference, even unwittingly.

➤ProLiteracy Worldwide provides a network that helps adults and their families gain the literacy skills necessary to live and work effectively in society. In the United States, an estimated 40 million adults (21–23 percent of the American adult population) are functionally illiterate, unable to fulfill simple tasks such as reading maps and completing basic forms. But every day, over 113,000 volunteers are helping them out of the darkness.

Since 1995, donors have made possible the distribution of $1.9 million worth of books and literacy materials to 927 family literacy and English-as-a-second-language programs. Over 1,200 affiliates in all 50 states advocate for the needs of those who cannot read. This group relies mostly on generous individuals, corporations, and community groups for funding.

If you can read this, HELP! Contact:

ProLiteracy Worldwide
1320 Jamesville Ave., Syracuse, NY 13210
Phone: (888) 528-2224 I Fax: (315) 422-6369
E-mail: info@proliteracy.org I Web site: www.proliteracy.org

Part 2

Passionaries for Youth

INTRODUCTION BY DR. BETTIE B. YOUNGS

Dr. Bettie Youngs is the best-selling author of Gifts of the Heart: Stories that Celebrate Life's Defining Moments, Woman to Woman Wisdom: Inspiration for Real Life, *and the* Taste Berries for Teens *series.*

S OMEONE ONCE SAID that God hears the prayers of mothers first because their pleas almost always concern children. Certainly, children hold favor with God, and a mother's heart is always wrapped around her children—and all children. That is what makes this section so special: Those profiled herein have wrapped their hearts around the needs of children, becoming the answers to the prayers of so many. They strive to make the lives of our youth better. And succeed they do.

Children are perhaps the most vulnerable members of our society. They have little voice of their own and depend on us to meet their basic needs—from clothing and housing to nutrition and health care—for acceptance and love. The goal is for every child never to want for these things, and the passionaries in this chapter have all taken the initiative to make the lives of children safer, better, and brighter. From Mary Kay Beard reaching out to the children of prisoners to Nann Gonzalez rescuing abandoned Romanian infants;

from actor Hugh O'Brien's student leadership weekends for teens across the country to the miracles granted because of a young boy named Chris whose dreams evolved into the Make-A-Wish Foundation, thousands upon thousands of children's prayers are being answered. Their lives are getting better.

Can our own hearts be as generous as the passionaries profiled here? Can we, too, learn to see the needs of children through the eyes of our hearts? The answer within this chapter is a resounding "absolutely!" May these inspiring stories launch a wave of heavenward prayers and call our children's keepers to action.

10 : Mary Kay Beard
Angel Tree

BANK ROBBER, SAFECRACKER, MOST WANTED

THEY COULD HAVE BEEN Bonnie and Clyde. A striking, well-dressed woman accompanied by a neatly dressed man entered a small bank in the South and walked up to the lone teller. At first glance, the bank teller noticed only the flaming red hair. Then he saw the shotgun in his face.

"Just give me the money, Hon," the attractive redhead drawled, and the teller handed it over. This "Bonnie" was Mary Kay Mahaffey: bank robber and safecracker. Her photo hung in post offices, on the FBI's "Most Wanted" list.

Mary Kay was on the run for the next five years. First she was evading the police with her husband, Paul, who taught her everything she needed to know about guns, safes, and bank alarms. A couple of years into their life of crime, Paul ditched her and she teamed up with a couple of buddies to pull bank stickups and other thefts across the southern part of the United States. Eventually, the FBI caught up with her, and she was arrested in Peoria, Illinois.

Within a few days, the warrants began arriving at the jail. In addition to 11 federal indictments, 4 different states filed 35 charges against her, ranging from grand larceny to armed robbery. She was told she could spend between 75 and 180 years behind bars.

But she didn't. Released after serving fewer than six years, she married ex-prisoner Don Beard and went on to start a program that has touched the lives of more than 6 million children of prisoners over the next 25 years. How did she do it? How did Mary Kay go from America's Most Wanted to the founder of Angel Tree?

It actually started before her incarceration, when she grew up in a severely dysfunctional family situation. The middle child in a family of 9 children, Mary Kay had been hospitalized 13 times because of her abusive father by the time she was a teenager. A downward spiral of activities enveloped the ensuing years until she found herself sitting in a jail cell facing life in prison.

Mary Kay remembers thinking, "I wanted my life to be different, especially if I was going to spend the rest of it behind bars." Picking up a Bible, she stumbled upon verses her mother had taught her when she was a child. She read, "I will give you a new heart and put a new spirit in you; I will remove from you your heart of stone and give you a heart of flesh. I will cause you to walk in my statutes and keep my commandments" (Ezekiel 36:26–27). She said, "What that meant to me was God would empower me to do all he asked of me. With God doing all the work, I would not fail."

A new inner-peace replaced her bitterness; Mary Kay stopped fighting with other inmates and asked their forgiveness. Though her sentences totaled 180 years, she pleaded guilty to all the charges and, miraculously, she was sentenced to only 21 years in an Alabama prison. Even more amazingly, one by one, the other states began to drop their charges.

Mary Kay recalled, "In my sixth year at a halfway home, an officer appeared at the door with my release papers. It was a miracle. Even the parole board isn't real sure how it all happened. I never met with the parole board, yet this officer was standing there asking me to sign my release papers. To this day I believe my papers must have gotten mixed up with someone else's."

Unexpectedly released in April 1982 with no place to go and no money, she called Chuck Colson, who had touched her prison life through his Prison Fellowship (PF). He gave her a job, which she eventually parlayed to becoming the state director for the Alabama PF.

One of her first tasks was to come up with a Christmas project. She remembered the six Christmases she had spent behind bars. "Some Christian groups would come to the prison and they would bring little trial-size tubes of toothpaste, bars of soap, and bottles of shampoo. I saw the women bring the items back to their cells, organize the stuff, and trade with each other. Then they would divide up the items into small piles. I realized that each pile was for one of their children. They would gather bits of colored paper and wrap those items to give to their children as Christmas gifts. It was all they had. And I thought, just because she's a thief or a drug addict, or possibly even a murderer, doesn't mean she doesn't love her children.

✦ *"Children don't care about things if they know they are first of all loved."*

"The week before Christmas, the children would come to the prison for their annual visit with their mothers, and they would receive these little gifts. They would gleefully tear the wrapping off and barely glance at the gift but they would throw their arms around their mothers and say, 'Oh, Momma, thank you, thank you.' You see, children don't care about *things* if they know they are first of all loved."

That Christmas, Mary Kay went back to the same prison where she had spent six years and gathered the names and addresses of the inmates' children. Then she, her sister, and a handful of volunteers put up Christmas trees at two Alabama malls, one in Montgomery, and the other in Birmingham.

"We made paper angels—red for girls and green for boys—and on each angel we wrote the name and age of a child and what they would like. The gifts were to come wrapped with a tag from their incarcerated parent. Then we put these paper angels on the tree . . . an Angel Tree! That's how we got the name. I had no idea what God would do with that project. But within six days we were out of names, and I had to go back to the prison to get more. At the end of that first Angel Tree project in 1982, 556 children had received up to four different gifts each," Mary Kay shared.

Then Mary Kay saw something else happen. "In January, all of my Bible study groups at that prison doubled or tripled. The newcomers were the inmates whose children had received gifts. They said, 'Anyone who would give my child gifts from me for Christmas is someone special, so I decided to come and listen to this Bible study.'"

She also saw other results, like the reuniting of family ties as children who had not heard from Dad or Mom for a while received gifts from them. "Angel Tree was not my project; it wasn't even my idea. It was God's idea. He just allowed me to be the instrument that he used to plant the seed."

The following year, her program branched out to 12 states and soon developed into a nationwide church-based program. Since Mary Kay first thought about those little tubes of toothpaste while she was in prison, Angel Tree has exploded. In 2004, more than 550,000 children received gifts from generous volunteers, bringing the cumulative total to more than 6.5 million children touched by angels.

Angel Tree continues to "branch" out in new directions as well. In 2003, they started Christian summer camps that a growing number of Angel Tree children can attend, structured just for them and their special needs. And in 2004, churches began opening their doors to provide a quiet environment where Angel Tree children can do their homework. Mentoring programs give these children adult guidance from church members who care and volunteer their time.

When the now silver-haired Mary Kay Beard visits women in prison, she connects with them in a way that few can. She's one of their own and she cares for their kids. They also see that a woman in their position can still change the world. When she sees how Angel Tree has flourished in just 25 years, Mary Kay smiles. "I am both awed and humbled to have been part of something so enormously effective. Being there at the beginning—I consider it one of the highest privileges of my life."

≈≈*Ripples*

José and Mayra Abreu

It was Christmas Eve 1989, and Mayra Abreu had no gifts for her three children. Her husband was in prison and she had spent all of her money on cocaine. "I was such a mess," she thinks back, starting to weep. "I left my kids alone at night and went out on the streets getting drugs."

As she was bundling up the kids to take them to her sister's home, a UPS driver delivered a package for the children. Used to empty Christmases, they tore into the packages with delight. There was a doll for their daughter Mencia, a model space shuttle for Alex, and an animal farm for Ricky. The card read simply, "From Daddy." But Daddy was in prison, thought Mayra. How could he have bought gifts for our children? Then she remembered: José had signed the children up for the Angel Tree a couple of months earlier.

"When they opened that box and I saw the joy in my children's faces, I felt such conviction and guilt," Mayra remembers. "I fell on my knees and cried out to the Lord for forgiveness, asking him to take away my craving for drugs. And when I got up, I felt such relief."

Mayra and José had both come from the Dominican Republic to New York as teens. By the time they married, they were both heavily addicted to drugs. When their children had arrived, José was supporting his young family by breaking into homes. After each crime he'd say a little prayer: "Lord Jesus, have mercy on me, a poor sinner." José says, "My kids got used to having things today and not having them tomorrow." Furniture disappeared; food stamps bought no food, but were traded for drugs. Unable to pay rent, the family wandered from shelters to welfare hotels.

José was caught and convicted for one of his break-ins. In prison, he was touched by a counselor from Prison Fellowship, turned his life over to Christ, and signed up his children for Angel Tree. When he returned home in 1990, life changed for the Abreu family. "We did fun things together we had never done before," says Mayra. "We went to the beach, the park, and camping." And, to the children's relief, there were no more addicted friends, no more drug dealers, no more hiding and lying.

While visiting Rikers Island Prison in 1993, the Abreus were shocked to see that infants allowed to live with their birth mothers for the first year of life were taken away at age one. Moved by one mother's plea, they began arranging to personally take legal custody of some of these children, integrating them into the Abreu family until their mothers were released and allowed to reclaim their children. In 10 years, 12 children have spent time in their household—some short-term, others for many years—including Kiano, a one-year-old whose cerebral palsy was a special challenge.

Recently, José faced deportation because of his past drug conviction. With a courtroom packed with grateful PF friends and supporters, the judge granted him permanent legal status. Today, José conducts various PF seminars—including one called Free At Last where he uses his past experiences to help transform the lives of drug addicts. Mayra also works as a PF staff member, coordinating the entire New York City Angel Tree effort. Even their oldest daughter, Mencia, contributes by recruiting students from her high school to help purchase gifts for prisoners' children.

The Abreus faced their latest challenge when José's liver gave out after decades of drug use and alcohol binges and he needed an organ transplant. Mayra was a match and they both underwent surgery in April 2000. Part of Mayra's healthy liver was transplanted into José. Recently, doctors cleared him for a normal life. Mayra, whose own liver quickly regenerated to normal size, had saved his life. "A part of me is forever with him," she smiles.

➤In 2004, a million gifts were sent by volunteers to 535,000 children of prisoners, all sent in the name of their incarcerated parent. This brought the cumulative total to more than 6.5 million children touched by Angel Tree since Mary Kay Beard founded it in 1982. This program is now in 45 countries internationally. Angel Tree branched out in 2003 to also develop summer camps and after-school, church-based mentoring, both structured specifically for these special children.

Reach out in love to the more than two million children whose mothers and fathers are now in prisons, and help break the cycle where many of these children grow up to repeat the pattern and become prisoners. Angel Tree is making a difference.

Be a living angel. Contact:

ANGEL TREE PROJECT
P. O. Box 1550, Merrifield, VA 22116
Phone: (800) 55-ANGEL I Fax: (703) 456-4008
E-mail: webmaster@angeltree.org I Web site: www.angeltree.org

11: Chris and Friends
Make-A-Wish Foundation

SOME DREAMS CAN COME TRUE

BECAUSE HE WAS a very sick little boy, Chris Greicius's dream meant more to him than anything. In 1977, the four-and-a-half-year-old was diagnosed with leukemia and given three years to live. In all his short life, Chris wanted nothing more than to be a police officer. He was awestruck by the officers' strength and power. Becoming one of "the good guys" was his heart's desire. He couldn't have known that this simple dream would serve as the inspiration for the largest wish-granting organization in the world.

During his illness, Chris and his mother, Linda Pauling, had been introduced through mutual friends to U.S. Customs Officer Tommy Austin. An instant bond was formed upon their first meeting in Phoenix, Arizona, when little Chris looked up at Tommy and displayed his law-enforcement skills saying, "Freeze, I'm a cop!" Tommy had promised Chris a ride in a police helicopter in the spring of 1980 when Chris's condition worsened. Tommy went into action, contacting Officer Ron Cox at the Arizona Department of Public Safety (DPS) about making his young friend's wish come true. Ron was more than eager to oblige, recruiting other DPS members to create an even more magical experience for Chris.

April 29, 1980, was the special day. Chris called Tommy early in the morning just to make sure it was really going to happen. "You haven't forgotten? I've been up for an hour and I'm ready to go," he said excitedly. The helicopter picked up Chris and escorted him around the city of Phoenix before landing at the DPS. Then three squad cars and a motorcycle driven by another policeman, Officer Frank Shankwitz, welcomed their new recruit. The seven-year-old bundle of energy immediately greeted Frank and admired his "neato" motorcycle.

Chris' new law-enforcement buddies nicknamed him "Bubble Gum

Trooper" because he didn't go anywhere without his trusty pack of bubble gum. He even shared a piece of gum with the DPS director. To top off what had already been an incredible day for this little dynamo, he was sworn in as the first ever, and only, honorary state trooper in Arizona state history.

The following day, Officer Ron contacted his department's supplier, John's Uniform, about making a little outfit for Chris. The company was so moved by the request that the owner and two seamstresses worked on it all night. On May 1, several officers presented Chris with an official Arizona Highway Patrol uniform, likely the smallest ever made. But it was still missing one thing.

The motorcycle wings that Frank wore on his uniform had fascinated Chris, but Frank explained that they could only be presented to those who had passed a motorcycle proficiency test. So a handful of resourceful officers set up a special mini-course where Chris could take his own test on a battery-operated motorcycle. Needless to say, Chris passed with flying colors.

Just three days later, Chris was back in the hospital, but he had his uniform hung in the window and his motorcycle helmet and "Smokey Bear" hat placed on the dresser, a proud and happy junior patrolman. In the hospital, Frank surprised Chris by presenting him with the honor he had earned: his own, brand-new set of motorcycle wings. Chris's smile lit up the hospital room—his lifelong dream was now complete. The following day, Chris Greicius passed away.

Chris was to be buried in Kewanee, Illinois. DPS spokesman Allen Schmidt promised that two Arizona officers would make the trip to Illinois to represent the department in saying good-bye to their young fellow officer. Scott Stahl, a DPS officer and a native of Joliet, Illinois, joined Frank on the bittersweet mission. During the flight back to Arizona, Frank and Scott began to reminisce about how happy it had made Chris to see his wishes actually come true. They recalled how the entire experience turned some of Chris and Linda's pain into smiles and laughter. Maybe if one boy's wish could be granted, the same could be done for other children. They concluded, "There must be other children out there."

Upon returning to Phoenix, the two officers approached some of the people who had been integral in making Chris's wish come true and presented the idea of granting wishes to other sick children. Linda and others quickly endorsed the plan, and The Chris Greicius Make-A-Wish Memorial was born. It would later grow into the organization known today as the Make-A-Wish Foundation.

Of course, the founders of the Make-A-Wish Foundation had families and jobs (some had more than one job) outside of their new endeavor. Their determination to honor Chris took time, but it never wavered, and this goal was enhanced by their involvement in the community. When he was off-duty, Frank Shankwitz provided undercover security. One evening while Frank was making his rounds at a grocery store, the manager asked him how much money had been raised so far. At that point, the fund they had set up didn't even have a bank account. When the manager learned this, he pulled 15 dollars from his wallet and suggested the organization open an account at the bank branch in his store. That was the foundation's first donation.

Later that year in November 1980, the Make-A-Wish Foundation received its tax-exempt status as a nonprofit organization, and fundraising began in earnest. Phoenix newspapers and television stations interviewed members of the founding board, introducing the community to the new nonprofit organization and broadcasting their needs. Generous people all over the state of Arizona stepped forward to offer their support. By March 1981, more than $2,000 had been raised—enough to grant another child's wish.

The first formal "wish child"

Now officially a foundling nonprofit, the small group of new friends learned about Frank "Bopsy" Salazar, a quiet, thoughtful, and religious seven-year-old. Two years earlier, Bopsy had been diagnosed with leukemia, but he did not allow the illness to deter his joy for life.

At its inception, the philosophy of the Make-A-Wish Foundation was to grant one wish for a child facing a terminal illness, but Bopsy couldn't make up his mind. He had three wishes: be a fireman, ride in a hot-air balloon, and go to Disneyland. Physically, Bopsy's health was deteriorating rapidly. So the group determined that he would receive all three wishes. One phone call to the Phoenix Fire Department and the wheels were in motion to make the first wish come true.

Bopsy had an experience truly befitting a firefighter. A full uniform was custom-made just for him, complete with a yellow coat and helmet, and he was made the first honorary fireman in Phoenix history. On his wish day, Bopsy scrambled around the back of Engine Nine's ladder truck, pressing on the horn. After the ride, he doused a few cars with water from a 75-pound hose. The day was complete when Bopsy was pinned with an official firefighter's badge. Now Bopsy was a full-fledged fireman—but his wish experience was far from over. With another phone call to hot-air balloon pilots Chris and Bob Pearce, Bopsy's second wish of floating high over Phoenix with his mom, Octaviana, was also granted.

Only one wish remained. Frank Shankwitz contacted representatives at Disneyland and informed them of Bopsy's situation. The park agreed to create a special day for Bopsy and his family, complete with private tours, meals, gifts, and other amenities. This marked the beginning of the Make-A-Wish Foundation's "magical" relationship with Disney. Now 25 years later, visiting a Disney theme park remains the most requested wish, and The Walt Disney Company continues to be one of the foundation's largest supporters.

Not long after returning from his wish-granting trip to California, Bopsy's condition worsened, and he had to return to the hospital. Asleep in his third-floor room, he was awakened by the sound of someone suddenly knocking on his window. It opened wide and in came five of his fellow Phoenix firemen, crawling in one by one. His "colleagues" had parked their ladder truck below and climbed up to his window to surprise him. Bopsy shared laughs with his buddies and drifted back to sleep with a smile on his face. Later that evening, Bopsy passed away—fresh with the memories of all three of his wishes being granted.

In the year that followed, the fledgling Make-A-Wish Foundation had granted wishes to eight more children in the Phoenix area when it caught the attention of *NBC Magazine,* a nationally broadcast newsmagazine program. Their coverage began with Tommy Austin and Chris's mom, Linda, sharing the story of how the little Bubble Gum Trooper's dreams came true. The reporter highlighted the beginnings of the foundation's dreams and told the stories of how the lives of the other children and their families had been moved.

Millions of people saw the profound impact of granting a sick child's wish. Phone calls poured into the NBC offices asking for more information about the Make-A-Wish Foundation and how individuals could start a chapter in their area. People donated thousands of dollars to help grant more wishes. On May 13, 1983, a year after NBC's story, the Make-A-Wish Foundation was officially incorporated with six chapters operating around the country. By the following year, 22 more had been established.

In 2005, 25 years after Chris donned his child-sized police uniform, the Make-A-Wish Foundation granted its 135,000th wish. Today, nearly 25,000 volunteers have become involved wish-granters nationwide, and the foundation grants a wish every 41 minutes to a courageous child with a life-threatening medical condition.

You give children the will to push forward. You give them something to look forward to and cherish. I don't think there is anything greater for a child who suffers for life and fights to live than for angels to grant wishes. — Darlene, "Wish mom"

≈≈*Ripples*

From a Wish: Dale Earnhardt

THE MOTOR-SPORTS WORLD lost a legend on February 18, 2001. With Dale Earnhardt's tragic passing, his family, friends, and millions of fans lost a hero. His aggressive, take-no-prisoners approach to racing on the NASCAR circuit earned him sole possession of a standard-bearing nickname, "The Intimidator." But to the scores of Make-A-Wish children whom he personally befriended over the years, Earnhardt was anything but a menacing presence.

"Our wish was that children were truly privileged to experience someone far more impressive than Dale Earnhardt, the racing champion, and that was Dale Earnhardt, the man," said Paula Van Ness, then president and CEO for the Make-A-Wish Foundation. "And he helped so many children. They got to share in the life of an engaging, selfless person whose caring for others knew no bounds."

But to Mr. Earnhardt, the lasting memories were clearly a two-way street. This was perhaps most evident in 1998 at Daytona International Speedway, where amid frenetic preparations for a race he had never won, he took time out to meet a Wish child named Wessa. "This little girl was tiny, but she had a pretty voice," Mr. Earnhardt told The Associated Press soon after. "She gave me this penny and said, 'I rubbed this penny, and this is going to win you the Daytona 500.' I glued that penny to my dash-board."

The next day, Mr. Earnhardt broke his 0-for-19 string in stock-car racing's showcase event while ending a 59-race Winston Cup losing streak. As required of all Daytona 500 winners, Earnhardt turned over his winning black No. 3 Chevrolet Monte Carlo to Daytona USA, the motorsports attraction at Daytona International Speedway, where the car was to be displayed until the next year's winning car was wheeled in. The agreement called for the car to remain exactly as it was when the driver climbed out in Victory Circle.

Ever the competitor, Mr. Earnhardt was determined to fight for one exception to that rule. He wanted his lucky penny back. It was the penny that brought together an unlikely pair—Dale Earnhardt the racing legend, and Wessa, the adoring fan whose good-luck charm helped him break through 19 years of bad luck to make his own wish come true.

Mr. Earnhardt was always admired for his winning spirit, but the Make-A-Wish Foundation will forever remember him for something more important—his giving spirit. "He was a gentleman, but a truly gentle man toward the children," said Dottie Rollins, then director of NASCAR wishes for the Make-A-Wish Foundation. "He was and always will be remembered as what NASCAR racing is all about. When he met the children, he went to the extremes, doing all the little things to make them feel special. He was as focused on the children as he was on his racing."

►The Make-A-Wish Foundation grants the wishes of children with life-threatening medical conditions to enrich the human experience with hope, strength, and joy. Born in 1980 when a group of caring individuals helped a seven-year-old boy named Chris fulfill his dream of becoming a police officer, the foundation is now the largest wish-granting charity in the world, with 71 chapters in the United States and its territories. Serving every U.S. community, the Make-A-Wish Foundation grants more than 12,500 wishes a year and has granted more than 135,000 wishes nationwide since its inception.

Any child between the ages of 2 and 18 who has a life-threatening medical condition, such as a progressive, degenerative, or malignant medical condition that has placed the child's life in jeopardy, may be eligible for a wish. A child can be referred to the Foundation by a medical professional, a parent, or legal guardian, or children can even refer themselves. Generous donors and nearly 25,000 volunteers help these courageous kids "share the power of a wish."

Make dreams come true. Contact:

MAKE-A-WISH FOUNDATION
3550 North Central Avenue, Suite 300, Phoenix, AZ 85012-2127
Phone: (800) 722-WISH (9474) I Fax: (602) 279-0855
E-mail: mawfa@wish.org I Web site: www.wish.org

12: Nann Gonzalez
ROCK Ministries

LOVE AND LOSS IN ROMANIA

FALLING IN LOVE is an occupational hazard for Nannette Gonzalez. So are lice, scabies, HIV, hepatitis, and the psychological burnout that comes from helping children with lots of problems and precious little hope. In the seven years that this California native has spent nurturing abandoned babies in Romania and helping them find homes, she has been spared most of these liabilities—except for the problem of love and its attendant loss.

His name was Carlos and he even looked like her. Seven months old, he weighed only 10 pounds when his mother brought him to Victor Gomoiu Hospital in Bucharest. He had acute bronchitis, scabies, showed signs of neglect, and was severely malnourished. While most mothers would have stayed close by, Carlos' mother left and didn't check back for almost three months. During that time, Gonzalez nursed the frail infant back to health, helped him learn to sit up, and loved him as if he were her own. Then, when the mother returned, Nann handed little Carlos back and prayed.

In Romania, baby abandonment is not only legal—it's also state-assisted. Carlos is just one of the hundreds of infants and children a year who come to ROCK (Romania Outreach to Christ's Kids) Ministries, a non-profit organization Gonzalez founded in 1997. Based in a 40-bed ward of a state-run hospital, ROCK's mission is to get kids out of the institution and to reunite them with their families. That failing, they look to foster care or to permanent homes through adoption.

To pull all this off, Gonzalez, 44, single, and childless, must juggle the hats of social worker, detective, nurse, and spokesperson. But mostly she considers herself a missionary. "At first I couldn't understand any woman just giving up her baby," Nann shares, "but then I've never been that poor." She now understands that some mothers leave their babies out of genuine concern. They think if their baby has food and shelter that they'll be better off, because that's more than they can afford to give.

Mariana Clichici, for example, had three kids and no husband. She could provide for her family as long as her grandmother cared for the children while she worked. When her grandmother died, Mariana had to leave the children in a state-run orphanage, thankfully one that ROCK worked with. To put the family back together, ROCK bought Clichigi a home for $5,000 and gives her a stipend of $100 a month. That kind of money goes far in Romania, where the average family makes do on the U.S. equivalent of $110 a month.

So many children are abandoned in Romania for three distinct reasons: poverty, politics, and precedent. After the 1989 ousting and subsequent execution of dictator Nicolae Ceausescu that ended his brutal 24-year regime, Western media uncovered the horrific fact that more than 200,000 children were living in orphanages not much better than concentration camps. Many were the product of Ceausescu's maniacal goal of increasing the population to 30 million by the end of the century.

To that end, Ceausescu outlawed birth control and abortions and required every woman of childbearing age to have five children or be heavily taxed. Couples who had kids they didn't want or couldn't afford simply dropped them at the local hospital—no questions asked. Many of those castoffs were seriously ill and treatment was practically nonexistent. Though this mandatory birth policy and communism officially ended in 1989, poverty lingers along with the perverse mentality of recklessly bearing and discarding children. Until the government recently imposed restrictions, freed Romania had been an international magnet for orphan adoptions.

Because many abandoned children have either been adopted or have grown up, Gonzalez estimates that close to 80,000 abandoned children remain in institutions while 100,000 are street children. This is still a daunting number, but one that Nann and her staff work to reduce, one child at a time. Of the thousand or so kids who've come through ROCK, she estimates that 50 percent have been successfully reunited with their families, 30 percent have gone into a Romanian foster home, and 15 percent have been adopted. Some don't survive.

In many ways, Nann's strict upbringing prepared her for the grueling role she would choose as an adult. A third-generation Mexican, born and raised in Bakersfield, California, she attended missionary school, taking classes in the Bible and self-denial. Both have come in handy for the frustrating, pared-down life she lives in Romania—a country where hot water is a luxury, appliances are scarcer than thousand-dollar bills, and, as she puts it, "everything takes twice as long, except having babies."

She learned of the orphan problem firsthand in 1994 while doing missionary work in Seville, Spain. She was invited to visit a Romanian hospital to hold babies in desperate need of attention and human touch. "They didn't even cry," she recalls. "They'd learned how useless crying was since no one ever responded." Overworked nurses came by just three brief times a day to prop bottles in their mouths and change diapers. Some babies never left their cribs. Others were never held upright, so that at 14 months old they couldn't sit up, let alone walk.

"These kids weren't orphans," Nann said, the outrage still fresh in her voice. "Orphans don't have parents. These kids were abandoned. They could be in the institution from birth to 18 when the government tells them to fend for themselves and they become prostitutes or thieves or beggars."

In 1997, three years after her first visit to Romania, Nann founded ROCK. Her identical twin sister, Annette Gonzalez Elrod, handled logistical matters stateside while Gonzalez worked in the orphanages. Today ROCK headquarters is located in San Diego and has a staff of 30 Romanians, 5 American missionaries, and 2 more Americans working out of San Diego. "A lot of generous people in the United States make this possible," says Gonzalez. "Last year we received funding of $325,000. Operating expenses run up to $20,000 a month, with the rest going to the child-family reunification effort."

Several months after Carlos left the hospital, ROCK staff made a random home visit. They found Carlos with cigarette burns on his back and suffering other signs of neglect. At 20 months old, he wasn't even walking. Asking the mother if they could help, she at first resisted. Eventually she agreed to let them put her son in foster care, and ROCK found a good home for Carlos. Today he's thriving again.

"The mother didn't even cry when they took him away," said Gonzalez, who herself is tearful as she relives the story. "I wish I could adopt him." It's not the first time she's felt so attached.

Meanwhile, Nann has become a mother to hundreds. Working at the government level, she strives to make it more difficult for Romanian women to abandon their babies, as well as to improve the Department of Child Protection.

And she has an even bigger vision: Bedrock Falls Ranch. Nann already has the land: 10 acres, 25 miles outside Bucharest, which she bought for $2,000—and the plans are drawn. "It will be a haven outside the hospital for kids whose parents won't take them home, but won't give them up for adoption either," she gushes. "I want to build a place of hope where these children can dream. Romanians don't dream. They think they're stuck."

Though all Nann Gonzalez has is a rolled-up plan, a deed for some undeveloped land, and a heap of faith, her vision for Bedrock Falls is steadfast and full of promise . . . like a good parent for a child who has a real future.

➤Founded by Nann Gonzalez in 1997, ROCK Ministries cares for abandoned and orphaned Romanian children. Volunteers and staff train, employ, and disciple local individuals, who bathe, feed, clothe, and hold these infants. Just being held and exercised stimulates these discarded children physically, emotionally, and spiritually. ROCK also works to reunite and support families, facilitates foster care, arranges medical treatment for the severely ill babies, and assists in adoptions when Romanian bureaucrats allow. They work on a shoestring budget and lots of prayers. Romania has 180,000 abandoned children.

Volunteer in Romania or stateside or donate: you'll ROCK!

ROCK MINISTRIES
P.O. Box 1651, Rialto, CA 92377
Phone: (909) 877-3323
Web site: www.rockministries.org

13: Brandon Keefe
BookEnds

A LITTLE BOY WITH AN INFECTIOUS SPIRIT

BRANDON KEEFE never thought that staying home with the sniffles could be a positive thing until a cold kept him home one day in 1993. An idea came to this eight-year-old that day that would change his life and turn his cold into a "positive infection" that spread to countless other kids. This story is about the infectious rippling of a good idea, and of the power of a determined child.

Not wanting to leave her sick son alone, Robin Keefe brought Brandon with her to Hollygrove Children's Home, a residential treatment center for abused and neglected children where she served as president. She bundled sniffling Brandon in a corner and convened a meeting about how to build a library for the more than 60 kids who lived at the 100-year-old Los Angeles children's orphanage. Throughout the discussions, various problems were raised: Books were too expensive, volunteers were scarce, and the budget couldn't be stretched any further. Brandon played with his handheld videogame. "I really wasn't paying much attention, but I heard them talk about needing books for the library."

The next day, providence stepped in. Brandon's third-grade teacher spoke to her class about the value of community service—that even eight-year-olds could reach out and make a big difference. Then she asked if anyone had suggestions on what to do. Brandon's hand shot up. "Hey, my mom's orphanage needs books. Why don't we run a book drive? Everybody has books on their shelves they've outgrown. Why don't we give the ones we've already read to kids who need them?"

The other children got excited about his idea, and over the next few months Brandon organized a school-wide book drive. With the assistance of friends, teachers, and school administrators, he distributed flyers, spoke to every class in the school, and gave speeches at morning assemblies.

Soon students at Willow Elementary School had amassed 847 new and slightly used books. The collection included every type of children's books imaginable: biographies, mysteries, science fiction, fairy tales, picture books, and bestseller series ranging from *Goosebumps* to *Nancy Drew*.

On the last day of school before winter vacation, Brandon waited eagerly for his mom. As Robin drove up, a grinning Brandon stood on the sidewalk surrounded by dozens of boxes of books and exclaimed, "Merry Christmas, Mom!"

✦ *"I think a lot of people are blind to need because there is so much out there. But if you're able to show them simple ways to help, they are more than willing."*

"That was one of the best days of my life," said Robin. She had no idea of what her son had been up to, or that he was so good at keeping a secret.

Even gathering 847 books wasn't enough to stop young Brandon—he had bigger plans.

Now with his mother as a partner, Brandon saw his idea transformed into a formal nonprofit organization called BookEnds: Student-to-Student Solutions for Literacy. He and his classmates continued to hold book drives, and within two years had gathered 2,500 new and used titles for Hollygrove's library. As BookEnds thrived, Brandon moved to a large, private middle school where they held a new drive that collected more than 7,000 books in a single week.

Community groups joined in the excitement at Hollygrove and helped convert an old meeting room into a new library. They raised money for shelving and catalogued the books. Even a dilapidated old library cart was donated and restored. Every night, volunteers would fill up the cart and make the rounds so that the children living in the orphanage would be tucked into bed with something good to read.

"We knew we were on to something," Brandon said. "There was such a great need in Southern California for books, the program just kind of erupted." Since that fateful day when Brandon stayed home with a cold, BookEnds has expanded. In 2003, volunteers collected for more than 40 libraries in Los Angeles–area schools and community homes. Still run by Brandon and Robin—but with the vital help of over 101,000 student volunteers—BookEnds has accumulated more than 750,000 books that have enriched the lives of at least 100,000 children.

More than anything, Brandon's efforts showed him that helping the less fortunate could be as simple as common sense. With BookEnds, making a difference didn't require moving mountains—people just donated their old books that were still in good condition instead of throwing them away, thus giving the books a new life. "Most people hesitate to throw them away because they're expensive and treasured," Brandon said. "We offer a way for people to get rid of their extra books without the guilt of trashing them . . . and at the same time help children."

Throughout his teens, Brandon continued to spend much of his free time speaking at local elementary and middle schools, drumming up support for more book drives. "I think a lot of people are blind to need because there is so much out there," he said. "But if you're able to show them simple ways to help, they are more than willing."

Brandon Keefe's BookEnds story has been featured on the Amazing Kids Web site, which also gives touching accounts of thousands of other remarkable kids who are making the world a better place to live. To Brandon, the most amazing part of BookEnds is that children get excited about doing something to help others. "It's neat how you can empower kids," he said. "As corny as it sounds—one person *can* make a difference. But not one person by themselves . . . one person who connects with other people who want to get involved."

≈*Ripples*

THE RODSTEIN FAMILY

As a friend of Brandon's, Josh Rodstein literally grew up with BookEnds and went on to encourage the involvement of his entire family. At Taft High School, where he was a student, Josh organized drives that brought in more than 3,000 books. Upon his graduation, he asked his younger brother, Joel, to continue his work for the BookEnds drives while Josh went off to college to duplicate the idea there. At the University of California at Irvine (UCI), Josh partnered with the UCI Volunteer Center to support their college book drive pilot program. More than 3,500 books were collected throughout the campus and distributed to youth organizations and homeless shelters in Orange County.

Laurie, Josh's mom and a dynamic fifth-grade teacher in Woodland Hills, decided to join Josh's commitment to BookEnds by encouraging her students to organize their own drives. The first year, a total of 1,400 books were collected, increasing to 2,200 books the second year. Laurie's students even took on new initiatives like selling snacks after school, raising enough to donate $500 to Fullbright Elementary School for additional books and $200 to purchase shelving for the Delano Teen Club.

Becky, Josh's younger sister, chose BookEnds for her Girl Scouts' Gold Award project, enlisting the San Fernando Valley scouts to help collect 10,000 books—and ended up collecting over 20,000 to hand out to those in need. For her bat mitzvah service project she organized a book drive collecting over 400 books. Becky even requested that guests donate books at her bat mitzvah celebration instead of bringing gifts. She gave each of the attendees a chance to participate in her dreams—inspired by Josh, Brandon, and thousands of volunteers—to spread the joy of reading.

➤In national reading tests, California fourth-graders ranked second to last; 2 out of 3 third-graders cannot read at their grade level. In Los Angeles, the ratio of books to students is 5 to 1 (3 to 1 if outdated and damaged books are purged). The national average ratio of books to students is 18 to 1.

The disparity in reading resources between the best- and worst-funded schools has contributed to the "rich get richer and the poor get poorer" cycle. Children who need the most help in reading—the poor and immigrants—have the least access to books.

To get involved, check out:

BookEnds
6520 Platt Avenue #331, West Hills, CA 91307
Phone: (818) 716-1198 | Fax: (818) 716-1126
E-mail: info@bookends.org | Web site: www.bookends.org
Check out other amazing stories at www.amazingkids.com

14: Wendy Kopp
Teach For America

EACH ONE, TEACH ONE

SENIOR YEAR AT PRINCETON brought a fresh urgency to Wendy Kopp's thoughts about her future. The year was 1988 and Wendy was part of what the world had dubbed "a selfish generation." Yet she found herself and her peers searching for a way to make a real difference in the world. Hers was the age-old question that often haunts young adults: "What am I going to do with the rest of my life?"

While working on her thesis for a senior paper, Wendy happened upon an idea that would put her in the middle of an incredible movement. "The dream was that every child growing up in this nation would have access to a high-quality education," she reflects. Her concept was to create a corps of top-notch, recent college graduates who would commit two years to teach in urban and rural public schools in low-income areas. Called Teach For America (TFA), this corps would mobilize some of the most passionate, dedicated members of her generation to change the fact that where a child is born in the United States largely determines his or her chances in life. Wendy's teacher at Princeton gave her thesis an "A."

"The more I thought about it, the more convinced I became that this simple idea was potentially very powerful," Wendy said. So, instead of going off to a two-year corporate-training program, Wendy began her own program: recruiting a corps of bright, civic-minded college graduates who would teach for two years in America's most challenged public schools. "If recent college graduates devoted two years to teaching in low-income public schools, they could take the insight and commitment gained through that experience and go on to become a powerful force of leaders dedicated to improving opportunities for all children in this nation."

Wendy was 21, a few months shy of graduation, with little money and no experience teaching or running a nonprofit organization when she embarked upon the path of creating Teach For America. Her dream: to recruit teachers for America's most challenged public schools. Wendy asked everyone she could think of for help, but found little guidance. She even wrote to President George H.W. Bush, suggesting that *he* start a teacher corps. The only response from the White House was a curious letter rejecting her application for a job. "It must have slipped into the wrong stack," she muses.

But Wendy didn't back down from her dream. She began to live and breathe the idea that one day all children would have the opportunity to attain an excellent education. Within her plan, her projected startup budget was $2.5 million. That kind of money didn't come to a young, inexperienced student without a lot of legwork—and begging. She worked day and night to find companies to fund her idea. She scrolled through books with the names of CEOs and started writing and calling them, one by one. She secured meetings with a half-dozen powerful executives, and some agreed to give her money.

Wendy's tenacity even led to a meeting with future presidential candidate Ross Perot, whom she was sure would jump at the chance to help fund her idea. Both were from Dallas, and Perot had said publicly that he was interested in education reform. She smiles when she talks about the day she walked into his office, sat down, and refused to leave without a financial commitment.

More than a few of those potential donors told her to get more experience, hire a seasoned leader, and get her head out of the clouds. But her persistence paid off, as did her grassroots recruiting campaign: More than 2,500 soon-to-be-graduates applied to join Teach For America that first year after she posted photocopied flyers at top college campuses. She and a few other staff members chose 500 of those applicants. With the help of more than two million dollars in corporate donations, Teach For America got off the ground, placing its first charter corps members in six different urban cities throughout the nation in 1990.

"The idea that all kids in our country should have the chance to obtain an excellent education inspired college grads to say, 'I want to be a part of that.' It magnetized people in the funding community to help get us off the ground . . . and motivated people in school districts to say, 'We want to hire these people.'"

Just one example from the 3,100 TFA corps actively teaching in 2003 is Bill DuFour, a pre-law, 4.0 grade point average, USC graduate who has postponed law school to teach in the inner city of Los Angeles. As of 2003, more than 12,000 outstanding college graduates have joined Teach For America and have been placed in schools in some of our nation's lowest-income urban communities. They have directly impacted the lives of 1.75 million students and form a growing force of civic leaders committed to ensuring that our nation lives up to its ideal of opportunity for all.

Many of these corps members stay in teaching even after their two-year obligation is complete. Others go on to pursue positions in school administration and education policy. Equally important, a great number of Teach For America alumni work in fields as varied as law and medicine and apply the insight they gained to effect the systemic change necessary to realize educational equity. They've developed a dedication to helping children and making change.

Teach For America draws thousands of eager applicants from schools such as Yale, Northwestern, Spelman, and UC Berkeley. By 2003, the group had corps members teaching in 20 communities across the country, including Atlanta, Baltimore, Chicago, Los Angeles, Washington, D.C., New York City, St. Louis, Detroit, the Mississippi Delta, Texas, and rural North Carolina.

Under the eye of Teach For America corps members, students in some of the nation's lowest-income communities are achieving at the same academic level as students in affluent suburbs. "We see in various schools across the country that it can be done, that kids have the potential, and when given the opportunity they deserve, they *can* and *do* achieve at high levels," says Wendy, as her dreams ripple through classrooms.

The waves come as each one teaches one, and the impact becomes even stronger. Despite her program's amazing success and growth, Wendy still feels she has a long way to go before achieving her ultimate goal. Her organization wants to expand to more cities and reach more classrooms so that every student in America has access to excellent, dedicated teachers.

Since 1990, Teach For America has not only established itself as a powerful corps of first-class teachers, but has also grown into a national movement with Wendy still leading the charge. Now married with three young children and the discipline to run every day, she devotes her amazing energy to making her dreams a reality. "Clearly, much more needs to get done, and we really believe we can get there," Wendy said. "I am convinced that we will see the day when all kids in our country have the chance to obtain an excellent education."

≈≈*Ripples*

KIPP's DAVE LEVIN AND MIKE FEINBERG

AFTER COMPLETING their Teach For America commitment, corps members Dave Levin and Mike Feinberg saw the children they loved and worked with go off to a less-than-mediocre middle school. They were determined that "their" kids would have a chance at excellence at the next level. So the two teachers decided to start their own schools. In 1994, Mike and Dave founded the Knowledge Is Power Program (KIPP) for 50 fifth-graders in inner-city Houston, Texas. Their students' academic success and interest in learning inspired Dave and Mike to expand the program beyond one classroom.

Mike and Dave launched the first two KIPP Academies in Houston and in the Bronx, New York. Based on their basic principles known as the Five Pillars—high expectations, choice and commitment, more time, power to lead, and focus on results—they have gained national recognition for outstanding academic achievement. Since the doors opened in 1995, 99 percent of KIPP alumni matriculate into top high schools and have earned more than $18 million in scholarships. In fall 2003, the first class of KIPP alumni started college.

In 2000, Doris and Donald Fisher, founders of The Gap, Inc., formed a unique partnership with Dave and Mike to replicate the success of the first two schools. Together they expanded KIPP into a national, nonprofit organization that recruits, trains, and supports outstanding educators to open and run high-performing college-prep public schools. In 2001, graduates of KIPP Leadership Program launched 3 schools, 10 in 2002, and another 17 in 2003. Current data shows these programs are making a positive impact on the lives of thousands of students in educationally underserved communities around the country. Their family of academies has grown into 32 top-performing public schools, serving over 4,000 students in 13 states and the District of Columbia. And the ripples go out from Mike and Dave.

➤ Teach For America (TFA) was founded in 1990 by Wendy Kopp, author of *One Day, All Children* (New York: Public Affairs, 2001). More than 12,000 high-achieving college graduates have gone through Teach For America's teacher-training program, directly impacting the lives of more than 1.75 million students. After 2 years in the classroom, more than 60 percent of Teach For America alumni remain in education as teachers, principals, school founders, and policy advisors. Others have gone on to work in other fields such as law, medicine, business, and social work.

TFA recruits from colleges and universities in all 50 states, looking for the best and brightest graduates. In 2003–4, the profile for the 3,100 corps members was: average GPA of 3.5, 92 percent held leadership roles in college, 37 percent are people of color, and all are young and energetic, with a mission to light fires in their students—teaching with commitment and hope in 22 low-income communities across the country. Currently, 3,500 corps members are teaching in over 1,000 schools in 22 regions across the country.

Think big . . . to teach treasures and reach the inner cities, you train the best. Call:

TEACH FOR AMERICA (NATIONAL OFFICE)
315 West 36th Street, New York, NY 10018
Phone: (800) 832-1230 ; (212) 279-2080 I Fax: (212) 279-2081
Web site: www.teachforamerica.org

KIPP
Phone: (866) 345-KIPP
KIPP's Motto: "Work hard. Be Nice"
E-mail: info@kipp.org I Web site: www.KIPP.org

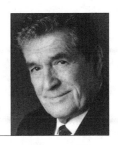

15: Hugh O'Brian
HOBY

From Gunfighter to Candle Lighter

"HUGH, what are you going to do with this?" Dr. Albert Schweitzer, humanitarian, doctor, and winner of the Nobel Peace Prize, took the hand of American actor Hugh O'Brian and looked him in the eye as he asked that question. After spending nine life-changing days at Dr. Schweitzer's medical clinic in Central Africa in 1958, Hugh was not surprised by the impact of the inquiry.

Over the course of those African days, O'Brian had helped build cribs for sick babies and pass out food to hungry patients, including lepers. Nights he devoted to sitting up with the doctor and hearing how the world needed help from America. At different times, the elder Schweitzer had told O'Brian, "The most important thing in education is teaching young people to think for themselves," and "The United States *must* take a leadership role in bringing peace to the world."

Just two weeks earlier, Hugh had been in Winnipeg, Canada, on a break from starring in his hit television show. Many over 40 will always remember him as gunfighter Wyatt Earp—the title character in one of early television's top-rated shows for seven years running. Hugh recalls, "I was headlining in a circus there that summer. I used to like to do rodeos, horse shows . . . anything to have fun and make an extra buck. When I got the invite to visit the world-famous Albert Schweitzer, I caught the first plane to join him in the deepest part of Africa." Nine days after his arrival, as he was leaving the small jungle village and saying good-bye, Hugh was boldly challenged by Schweitzer's "What are you going to do with this?" That question changed the direction of his life.

Hugh had a lot to think about and plenty of time to ponder on his trip home. In those days, before the age of jets, the flight took 45 hours. During the long journey, the challenge of how *he* might impact the world percolated, and a vision started to emerge. He wanted to somehow gather young people throughout the world together to teach and learn from one another. "I started thinking about who I was, what I was doing. Two weeks after I got off the plane, I had gathered my first group of kids," recounted Hugh.

+ *"Find something that makes you want to get up in the morning, and then go make it happen."*

Following his visit with Albert Schweitzer on the bank of the Ogowe River, O'Brian created HOBY, or Hugh O'Brian Youth Leadership, a program that would teach America's young people to think independently and become the leaders of the generations to come. Little did this Hollywood idol anticipate that more than 45 years later he would have more than 335,000 kids who call him "Big Daddy." These teens—who really have become his family, albeit a big family—respect and admire this man who has given most of his life to love and encourage them.

"I focused on 15-year-olds because when I was that age, in tenth grade, that's when I personally had to decide to fish or cut bait. You've got two years left of fun and games, and then there's an old tough world out there, and you have to focus on who you want to be," mused Hugh. "The goal is to expose the cream of the crop of our youth to the best motivational leaders in the country and let the two groups interact. Then the students take what they've learned and spread the vision to others for their last two years in high school."

With unwavering cowboy determination and focus, Hugh's vision to corral and spur on great kids has grown every year since its 1958 inception. In 2003, more than 14,500 high-school sophomores participated in 3-day HOBY leadership seminars held in 70 different cities within each of the 50 United States. High school sophomores take note: One student leader is invited from each high school . . . and it's totally free. These electric, three-day weekends are run completely by committed volunteers, many of whom are past HOBY graduates. Funds to run HOBY come from the generous hearts of individuals and corporations.

Imagine the wild excitement as more than 200 top students join together for one weekend at a HOBY regional conference. With sparks flying, a variety of world leaders including CEOs, astronauts, doctors, politicians, and others challenge the thoughts of the next generation's leaders. The group catches the fire and thrill of their potential power to change the world.

As Hugh's "kids" participate in HOBY, they discuss themes of peace, justice, leadership, media, and communications, and how to become strong members of society. Many alumni are now judges, business leaders, scholars, and politicians. Their vistas have been expanded, smoldering fires ignited, and now they're giving back to the world by inspiring future generations of leaders.

HOBY also has an annual weeklong "super-round-up." Their World Leadership Congress takes place each July and is coordinated by a major university. Four top students from each of the 70 spring conferences are chosen to attend, and they are able to interact with world-class leaders and top international students brought in from more than 30 countries. Again, this program is totally free to the students. Each of these HOBY Ambassadors is asked to give back 100 hours of community service after the program. Additionally, each one is encouraged to create a service project. Miracles and motivation abound following this super-charged annual event.

Through generous corporate sponsorships as well as the efforts of more than 5,200 volunteers, HOBY operates at no cost to taxpayers, parents, or students. "No money is requested or received from any government source. HOBY is considered a great example of our free-enterprise system. I'm very proud of that," says O'Brian.

Hugh O'Brian is thrilled. "I'm excited about today. I enjoyed yesterday, I've pretty much forgotten the day before, and I'm looking forward to tomorrow. I get up in the morning and get on the phone. I enjoy it, and I feel that I'm doing something that makes a difference. I tell my kids, 'Find something that makes you want to get up in the morning, and then go and make it happen.'" This is Hugh's fulfillment of the dream inspired by Dr. Schweitzer—providing strong leaders for tomorrow.

Beyond those nine all-important days in Africa with Schweitzer, the best advice Hugh ever received was from his father. He had tried out for his high school varsity football team when he was a freshman, but lost the position to a senior. He told his father that the other boy had just been lucky. His father said, "Luck is a thing that happens when preparation meets opportunity." In other words, Hugh needed to prepare himself better, and he did. The next year he became the only sophomore to make the varsity team. Says Hugh, "That simple lesson is something I've never forgotten."

Hugh says he isn't concerned about his legacy, but only that the program he created survives and grows through HOBY graduates. "Of our 70 seminar sites each year," Hugh says, "62 of the chairmen are our alumni; that is, they went through the program when they were 15 and today they are in their 40s, 50s, and 60s. So we're going to be okay even when I'm not around to push or pull the wagon. I think Dr. Schweitzer knows what we are doing and he's smiling down on us from his heavenly perch saying, 'Hey, it was worth the time that I spent with that boy.'"

While an older generation remembers Hugh O'Brian as Wyatt Earp, a younger generation knows him as the man who taught them to be caring leaders. As Hugh puts it, HOBY "is where 'old Wyatt' has all of his guts, bucks, and time. Rather than curse the darkness, I decided to light a candle. Well, I've got so many candles out there now that there aren't enough sprinkler systems to put out their fire!" While Wyatt Earp might have been famous for the *Gunfight at the OK Corral*, the gunfire we hear coming from Hugh O'Brian's HOBY corral is "OK," too: It's the sparks from his kids lighting thousands and thousands of candles across the world.

≈≈*Ripples*

Kristi Benson and Governor Mike Huckabee

Receiving over 30,000 letters a year, Hugh picks up one from HOBY alumna, Kristi Benson, who attended the 2001 HOBY World Leadership Congress and returned home to create her own charity organization in Montana. Her project, the Beaverhead County Angel Fund, helps buy books, backpacks, and equipment for local children who can't afford school supplies. Writes Kristi, "The Angel Fund would never have happened without inspiration from HOBY. Hugh, I want to thank you for inspiring me to take the risk and try to reach my goals."

For O'Brian, turning HOBY into something that inspires young people like Kristi took patience, perseverance, and an attitude that would not let him quit. "First, you crawl; then walk. Next you run, and then you fly," says O'Brian. "We are flying now with HOBY, and there are thousands of people on board enjoying the trip. They truly enjoy putting their arms around the tomorrows of these future leaders."

Another of those on board with a first-class seat is Arkansas Governor Mike Huckabee, a 1971 HOBY alumnus. He wrote to Hugh, "The HOBY seminar was life-changing for me. I'm certain that had I not had that experience, I would not today be governor of my state."

► In 1958, famous Wyatt Earp television star Hugh O'Brian created Hugh O'Brian Youth Leadership (HOBY) to "spur on" youth leadership, corralling outstanding sophomores together regionally and having them interact with world-famous adults. Since 2000, every public and private high school in the United States has been invited to select one outstanding student to attend one of its 70 different yearly HOBY leadership seminars.

HOBY excels at fulfilling its mission to develop leadership skills and independent thinking among outstanding high school students. By 2003, more than 325,000 tenth-graders had participated *at no cost*. Each year, 14,500 new HOBY Ambassadors attend the conferences. In addition, more than 30 countries are represented annually at their World Leadership Congress.

For the past 45 years under Hugh's leadership, a dedicated group of more than 5,200 committed volunteers donate over 1 million hours a year to run HOBY programs at the local level. This program would not be possible without the generous gifts from big business, small business, and individuals.

Join the "posse" roundin' up the future leaders of tomorrow, and contact:

HUGH O'BRIAN YOUTH LEADERSHIP (HOBY)
10880 Wilshire Boulevard, Suite 410, Los Angeles, CA 90024
Phone: (310) 474-4370 I Fax: (310) 475-5426
E-mail: HOBY@HOBY.org I Web site: www.HOBY.org

16: Dr. Laura Schlessinger
My Stuff Bags/
Operation Family Fund

SMALL THINGS, BIG IDEAS

SOME PEOPLE WORK their whole lives to become famous, driven by money and power. From an early age, young Laura Schlessinger also dreamed of celebrity, but for a different reason—she wanted to leverage her fame to help those in need. "For years, I hoped to become really successful and well-known because that would give me the power to make important things happen," said Schlessinger, a licensed psychotherapist and spunky radio talk show host, better known simply as "Dr. Laura."

✦ *"Whatever you decide to do, find a way to contribute even in a small way to the welfare of all children. We owe that effort to our kids and our future."*

Dr. Laura started out as a no-nonsense psychotherapist. She went into radio in the late 1970s and became the fastest-growing and most outspoken radio talk show host in broadcast history. Her daily three-hour program, which focuses primarily on basic family values and childrearing, has gained a worldwide audience of more than 15 million listeners. In addition to becoming a fixture in the American radio scene, Dr. Laura has garnered dozens of awards from women's groups and broadcasting associations. Dr. Laura is the first and only woman to be awarded radio's prestigious Marconi Award and was a nominee to the Radio Hall of Fame. Nevertheless, she hasn't rested comfortably with her successes. Instead, she has made good on her promise to use her fame for worthy causes— especially helping abused and neglected children.

In 1998, when Dr. Laura learned that every year 300,000 children are rescued from abusive homes, and more than 550,000 are placed in foster care, her heart broke. She wondered what life must be like for them with very few belongings to call their own. "I'm a creature of habit. When I travel, little personal belongings always come with me—my tea cup, my files, my stapler, my pens . . . *my stuff.* We all need our special comforts. It makes us feel at home." Unwilling to ignore the desperate need of these children, in 1999 she started the Dr. Laura Schlessinger Foundation and a program called My Stuff Bags.

The My Stuff Bags program aims to give thousands of displaced children a duffle bag of personal items to carry with them to shelters and foster homes, replacing the beat-up garbage bags they often use. A typical bag includes a stuffed animal, a blanket, some toiletries like a toothbrush and toothpaste, books, crayons, toys, school supplies, and more for kids to call their own. "When I started this program, I wanted to make it personal, as human-to-human as possible," Dr. Laura says. "I didn't want to just take money and buy items. The kids needed to feel *somebody* cared for them, even if their families didn't."

Sharing her idea on the air, Dr. Laura asked her listeners for their help. Rather than just buying items, she asked them to make things to contribute in order to create a more personal connection between the children and those who care about their well-being. To her delight, thousands of people from all over the country responded by donating and making blankets—the beginning of what became known as the Dr. Laura Blanket Brigade. One woman even committed to making one quilt a week for an entire year and wrote in: "Hopefully, I will have done my small part to comfort 52 children by the end of the year."

Dr. Laura found a way to raise the much-needed funds to keep her foundation afloat. "At that time, there was a lot of pain and difficulty in my life," Dr. Laura says. "Then my son said to me one day, 'Mom, you need a hobby,' because, as he put it, I was 'either working or sad.' And I thought, oh my gosh, he's right." At first, she started making jewelry as a distraction, and then she was inspired. "I went out and bought 50 books on jewelry-making and stayed up late at night, first reading them and then fiddling with my own designs. I discovered that I'm somewhat artistic. It all came together very fast."

Soon Laura brought her creations to the office and her colleagues raved. "Somebody said, 'You know, you should sell these on the Web site. People would love to have something made by you.'" They were right. The first jewelry collection of 15 pieces made $32,000 for the foundation. "I buy all the materials and then create and donate the necklaces," Dr. Laura shares. "We conducted boutiques for Valentine's Day, Mothers' Day, summer, and Christmas, and made over $30,000 for each event."

In 2003, the program provided almost 100,000 My Stuff Bags to centers all over the country. "My goal is to provide 300,000 bags per year," says the ambitious family advocate. She has every reason to be optimistic. The response from both children and their caretakers has been overwhelmingly positive. One foster parent who received bags for a 10-year-old boy and 13-year-old girl in her care believes the My Stuff Bags is a pure act of kindness. "These children entered my life without anything they could remotely call their own. The little things we consider ordinary, such as shoes, clothes, a jacket, or something as great as a toy, are almost beyond what they can comprehend."

Dr. Laura has closed her foundation and has moved on to supporting another tremendous need: members of our military and their families. Through Operation Family Fund, her now-famous necklace collection has helped raise over $235,000 to benefit the families of military personnel who have died or have been severely disabled in the fight against terrorism.

Dr. Laura also uses her success to encourage people to help kids and families in other ways. She promotes strong and lasting marriages, sexual abstinence before marriage, involved parenting, and swifter government action in cases of child abuse. The author of nearly a dozen books for parents and kids, she has won awards from radio industry associations and family organizations for her promotion of family values. However, no award means as much to her as touching the lives of even one abused child.

"I think each person needs to look into their hearts and see what they can do. Maybe you're suited to becoming a foster or adoptive parent. If not, encourage your friends to stay married, tutor at your local school or library, or help the military who are fighting against terrorism on our behalf. Whatever you decide to do, find a way to contribute, even in a small way, to the welfare of others. We owe that effort to our kids, our military, and our future."

> I would like to take the opportunity to thank you for the bag. I am in a hard situation right now and it is a relief to know that some one actually cares. That, I will keep in mind through my struggles in work and every day life. I hope one day to make a difference in some one else's. Thank you

A letter from Dan G. to Dr. Laura

➤In 1999, Dr. Laura founded My Stuff Bags and in 2003, her program provided almost 100,000 My Stuff Bags to centers all over the country.

Dr. Laura is now supporting Operation Family Fund with her energy and handmade necklaces. Operation Family Fund is a 100 percent volunteer-driven non-profit founded in 2003. It is giving help and hope to the families of fallen and injured military personnel.

Dare to care. Contact:

OPERATION FAMILY FUND
P. O. Box 837, Ridgecrest, CA 93556
Phone: (760) 793-0541 | Fax: (760) 375-8067
E-mail: support@oeffamilyfund.org | Web site: www.operationfamilyfund.org

Foster care statistics from www.afc.hhs.gov/programs

17: Domingo Guyton
YMCA

TEENS AGAINST GANG VIOLENCE

WITH BLOOD OOZING from four knife wounds, Boston teenager Domingo Guyton made an unusual decision—he did not want his mother to see him this way. The pain in her tears was too much to bear and the pain in his conscience was too heavy a load. So he walked to a friend's house and sat on the front steps while they waited for an ambulance. By 1990, the 14-year-old had already been in and out of trouble with local street gangs for three years.

Growing up in a loving home with his mother and grandmother, Domingo had never experienced alcohol, drugs, swearing, abuse, or neglect. He sang in the church choir, played the drums, and his mother read Bible verses to him every night. Stepping outside their house, however, was like "entering a different world." His neighborhood was "hardcore," and fights, drugs, and gangs dominated the streets. "Every day, someone got shot or stabbed," he recalls.

"I started carrying pocket knives at the age of 11, then my grandmother's kitchen knives. My aunt from Tennessee thought it would be nice for a fine young man like myself to have a BB gun like my other cousins in the south. She didn't think I would start carrying it around the streets doing stupid stuff. It was taken from me when I got stabbed," explained Domingo.

When released from the hospital with his wounds bandaged, Domingo was scared, bitter, and angry. "I didn't feel safe, so I purchased a .32 with a bunch of bullets from some guy on the street for $150. It was always with me. I was so full of rage. Everything I hated and feared about the other guys—their violent nature and unreasonable grudges—now fit me. I was no different than my enemy."

Domingo began looking for trouble. He'd sit in the back of a bus counting up a handful of money just to tempt someone to take it. With the gun in his pocket, he just wanted a reason to pull it out and use it.

When Domingo finally found trouble, it wasn't what he expected. An eight-year-old girl was watching TV when a stray bullet went flying through her window, just passing her head. Domingo had been standing nearby with "friends" who later lied, telling police that he had pulled the trigger.

With a court date looming, Domingo was frightened. Boston City Hospital and the Violence Prevention Program strongly recommended that he meet with Dr. Ulric John-

✦ *"Every time I told my story, I learned more about myself."*

son. Dr. Johnson had started Teens Against Gang Violence (TAGV) in 1990 and Domingo Guyton was one of his first recruits. "I met with Ulric a few times and he saw an inner glow in me. He believed in my potential and didn't just look at some of the dumb things I was doing."

After hearing both sides of the story, the judge uttered words that would torment Domingo for his entire life: "Domingo is clearly guilty." Behind the trembling 15-year-old, Dr. Johnson stood up. He gave the judge his personal guarantee that Domingo could be saved and would turn his life around if released under his care. The charges were dismissed and Domingo knew how close he had come to throwing his life away.

Though he wanted to change, it would take one more fight and his expulsion from the school system for Guyton to embark on a new road. His transformation started when he realized Dr. Johnson wasn't about to give up on him. "Ulric reminded me of my friends who were in jail or in hospitals and gave me the option of a different life," recalls Guyton. "I remained in the program and started speaking to youth groups about nonviolence. Every time I told my story, I learned more about myself."

Dr. Johnson's Teens Against Gang Violence gained an impressive reputation in the Boston community. While membership is small, the impact of the program has spread through schools and neighborhoods where members have been invited to speak. By role modeling nonviolence and behavior based on love and respect, TAGV works to change youth culture.

"Slowly," remembers Domingo, "my anger burned away and a sense of purpose and peace enveloped me. The need to fight was gone. My priorities became helping young people in the community and appreciating my own family."

Domingo has come a long way from lying in a hospital bed plotting revenge. He went through college and today is the Teen Director at his local Boston YMCA. Now 27, he says, "I try to teach my 'Y' kids to respect older people and to listen to what they are saying." The love and respect he learned from Dr. Johnson ripples out through Domingo to his "Y" kids, many of whom are experiencing the anger and purposeless he remembers so well. He shares himself and gives hope to a new generation in Boston, now knowing that "character counts."

Domingo made a wise choice in selecting the YMCA as his vehicle to change the lives of young people headed for trouble. YMCAs are at the heart of community life in neighborhoods and towns across America. Each year, YMCA staff and volunteers are at work in more than 120 countries around the world and serve more than 45 million men, women, and children. YMCA provides lots of activities that kids like, where they can have fun and hang out in a safe place, and be off the streets.

Across the United States and abroad, YMCA teaches kids to swim, provides exercise classes for people with disabilities, and leads adult aerobics. They offer hundreds of programs in response to community needs—including camping, childcare, teen clubs, environmental programs, substance-abuse prevention, youth sports, family nights, mentoring, job training, and international exchange.

"We have hundreds of kids in our Boston programs," notes Domingo. As a musician who writes his own songs, he sings and plays the drums as one way to reach young people. "I have a Leaders Club that meets every Thursday night, and our teens volunteer 12 hours a month to help out in the community—like the big spaghetti dinner we just did at a nearby retirement home. They love helping others."

Guyton learned from his own life-changing experiences to believe in his kids. "I have hope in them because they have hope in themselves. Sure, you know there will be some who won't listen and will have to learn the hard way like I did," he says. "But overall, most of the teens I deal with are going to turn out okay."

➤Across the United States, 18.9 million members are part of more than 2,500 YMCA branches and camps. They are run by 55,961 volunteer policymakers serving on their boards and committees plus 540,672 volunteer program leaders and uncounted other volunteers, all of whom work with paid professional staff members. They are at work in more than 120 countries around the world, serving more than 45 million people. YMCAs have total revenue of $4.1 billion.

The YMCA was founded in London, England, in 1844 by George Williams and some friends to help young men like themselves find God. The first U.S. YMCA was started in Boston in 1851, the work of Thomas Sullivan, a retired sea captain and lay missionary. From there, YMCAs spread rapidly across America, many of which started opening their doors to boys and men of all ages.

Believe it or not, these things were all invented by or started at a YMCA: volleyball, basketball, racquetball, Father's Day, Toastmasters, Gideons, and professional football. YMCA inspired the founding of Camp Fire Girls, Boy Scouts of America, the Peace Corps, and the USO. Additionally, YMCA helps people develop values and behaviors that are consistent with Christian principles. At every YMCA, "character counts."

Calling the young and young-at-heart—get involved. Contact your local YMCA or check out www.ymca.net

TEENS AGAINST GANG VIOLENCE (TAGV)
1486 Dorchester Avenue, Dorchester, MA 02124
Phone: (617) 825-TAGV
E-mail: teensagv@aol.com I Web site www.tagv.org

18: Joani Wafer & Dawn Bodo
Kids Korps USA

Two Sisters' Assignment from God

WHEN MEALS-ON-WHEELS volunteers realized the people they were serving were splitting their sparse meals with their pets, help came from a surprising source: kids. A chapter of Kids Korps USA was enlisted to put together special pet treats like dog and cat biscuits packed in hand-decorated brown paper bags to accompany each Meals-on-Wheels delivery. Other kids in Kids Korps write letters to teens in prison or deliver homemade window boxes spilling over with bright flowers to nursing homes. Aged 5–18, they come from myriad backgrounds, united by a common compassion for others. Unbelievably, these kids may *choose* to spend time with an octogenarian rather than play Nintendo.

There is no greater power than a child's capacity for caring. This was evident to sisters Joani Wafer and Dawn Bodo, who, despite living thousands of miles apart, founded Kids Korps USA together in 1995. Their goal is to tap the natural compassion of kids. "They come into this life with a love for others that, when encouraged early, doesn't go away," says Joani, who started the first chapter in Rancho Santa Fe, California.

When God's assignment for this venture came, it was literally from the sky above. Joani even remembers the date—July 25, 1994. "The kids were swimming in the pool, and I was doing dishes while looking out the window. The San Diego sky was so beautiful, all reds and purples. Something tugged at me to go outside. That's when a distinct voice spoke in my ear: *children for charity*. I heard it over and over. *Children for charity*. I looked up at the striking sky in awe. Then I heard one of my kids crying and went back in. The boys were playing Nintendo and fighting. It was suddenly clear—they need a sense of purpose beyond our affluent lifestyle." Joani wanted rational advice from the friend she trusted most—her older sister, Dawn.

"I felt goose bumps the moment Joani called," Dawn remembers. "I had waited years for a meaningful assignment from God." After raising two boys, and earning her degree in theology, she was ready for a new challenge. When Joani pitched her idea of a charity run by children, Dawn knew her prayer had finally been answered. Joani gave up her lackluster jewelry business and never looked back. "God does not forget our prayers regardless of how long ago we asked."

Despite initiating Kids Korps USA on opposite ends of the country, their first endeavors couldn't have been more in sync. Joani and a few friends selected a San Diego nursing home for their first event. A nursing home was the last place some of the children wanted to be on a Saturday morning—with *old* people, some of them in wheelchairs. But as children stepped forward to lead an exercise session, smiles and laughter gradually spread through the room. The young and elderly genuinely enjoyed their shared time and simple activities. Now Joani had her proof—kids did like making other people feel good.

A week later in North Carolina, Dawn approached the Burlington Boys and Girls Club to help her set up a Kids Korps chapter. She chose a novel path that worked. Linking up with existing youth groups, they engaged with the Salvation Army and other charities such as Meals-on-Wheels, Habitat for Humanity, and Special Olympics, eventually becoming a United Way certified charity. "The exciting thing about Kids Korps is that it makes it possible for all kids to get involved," said Joani.

And kids came in droves. Kids Korps mushroomed into two new branches: Teen Korps and a mentorship program for young adults called College Korps. Joani and Dawn enlisted friends who in turn involved *their* vast network of friends. Through word of mouth and the news media, membership grew and many more families signed up for various community-service activities. Starting with a handful of moms and their children, today more than 15,000 youth have volunteered to work through Kids Korps to make a difference throughout our country. Eventually the sisters envision their little army of love growing beyond national borders. "We tacked 'USA' onto our name from the beginning because we foresaw operations in other countries—Kids Korps Japan, Australia, Mexico. As long as we're dreaming," says Joani, "we might as well dream big."

Raising funds is always a hurdle for any nonprofit, but Joani and Dawn employed creative and bold strategies. They have no compunction about approaching anyone with any request—from producing fancy golf tournaments to enlisting talk-show host Larry King and entertainer Wayne Newton to host their galas. Kids raise their own capital as well with car washes and bake sales.

A remarkable 1996 study printed in the *Independent Sector* showed that one in three teens in the United States started volunteering before the age of 14; teens were four times more likely to volunteer if they were asked; and 70 percent reported that doing something for an important cause gave them a new perspective. The 1993 "Search Institute Study" found that youth engaging in *two hours* of service per week are half as likely to engage in high-risk behavior such as fighting, truancy, smoking, drinking alcohol, and drug abuse. Just a bit of service every week improves self-esteem, increases personal responsibility, and connects young people to others.

Dawn and Joani have seen the real difference kids can make in their neighborhoods and for themselves. For example, in one disadvantaged North Carolina community, Kids Korps volunteers came up with the idea of writing upbeat letters to teens in prison. "We love you," they wrote. "We care about you. We'd like you to join Kids Korps when you get out of jail, but you can't commit any more crimes." Empowered and involved children no longer see themselves as disadvantaged.

Other Kids Korps chapters collect personal-care items for the homeless, create care kits for battered and abused children, start choirs to perform in hospitals and nursing homes, plant trees, apply fresh paint to community churches, and work with people with disabilities. When members volunteer, they're away from the negative pressures of the streets. "They're building character and leadership skills," says Dawn. "They're not being wooed by violence, drugs or the pressures of hanging out with the wrong crowd. By working with people from all backgrounds, our youth grow up more caring and responsible."

Kids Korps currently organizes 15 projects per weekend across 75 community chapters, in California, Colorado, North Carolina, Michigan,

New York, Massachusetts, and Illinois, conducting more than 2,500 community-service projects positively impacting 100,000 youth and 25,000 parents or adults. Since 1994, more than 15,000 volunteers have contributed over 525,000 hours of community service. They've stuffed more than 20,000 care bags for youth entering transitional facilities, built more than 50 homes, and assembled more than 500 bikes for less fortunate families, representing more than nine million dollars in-kind community value. That is "kid power."

Reflecting on the nine years since receiving their marching orders from God and founding their "charity for children," both sisters are still amazed and humble. "We started Kids Korps USA with an idea and a name that represented kids working together to help others," Dawn shares. "But every time we needed expertise—be it legal, financial, or administrative—the right people showed up at just the right time."

Our children need Kids Korps as much as the community does. Even the country needs them. When you see the effect that kids volunteering their own time and efforts have on people, especially the involved children themselves, you know you have to keep going.

≋*Ripples*

FROM DAWN AND JOANI

EIGHTEEN TEEN KORPS MEMBERS traveled to Ensenada, Mexico, during the weekend of November 16, 2002. Their purpose was to assist Homes for Hope, a Youth With A Mission (YWAM)-affiliated organization that builds homes for desperate, low-income families in Mexico. Most of those in need have more than three children and sometimes live in trash dumps or with little more than cardboard, scraps of wood, and tarps as shelter. In a single weekend, Teen Korps volunteers built a home for their assigned family of five. Within two days, what started as a bare concrete slab ended as a little house complete with drywall, electricity, windows, a door, and a roof. Just two small rooms, it wouldn't seem like much to most people, but to them it was an expansive mansion, the first real home this family had to call their own.

Although the work was hard and tedious and the accommodations not quite "resort level," the experience had an unforgettable impact on all those involved. Teen Korps volunteers were deeply affected by seeing how other people live and how much we all take for granted. The family's excitement and gratitude were continually, even tangibly, expressed as the father and mother worked alongside the team while the little children's laughter was heard throughout the weekend.

Through the endless stories, trials, and jokes, the group bonded, seizing the opportunity to make new friends and learn more about each other. Above all, what made the weekend most rewarding was the gift of giving a family something that had surpassed all of their wildest dreams. Through helping others, Teen Korps volunteers learned more about themselves and more about what is truly important! These kids can't wait to build another Home for Hope.

➤Founded in 1995 by Dawn Bodo and Joani Wafer, two sisters living thousands of miles apart, Kids Korps USA is a national, nonprofit youth-volunteer organization. Their mission is to engage young people aged 5 to 18 in charitable activities and community-based services, instilling a sense of giving in children while providing teaching and leadership skills. Kids Korps' 75 chapters (in California, Colorado, North Carolina, Michigan, New York, Massachusetts, New Jersey, and Illinois) conduct more than 2,500 community-service projects impacting 100,000 youth and 25,000 parents or adults. Since 1994, more than 15,000 volunteers have contributed over 525,000 hours of community service, representing more than nine million dollars in-kind community value. That's "kid power."

Child power + charitable endeavors + you = a better world. Contact:

KIDS KORPS USA
265 Santa Helena, Suite 112, Solana Beach, CA 92075
Phone: (858) 259-3602 | Fax: (858) 259-3603
E-mail: info@kidskorps.org | Web site: www.kidskorps.org

Part 3

Passionaries for Health

INTRODUCTION BY DR. ART ULENE

Dr. Art Ulene is a medical doctor and author who appeared on NBC's Today Show *for 23 years promoting nationwide medical and public-health news.*

S INCE MY CHILDHOOD DAYS, I've wanted to direct my path toward serving and loving others through medicine. Starting out as a doctor in obstetrics and gynecology, I expanded my calling in 1975 through television and books. I was suddenly able to help millions of people stay on the cutting edge of a variety of medical and health issues, including obesity, heart disease, and women's health care.

Those profiled in "Passionaries for Health" have all shared this same noble purpose of reaching out and serving those with various unmet medical needs. With big dreams that match their big hearts, they fill in the voids within medical systems in America and around the world. Many have personally experienced loss or physical challenges that led them to discover these voids first-hand, and turned their experiences into a single-minded focus on making the world better for others. Along the way, they have attracted like-hearted supporters who pick up the torch and willingly give extensive time and energy to their cause.

Medical miracles are happening through these passionaries and their supporters. When you read the stories of Mark Plotkin's quest for sources of new medicines from the Amazon or Nancy Brinker's drive to cure breast cancer or James Jackson's tale of amassing huge amounts of medical supplies shipped to third-world countries, you will be moved and inspired. You might be touched by the vulnerability of Betty Ford or by Dr. McConnell's challenge to retired medical personnel, which channeled valuable expertise into a growing network of free medical clinics. These heroes are all compassionately committed to a "magnificent obsession" of healing, and turning their visions into reality.

Identify each passionary's main strength, and you will find a bit of yourself. Then you can look in your heart for the answer to the question: Can one person really make a difference in this rapidly changing, fraught-with-needs world? You might just find how you fit into the equation of healing our world, one person at a time.

19: Jimmy Murray
Ronald McDonald House Charities

A DREAM HOUSE FOR KIDS

WHEN YOU LOOK AT JIMMY MURRAY, you can see his heart in his smile. A round, affable Irishman from Philadelphia, his second love is athletics, but his first love has always been children. At one time, he thought of becoming a priest, but was kicked out of seminary in 1956. After graduating from Villanova in 1960, Jimmy worked his way through a series of sports-related positions with minor league baseball teams. In 1969, he hit the big time by beating out 127 other applicants for the position of assistant public information director with the NFL's Philadelphia Eagles. Eventually, owner Leonard Tose would promote him up through the ranks to general manager.

During his first season managing the Eagles, Jimmy received a challenge that would change his life, and it had nothing whatsoever to do with sports. A new recruit from USC, tight end Fred Hill, approached Jimmy with a problem. His bright, bouncy, three-year-old daughter Kimberly had just been diagnosed with leukemia. Fred had met with Dr. Audrey Evans, head of pediatric oncology at Philadelphia's Children's Hospital, a national cancer-research center. She had a long list of necessities required to get their children's cancer center up to standard. Hill needed his football team's help to fight the disease before it got a chance to take his daughter's life.

Without hesitating, Murray and Tose got together, and Tose offered: "Team, stadium, anything it takes." This led to the creation of "Eagles Fly for Leukemia," which still serves as the team's principal charity. Tose also pledged the Eagles' help to raise one million dollars and told Jimmy Murray to "go and get it!" He had his marching orders.

With help from the players' wives, Murray staged fashion shows, ran a radio-a-thon, collected money from fans at a game, and held a $1,000 per

person gala. Soon Murray was on his way to Dr. Evans with a first install-
ment check totaling $125,000. Check in hand, the doctor already had a
new request: "Wouldn't it be great if we had a house where parents could
get help, too?" Jimmy Murray will always remember that at that moment
his life was changed.

Fred Hill and his wife, Fran, knew exactly what Dr. Evans had in mind.
They had spent many nights sleeping on cots and eating out of vending
machines at the hospital to be near Kim. Hotels were expensive, rarely
within proximity to the hospital, and parents of sick children were often
uncomfortable with the stares of hotel staff and patrons, especially when
their child had lost hair due to chemotherapy.

"I prayed about it," Murray remembered. "It just came to me to call
Don Tuckerman, a Jewish friend of mine who was in advertising. That call
was 'a Federal Express message from God' because the next big promotion
they were handling was a St. Patrick's Day green milkshake for McDonald's. Green and white are the Eagles' team colors, and I'm Irish. It was
fate." When Murray asked the local McDonald's if they would donate a
percentage of the profits from this shake from their Philadelphia fran-
chise, he was called the next day and told they could have "*all* the profits." Eagle quarterback Roman Gabriel promoted the milkshakes, and
McDonald's donated more than $35,000 toward the purchase of a house.

One of McDonald's executives suggested that the house be named after
their clown-mascot, Ronald McDonald, because children would identify
with him in a fun and happy way. "Done!" shouted Murray, and in a
Philadelphia minute, the idea of the Ronald McDonald House was born.

It took another sick child to see the project through to reality. In 1974,
when Philadelphia builder John Canuso's daughter, Babe, was stricken
with leukemia, she also came under Dr. Evans' care. The doctor put Canuso in touch with Murray, and together, they found a house. Spending
$150,000 of their own money, the Canuso family renovated it from top to
bottom. In October 1974, with McDonald's founder Ray Kroc in atten-
dance, the first Ronald McDonald House opened its doors. "That house
changed my life forever," Jimmy remembered. "I try to go by that address
on the anniversary every year just to say a 'Hail Mary.'"

There was no goal, at the time, to create additional houses; it hadn't even been a thought. This was seen as a one-time-only project, exclusive to Philadelphia. That changed 18 months later when Chicago attorney Charles Marino and his wife visited Jim Murray and the Philadelphia Ronald McDonald House. Their daughter had also been diagnosed with leukemia. Murray, the Marinos, family members of several other Chicago-area children facing serious illnesses, and McDonald's dealers from the Chicago region sat down with representatives of the NFL's Chicago Bears and discussed the idea of replicating the Philadelphia model. Another milkshake ("Orange Crush" for the Bears), along with several other activities, raised one million dollars to transform a former convent into the Chicago Ronald McDonald House.

◆ *"Those houses are places of hope. The real things that are inside us are demonstrated there."*

With the ribbon cut on a second house, the concept caught on. Houses started going up in other cities around the nation at escalating rates. After that first Ronald McDonald House opened in Philadelphia in 1974, 10 more houses opened within 4 years. By 1984, McDonald's restaurants had partnered with local communities to found 60 more houses. Then 53 more had opened by 1989. In 2004, nearly 240 Ronald McDonald Houses were operating in 25 countries around the world, and over $400 million in grants had been given. The program continues to expand.

Each house has a local volunteer board, which comes under a national Ronald McDonald House Charities advisory board that is independent of the restaurant chain. The global office provides seed money and expansion and emergency grants. However, each house relies on its own people and businesses to provide the additional funds and services needed. Over the years, McDonald's has contributed more than four million dollars to the charity.

The Ronald McDonald Houses, now synonymous worldwide as a home for families with seriously ill children, are supported by more than 30,000 volunteers. Each year these compassionate volunteers donate a combined total of one million hours of their time to maintain the buildings in order to keep them ready and available for families in need. Families with sick children may stay free, but they regularly donate up to $20 a day.

Shortly after the first houses opened, Jim Murray and others saw an unexpected side-benefit to their project. It wasn't only the children who formed warm relationships. Parents bonded with each other as well, establishing lifelong friendships and support systems based on a common problem. If a child died, the other families quickly stepped in to provide solace, transportation, assistance with funeral arrangements, and personal understanding that no one else could comprehend.

Jim Murray has long since left the Philadelphia Eagles and today runs a sports marketing company. For many years, he served as president of the international advisory board overseeing the Ronald McDonald House Charities. As a result, he has a thousand stories to tell about his role in the Ronald McDonald House program. But Kimberly Hill, whose illness proved the catalyst for the Houses, remains his favorite.

By the time she was 15, Kimberly was jogging five miles every day and was a member of her school's track team. She ran cross-country and rode horses. Since the age of seven, she has been off medication and loves every minute of her healthy life. Her father, Fred Hill, told Murray that God put Kim on Earth for a very special reason. Jim is quick to agree, adding, "Those houses are places of hope. The real things that are inside us are demonstrated there."

≈≈*Ripples*

Norfolk, Virginia's Ronald McDonald House
by Eleanor Muhly, director of Ronald McDonald House

Though we experience heartbreaking times in our house, we also experience the joy of miracles. One of those took place at our Ronald McDonald House in Norfolk, Virginia, where Jennifer Williams, affectionately known as "our Jenny," was staying. Jenny had a brain tumor that was cancerous. The prognosis for a child in her condition is all too often grim.

Our paths first crossed in September 1989 when Jenny came to stay with us. She was just eight years old, but she had personality plus, a warm and loving heart, and a compassionate nature. The idea of someone being a stranger was alien to her. Every year, Jenny and her mom would stay with us anywhere from 2 to 13 days for tests and checkups.

One day, without warning, Jenny contracted a virus that actually consumed all the cancer cells in her brain. Ever since, she has been cancer-free. How did this phenomenon occur? I believe that Jenny's support system was strong—her doctors, nurses, family, friends, Ronald McDonald House staff, and the other families staying at the House. They all bombarded the heavens with their prayers. Jenny continues to visit our Ronald McDonald House every year for check-ups.

The dictionary defines the word *miracle* as "an extraordinary and astonishing happening attributed to divine power." Every time we see our Jenny's beaming smile, we know that, in our minds, nothing could have explained her still being alive but a miracle. That's the bottom line.

➤Since opening its first house in Pennsylvania in 1974, Ronald McDonald House Charities has helped more than 10 million families. These families have called a Ronald McDonald House a "home-away-from-home," saving them over $120 million in housing and meal costs. More than $400 million in grants have been dedicated toward making an immediate, positive impact on those children who need our help most.

More important, through the Ronald McDonald House Charities, countless smiles have been shared, lives touched, and connections made. There are 212 Ronald McDonald Houses in 20 countries, with 6,000 bedrooms available for families. An amazing 30,000 volunteers donate 1 million hours annually, serving families during their children's treatment.

Be a clown's best friend! Make a sick child and his or her family feel at home.

RONALD MCDONALD HOUSE CHARITIES
One Kroc Drive, Oak Brook, IL 60523
Phone: (630) 623-7048 | Fax: (630) 623-7488
Web site: www.rmhc.com

20: Nancy G. Brinker
The Susan G. Komen Breast Cancer Foundation

A SISTER'S LOVE CHANGES THE FACE OF CANCER

THERE WAS A TIME when women could scarcely utter the word. They called it "The Big C" and assumed you had to die from it. That fear kept Nancy Brinker's sister, Susan G. Komen, from seeking more aggressive treatment for her breast cancer. After nine operations and three courses of chemotherapy and radiation, Suzy lost her three-year battle in 1980 at the age of 36. Just before she died, Suzy turned to her sister and best friend, Nancy, and said, "Nan, as soon as I get better, let's do something about breast cancer."

"Terror, rage, sadness, and above all, a feeling of complete and utter helplessness invaded me," Nancy shared. In the beginning, Nancy wasn't sure how she could honor Suzy's request. "The first thing I had to do was make it a subject that people could actually talk about." From her living room, she set to work at getting the conversations going.

It certainly wasn't the ideal time to take on a new cause, but such calls to action are rarely convenient. Not only had Nancy lost her sister, her private life was in dramatic transition including a recent job loss. But Nancy proclaims, "Among the many things my sister taught me was this life lesson: there's no time like the present. So I set to work channeling my anger and sorrow to honor her dying wish."

Not long after Suzy succumbed to breast cancer, Nancy approached her husband, Norman, who had lost his first wife to cancer and understood her passion. Nevertheless, this bottom-line businessman wanted to see hard numbers before giving his full blessing to her idea of creating a foundation. Nancy did her homework and came up with profound comparative data: the whole Vietnam War had claimed the lives of 59,000 American soldiers. During that same period of time, a silent tragedy also took its toll—approximately 244,000 American women had died from breast cancer. Regardless of the alarming statistics, little funding was directed toward women's health.

In 1982, with a handful of friends, a shoebox crammed with ideas, and a few hundred dollars, the Susan G. Komen Breast Cancer Foundation was born. Astoundingly, just a little over a year later, Nancy discovered a lump in her own breast. Now she had her own fight to forge. Thankfully, by the time her cancer diagnosis was made, she had gained the wherewithal to seek and demand the aggressive treatment that had eluded her sister. Nancy was lucky. By knowing the vital role early detection plays in prognosis, she survived.

✦ *"It happened one step at a time. That's why the Race for a Cure is so symbolic—it represents many people taking many steps all in the same direction to fix something that's very wrong."*

Today the Susan G. Komen Breast Cancer Foundation is one of the largest of its kind with more than 75,000 active volunteers working in 15,000 communities throughout the world. Collectively, they have invested more than $630 million in breast cancer research and community-based outreach programs including education, screening, and treatment. By 2003, Komen Race for a Cure events were being held in more than 100 cities, attracting more than 1 million participants.

The Komen Foundation provides millions of dollars in research grants each year to help find a cure for the disease. It was also the first organization to fund specific research that led to the discovery of two genes that are known to be involved in breast cancer, BRCA1 and BRCA2. The Komen Foundation also provides resources and a variety of education materials for anyone affected by breast cancer, with a special outreach to minority populations. Nancy knows that every year more than 200,000 people will be diagnosed with breast cancer and 40,000 will die from it. Until a cure is found, the Komen Foundation's work will continue.

"Although what we've accomplished sounds staggering, and it is, it didn't happen overnight," Nancy shares. "It happened one step at a time. That's why the Komen Race for a Cure is so symbolic—it represents many people taking many steps all in the same direction to fix something that's very wrong."

Volunteer efforts remain a cornerstone of the Komen Foundation. "The government cannot fix everything that ails us," Nancy says. "Americans, not the government, are the creative problem solvers. For the future of this country, our charities must have dedicated volunteers." Having a group of people whose commitment is steady and whose compassion is limitless is what keeps any foundation operating to its potential—even more than money.

The innovation Nancy Brinker sees from Komen Foundation Affiliates continues to astound her. Today, in addition to the Komen Race for the Cure, several other of their events and programs have sprouted across the country: Cook for the Cure, Ski for the Cure, Rally for a Cure, a golfing event, and even Shop for the Cure. The Komen Foundation also provides an opportunity to drive change in public policy through Champions for the Cure, which helps generate letters to Congress asking for support of breast cancer research and funding. The overall theory is simple: Together we can make a difference.

Nancy Brinker's call for volunteers is not simply directed to those who want to help find a cure for breast cancer. Volunteering to live abroad as President George W. Bush's Ambassador to the Republic of Hungary for three years, Nancy energetically tackled Eastern European needs. She would like nothing more than to inspire both men and women to find their own cause, and to "stop complaining and start fixing."

What Nancy Brinker envisions is a better America with better schools, fewer hungry and homeless people, declining drug abuse and domestic violence, a cleaner environment, and a lower crime rate. "If that happens," she says, "I assure you it won't be due to government intervention, but due to the power of volunteerism. And I truly believe it's all within our reach because I've seen what happens when—just as in our Komen Race for the Cure events—a lot of people take a lot of steps in the same direction."

≈≈*Ripples*

FROM THE RACE: "WHY I AM RUNNING" BY CHRISTINE ADAMS

I HAD AN AWESOME EXPERIENCE at the Komen San Diego Race for the Cure this past weekend! At past races, I had not taken the time to really be with cancer survivors during the ceremony. This year was different—I was there when it started and could not leave until it was over. I bit my lip to keep my tears from flowing as I watched a husband and his wife (in her pink T-shirt and cap, letting the world know she's had cancer) huddled together and crying with their young daughter.

Then another woman in a pink shirt, who appeared to be no older than I, impressed me with her strength and composure. She smiled for the camera as her husband snapped several commemorative photos. I was happy to be there to snap a photo of them together. It's impossible not to wonder what power or meaning this photo will hold for them in the future.

It was after taking the photo of this young couple, who looked to be just starting a life together, that I noticed a woman standing alone. Her eyes were red and swollen—she was trying so desperately to hold it all together. I waited, hoping that her family would be right back. Maybe the two women standing in front of her were with her, and not just other strangers. My hopes vanished as time passed and nobody came to be with her. After what seemed an eternity spent wondering "should I or should I not?" I walked over. No sooner had I placed my arm around her and asked, "Are you all right?" than her emotions began to flow. She hugged me back and began to sob. She confided that her cousin had been buried the day before the race. The service was on the East Coast, and she was not able to attend. My heart ached for her and as I began to cry, she added further that both she and her cousin had been diagnosed only one day apart.

I could only manage a steady stream of "I'm so sorry's." We did not want to let go of one another. We hugged throughout the rest of the ceremony and she walked away from me to line up for the race. I will never forget this woman. I only wish I knew her name. I will wonder about her and hope she is able to line up for the race next year.

➤The Komen Race for the Cure is a vital event for so many. Not only does it raise money to help in finding a cure for breast cancer, but it also creates a sense of community. For those who are battling this terrible disease, as well as their frightened and worried families and friends, it provides the knowledge that, even if only for one day, they are not alone. We should all be very proud. What we do makes a difference; how and why we do it makes us special. In 2006, Susan G. Komen Race for the Cure events will be held in more than 100 U.S cities and 3 foreign countries with more than 1 million participants. Since its founding in 1982 by Nancy Brinker to honor her sister, the Susan G. Komen Breast Cancer Foundation and its affiliates have invested more than $630 million in breast cancer research, education, screening, and treatment. Today, the Komen Foundation is one of the largest organizations of its kind with more than 75,000 active volunteers. It is credited as the nation's leading catalyst in the fight against breast cancer.

More than 200,000 individuals will be diagnosed with breast cancer this year and 40,000 will die from it. And because no one knows exactly what causes breast cancer, there are no sure ways to prevent it. Research remains critical not only to the treatment of the disease, but also to its prevention.

To join the fight against cancer: walk, run, golf or shop—but contact today:

SUSAN G. KOMEN BREAST CANCER FOUNDATION
5005 LBJ Freeway, Suite 250, Dallas, TX 75244
Telephone: (972) 855-1600 I Web site: www.komen.org
You can also call the Komen Foundation's National Toll-Free Breast Care Helpline at: (800) I'M AWARE (462-9273)

21: James Jackson
Project C.U.R.E.

THE DEAL MAKER

"WHEN I WAS A LITTLE GUY, Dad told me and my two brothers that he would never be able to give us much financially, but he could show us how to get anything we wanted," recalled James Jackson. How right he was.

The Jackson boys' first lesson in "deal making" began when their dad brought home a big, fuzzy, extremely pregnant New Zealand rabbit. To teach the boys the fundamentals of bartering, their dad first demonstrated the importance of marketing, filling a bright red wagon with fresh grass clippings on which he nestled three tiny white bunnies. Next, he led his boys through the neighborhood and showed them how to trade their "wares" for other things. They exchanged the first bunny for a collection of marbles, complete with the steely shooters. Those marbles and the second bunny were swapped for a tricycle. The tricycle and the last bunny in their wagon landed them a bicycle. That was the beginning of an apprenticeship that would pay incredible dividends.

By the time the Jackson brothers reached junior high, they had become so well versed in the art of bartering that they were trading for automobiles—and neither one of them had a driver's license. More than once, they telephoned home with the news: "Hey, we just got a Pontiac, but could you drive it home for us?"

James resolved early on to be a millionaire by the age of 25. He and his brothers set their sights on Colorado, where they moved to set up a business in the leisure and entertainment arena. The IRS 1031 exchange clause, which had just come into existence, served as an incredible advantage, allowing them to trade "like for like," while postponing taxation. "We capitalized on that in the ski and recreation industry in Colorado," James recalls, "using our same old principles of bartering and trading rabbits, now trading up or exchanging properties among the already established network of popular ski resorts." The Jacksons accumulated enormous profits.

James liked getting what he wanted, but found that deal after deal, millions after millions, he was never satisfied. "I became addicted to deal-making, always needing to put one more big scheme together. Each one had to be bigger than the last. My brother went through three divorces. We'd all become good businessmen, but we weren't good men."

Financially, James had achieved all the wealth to which he had aspired, but he felt spiritually bankrupt. "Fortunately, my wife and I had a strong relationship. We were born in the same hospital room and dated during high school. We began to talk and realized, 'This isn't good.'" Despite beautiful homes and driveways lined with expensive cars, they weren't happy. "One day, I remember telling God that if he would just make me a simple man, I would never again use my talents and abilities to accumulate personal wealth."

So in the early 1970s, James and his wife quit their old life cold turkey. Within the next three years, they gave away everything—all $16 million (today's equivalent of $65 million)—and started over. The only thing they were not able to give away was their home. Every effort to give it away was blocked for some reason. Their new level of commitment led them to get involved in a local church where they began teaching a Sunday school class for newly married couples.

It became apparent to James that money troubles were at the heart of many young couples' marital problems. James saw both a need and a fulfilling way to use his talents. "I started teaching basic Economics 101 lessons on what the Bible says about finances." The response was positive enough that James decided to put his ideas in writing. Two years later, he had published *Whatcha Gonna Do with Whatcha Got*, which won the Gold Medallion Award.

Even before James' book came out, Dr. Bill Bright (founder of Campus Crusade for Christ) came to town and said, "Jim, this is really important. People need to understand good economics. Nobody is teaching this. Everybody's getting in trouble with credit cards and everything else." Using his economic principles, James began to train the staff of Campus

Crusade across Canada and the United States. From there, he went on to teach over 10,000 leaders from other denominations so they could instruct their parish groups.

As a result of this success, a Chicago think-tank asked James to share his concepts. He found himself speaking to heads of giant, multinational corporations including Sears, IBM, and Xerox. Executives across the nation believed his knowledge of trade and barter could be used to expand the market share of under-developed countries, allowing them to achieve financial independence using his principles.

The International Monetary Fund and World Bank asked him to create a bartering model for developing nations. James was back in his element, and he'd stumbled on a way to use his acumen for a worthy cause. The international cause became a practical challenge when a woman representing the newly formed government of the African nation of Zimbabwe convinced James to help her country. "We have a desire to do good," she said, "but we do not know how to make the economy work." Before embarking on this new journey, James couldn't have located Zimbabwe on a map. But once there, giving it economic CPR was simple for a man who'd gone from trading bunnies to making millions by the time he was 30. "Zambia had copper, but the world price had fallen," James recalled. "Zimbabwe had huge bumper crops of maize, but nowhere to put them." James arranged a successful barter. Copper was exchanged for maize. News of his abilities traveled quickly, and from Africa he traveled on to Ecuador, Peru, Venezuela, and Brazil, setting up similar trade opportunities.

James felt good about the economic help he was providing to these nations, but he was troubled that there was no magic bullet for their crushing poverty. As one man, he could do little, but then God led him to Brazil and Dr. Heraldo Neves. "I visited the doctor's dilapidated house that served as the only clinic for a rural area of 350,000 people. His emergency ward had an empty canister of oxygen and an old gray metal cabinet with a glass front, containing dirty re-rolled bandages—and that was all. People were lined up to get into his clinic, but there was little Dr. Neves could do to help them." Without knowing how he would do it, Jackson made a promise to help the doctor stock his clinic with medical supplies.

Back home in Colorado, James gathered a few friends for lunch and told them what he needed. Right away, a new friend, Greg Lowe, spoke up. "Jim, my company buys from manufacturers. We supply hospitals and clinics on a bid basis every year, and I always have to buy overstock. Come to my warehouse, and I'll see what we can do." Greg pulled more than $50,000 worth of supplies from his shelves that James and his wife loaded into their old Dodge truck. It didn't stop there. Greg called more friends, and in one month's time they were able to collect over a quarter-million dollars' worth of donated, surplus medical supplies. Fishing into his own pocket for shipping costs, Jackson was able to send an ocean-going cargo container to Dr. Neves in Brazil. That was 1987 and the beginning of Project C.U.R.E.

Since that first shipment in 1987, Project C.U.R.E. has grown exponentially. The first loads of donations were collected in James's garage in Evergreen, Colorado. It soon became apparent that this was not enough space. Local neighbors were recruited to assist in collecting, taking inventory of, and storing the supplies and equipment. Jackson located some space in the warehouse of an inner-city food distribution warehouse. The success of the project continued, and soon it became apparent that more space was needed. A local businessman offered his warehouse for use. Initially, these 17,000 square feet seemed huge, but soon the supplies were stacked wall to wall.

As more shipments were sent to developing countries, even more supplies were received. In 1996, Continental Airlines and the City of Denver arranged to let Project C.U.R.E. use a small portion of their giant hangar facility at the old Stapleton International Airport. The space that was formerly occupied by three mammoth jet airplanes was now packed with life-saving supplies and equipment waiting for shipment.

Project C.U.R.E. has joined forces with generous manufacturers and vendors with overstocked warehouses. Miracles flourished as needs from other countries poured in and were almost always met. Today, Project C.U.R.E. ships medical supplies and pieces of medical equipment into 104 different countries, and in just the year 2005 was able to donate over $45 million worth of aid. Presently, this pet project of James Jackson is approaching the $1 billion mark in their spectacular giving venture. Not one of their cargo containers has ever been lost or confiscated, thanks in part to relationships established with supportive governments around the world.

These 40-foot containers have helped earthquake survivors in Turkey, victims of war in Kosovo and Afghanistan, aided hurricane relief efforts in the Dominican Republic, and brought help to the sick and dying in remote villages throughout Africa and to the children of Iraq. Some of the greatest efforts and investments have gone to countries with the fewest advocates and the most urgent needs, such as the Congo where 65 percent of the population is infected with AIDS and yet there is little help for their sick.

From the efforts and donations of generous medical manufacturers, Project C.U.R.E. has expanded from a small warehouse in Denver to filling huge facilities in Los Angeles, Phoenix, Nashville, Houston, and London. The program anticipates opening its next warehouse in San Diego, California. The project runs completely on the steam of compassion, fueled by an army of over 5,500 volunteers who sort, take inventory of, and ship the donated medical supplies. Teams spearheaded by James travel across the world to remote areas to complete "needs assessments" of hospital facilities. They meet with department heads and even the ministers of health and finance to gain assurances that donated goods can be shipped without seizure or taxation.

✦ He lives by the belief that when you choose to make yourself available, all the forces in the world gather to help you do good.

Completing the circle of legacy, the eldest of James's two sons, an attorney with a Ph.D. in econometrics and finance, decided to continue in his father's footsteps. Douglas Jackson had just been offered the presidency of a university when he decided to re-chart his own life as his dad had done so many years before. Douglas took over as President/CEO of Project C.U.R.E. and left James to do what he did best—the international part. "Much to my delight," James shared, "I'm working with the most talented person I know. And another generation of our family has learned to use his great talents to serve God and to multiply his gifts to help people all over the world."

When James Jackson looks back on the detours his life has taken, he is amazed and humbled. He lives by the belief that when you choose to make yourself available, all the forces in the world gather to help you do good.

In giving up all that he was and turning it over to God and humanity, James Jackson embodies the words spoken by Florence Nightingale when she said, "And if I could tell you all, you would see how God has done it all, and I nothing. I have worked hard, very hard, that is all; and I have never refused God anything."

≈≈*Ripples*

THE BARONNESS AND ME BY JAMES JACKSON

Project C.U.R.E. was working on getting medical supplies into an area of the Balkans, where 80 percent of the male population had been killed in combat in the late 1990s. Baroness Caroline Cox, the deputy speaker of the House of Lords in the English Parliament, was there because the United Kingdom had sent aid. The Baroness and I met on an old, beat-up Russian helicopter that took us from Armenia. She was so intrigued with Project C.U.R.E. that she asked if she and her assistant could come to Denver and see our operation. Impressed and touched, the Baroness promised to get Project C.U.R.E. started in the United Kingdom. Thanks to a meeting she arranged in London in 1999, one organization gave us warehouse space and another helped get us registered through the Parliament as a recognized charity.

Baroness Cox took me into the House of Lords, put me in the seat of privilege, and introduced me to her peers. As a result, we now have a wonderful organization collecting things in the United Kingdom and shipping them directly from England to meet needs around the world. Shipments have been sent to earthquake victims in India with containers going right out of Rochester. The heart of this baroness has spread ripples of medical miracles far and abroad.

►Project C.U.R.E. founder James Jackson, a successful entrepreneur and award-winning author, was working as an international economic consultant with heads of governments in developing nations around the globe. His work led him face to face with the needs of the sick and dying.

Since 1987 when he founded the nonprofit Project C.U.R.E., it has grown from a handful of people to a corps of more than 5,500 volunteers sharing compassion for people in medical need in 104 countries. Their mission is to identify, solicit, collect, sort, and distribute medical goods according to the imperative needs of the world.

Project C.U.R.E. currently operates warehouses in five U.S. cities—Denver, Nashville, Houston, Phoenix, and Los Angeles—and across the Atlantic in London. Each week, they deliver an average of two, 40-foot ocean-going cargo containers filled with medical relief. In 2002, Project C.U.R.E. delivered over 100 cargo containers valued at more than $30 million to the world's most needy in over 100 countries.

If you want to help deliver this "cure" to the world, contact:

PROJECT C.U.R.E. INTERNATIONAL
9055 East Mineral Circle, Suite 200, Centennial, CO 80112
Phone: (303) 792-0729 | Fax: (303) 792-0744
E-mail: projectcureinfo@projectcure.org | Web site: www.projectcure.org

22: Roxanne Black-Weisheit
Friends' Health Connection

A CONNECTION OF CARING

TWO YOUNG WOMEN lie in hospital beds in two different New Jersey cities, both attached to feeding tubes and talking with each other over the telephone. Though they've never met, they are connected by a phone line, a new friendship, and shared experiences: They are each in the fight of their lives against cancer. They're also drawing strength from the caring heart of a beautiful brunette who has never met either of them. In 1988, then college student Roxanne Black founded the network that later brought the two of them together. This network has connected more than 10,000 people suffering from a variety of serious illnesses. She knows first-hand what it is like to face the trials of a devastating disease alone.

Roxanne Black began feeling ill one day in 1985 when she was a high school sophomore. The athletic teen from Atlantic City could never have imagined that she was soon to be diagnosed with a life-changing illness. Until then, she had gone to the beach every day and zealously rowed on her school's demanding crew team.

Doctors diagnosed Roxanne with lupus. She was shocked, scared, and sad. "Most people didn't know what lupus was," Roxanne remembered. "It wasn't commonly diagnosed. The symptoms mimic a lot of other diseases. They call it 'the body against itself' because your immune system attacks and destroys your own cells. It is a chronic and often crippling disease with no known cure. It can affect any organ—in my case, it affected my kidney function."

The Blacks happened to live in a modest house on the water. From Roxanne's bedroom, where she was confined for months at a time, she watched the crew team go by every day—her team. Tears fell from her cheeks as she longed to be out there rowing with her friends. "It was devastating," she said. No one around her understood what it was like to be

15 and so sick, to miss out on varsity sports, dances, first dates—all the exciting trappings of the teen years.

Roxanne might have remained trapped in her depression had it not been for just a few words of motherly advice. "Maybe you got sick for a reason," her mom said one day. "Maybe you were meant to help other people." Something clicked. For the first time since her diagnosis, Roxanne began thinking of her disease differently—not as a horrible disorder exiling her from the world, but as a way to reach out to people who were also suffering and alone.

"I called my local paper and said, 'I'm 15 years old, and I was just diagnosed with this disease called lupus. I want to start a support group in my home town.'" After her story was published, 25 enthusiastic lupus patients showed up at Roxanne's first meeting, held at a library in southern New Jersey. The group grew, becoming like a family, but Roxanne still didn't feel right. Because lupus often affects older adults, she could find no one her age with whom she could connect. At meetings, members would discuss how the disease affected their marriages, careers, and children. "They really couldn't relate to going through this disease from a teenager's perspective," she said.

By the time Roxanne went off to nearby Rutgers University, she still longed for someone her own age to talk with about her disease. Her health had taken a turn for the worse and she wanted a friend who could understand. While her fellow freshmen were out enjoying college life, Roxanne spent her days shuttling between classes and a dialysis clinic. Lupus had attacked her kidneys, and regular dialysis was the only way to filter out the toxic substances from her blood. Without it, she would die.

So from her college dorm room, Roxanne started another group. This time she connected people on a one-to-one, customized basis. "I decided anyone, any age, with any type of health problem could call me and I would connect him/her with someone else the same age with the same health problem," she shared. She sought out people afflicted with serious diseases, compiled personal information profiles, and then matched those with both common problems and common interests. Using index cards and an old filing box donated from the public library, Roxanne organized biographies of people suffering with illness and paired them together on a customized basis. The intricate network that began to evolve from her hours of work became known as Friends' Health Connection.

✦ *"Something miraculous happens when you put two people together and one can say to the other, 'Yes, I know what you're going through. Yes, I have been there.'"*

Still in her freshman year of college, Roxanne wrote to hundreds of newspapers and television stations to get the word out about her group. She conducted dozens of interviews, some right from her dorm room and many others from a hospital bed. "A *USA Today* reporter loved the idea and wanted to write a story about it. And from that first article I got hundreds of letters from people all over the country with all different types of health problems, from the most common diseases to very rare disorders," Roxanne said. News stations began calling her dorm phone. "It was a really crazy thing," she remembered. "I'd go sometimes from my hospital bed to CBS to a college class."

People whom Roxanne connected would write her back and say, "I've met my best friend. This person has helped me through the most difficult time of my life. I've finally found someone just like me." Roxanne later shared, "I knew I was on to something from the very beginning with those thank-you letters." Her diligence paid off, transforming Friends' Health Connection from a small collection of handwritten index cards into an international support network for people with hundreds of different ailments and needs.

Since its inception in the 1990s, Roxanne and a corps of dedicated volunteers have networked and interconnected about 10,000 patients. Each year, dozens of people donate their time, helping to sustain Friends' Health Connection by supporting this program in a variety of ways.

Dozens of hospitals now participate with the network, distributing materials to patients who may be in need of a friend. Additionally, Friends' Health Connection has added a statewide educational arm for patients and hospital staff. Not everyone copes with illness the same way. Some people don't necessarily want a friend, but do want to learn about the cutting-edge techniques and the medical leaders treating their disease. Roxanne explained, "We have become well known for our lecture series due to the high caliber of speakers we present. In fact, Hollywood's *Superman* star, the late Christopher Reeve, who was paralyzed several years ago in a horse-riding accident, spoke at one of our lectures in 2003."

Today, Roxanne Black-Weisheit is in her mid 30s. A kidney transplant from her sister 10 years ago gave her the gift of life, which has made her lupus more manageable. The disease will always be with her and she will never know when or where it will strike her body next. Now married, she still devotes much of her time and energy to running Friends' Health Connection. She has finally found a group of younger people with whom to chat about her disease, in whom to find understanding. "I have several people with lupus whom I've kept in touch with over the years," she says.

"Through all those years of pain, I thought that's how it would be for the rest of my life. I've learned that tomorrow can bring miracles—so you have to hang in there. I've also learned that something miraculous happens when you put two people together and one can say to the other, 'Yes, I know what you're going through. Yes, I have been there.'"

———

►Since its inception by founder and lupus patient Roxanne Black-Weisheit, Friends' Health Connection has networked more than 10,000 patients worldwide. In addition to networking, they also provide educational programs at hospitals for patients and staff about various diseases, often featuring prominent lecturers.

Roxanne and Friends' Health Connection are the recipients of numerous scholarships, honors, and awards, such as the Daily Point of Light Award from President George H. W. Bush and the Giraffe Foundation Award for people who "stick their necks out to help others." This award-winning organization helps individuals cope with illness through the power of friendship.

Make powerful connections happen; help this idea expand in your area.

FRIENDS' HEALTH CONNECTION
P. O. Box 114, New Brunswick, NJ 08903
Phone: (800) 48-FRIEND (483-7436) | Fax: (732) 249-9897
E-mail: info@friendshealthconnection.org
Web site: www.friendshealthconnection.org

23: Mark Plotkin
Amazon Conservation Team

THE MEDICINE MAN

IN A VAST, untamed place, far from civilization, thousands of medical secrets have lived for countless millennia, most never documented. "Medicine men," also known as shamans, use plants and spiritual tools to heal wounds and cure myriad diseases. These unknown miracles remain hidden under the thick canopy of South America's Amazon rainforests. At one time, only these shamans knew where to find these wonder cures and how to administer them—that is, until a young American named Mark Plotkin entered the forests.

On one of his first trips to the Amazon in the late 1970s, Mark sat in a thatched hut in the dense heart of the forest talking to a new friend, a Sikiyana Indian shaman. He had come seeking the medicine man's strange knowledge, hoping to find a cure for diabetes, the disease that had taken his beloved grandmother's life. The shaman was unfamiliar with the western term *diabetes*, but after describing the symptoms such as sores between the toes, incessant thirst, and fading eyesight, he grabbed his machete and led Mark deep into the jungle. Peeling off strips of bark from an unusual tree and adding other leaves and stems, the shaman weighed each ingredient, boiled it in an ancient clay pot and handed Mark the potion.

"It just so happened that a medical doctor traveling with me was treating a lady dying of classic type 2 diabetes who had a blood-sugar level reading over 500—a potentially fatal level," Mark recalls. "He had no medicine to give her. We asked the shaman for permission to try his brew. By the next morning, her blood-sugar level was almost normal. Within a week, she was back working in her garden." How Mark wished he had been able to try this magic brew on his grandmother.

Often dressed in little more than sandals and loincloths, shamans don't look much like modern Western doctors. Their patients are villagers who sit on the forest floor to be treated with plants, not pills. But the shamans are experts—in healing *and* in tropical ecology. They are the shepherds of the rainforest on which their people depend, in order to thrive and survive in every capacity, both physically and spiritually. Necessities like food, medicine, hammocks, clean water, and shelter for their families almost take a second seat to their spiritual bond with their environment. "They protect their forests because that's where the 'invisible people' live—the spirits of their gods and ancestors," Mark explained. "Shamans are the glue holding the tribal Indian cultures together."

Mark *is* the Indiana Jones of the Amazon. His adventures were the inspiration for the movie *Medicine Man,* starring Sean Connery, and later for the IMAX film *Amazon,* which received an Oscar nomination for Best Short Documentary.

A Louisiana native and a University of Pennsylvania dropout, Mark landed penniless at Harvard, working at their zoology museum while taking a few night classes through the university. It was through a class on the Amazon that his life mystically changed course and a new dream emerged. Being taught by the world's preeminent authority on ethnobotany, explorer Richard Schultes, Mark was mesmerized by his professor's experiences. Mark later recalled, "Can you imagine being an academic from the States dropped in the middle of the jungle? Living in the culture of the 'forest people' was like being on another planet: different reality, different language, different customs."

While at Harvard, Mark began studying in the Amazon, living there for months at a time, working with the shamans to preserve their knowledge by passing it on to their children and grandchildren. This started a lifelong quest to link up with indigenous tribes, to study the secret ancient mysteries of the rainforests. While there, he was able to observe a variety of plants and their uses. He was fascinated to see tribal elders using sap to cure infections and tree fungus to clear up earaches. He would recount these experiences in books and lectures to demonstrate to the world that the rainforests and their potential medical powers were worth saving.

"The shamans are the crucial link between the tropical rainforest and our neighborhood pharmacy," Plotkin wrote in his *Tales of a Shaman's*

Apprentice, one of several books he's written about the power and potential of nature as an almost limitless source of healing compounds. "They're also our greatest hope for finding cures to a host of diseases—cancer, AIDS, the common cold, as well as new ailments that will undoubtedly emerge in the future."

Just one example of how new drugs can be developed is the poison dart frog. Indians in Colombia extract a potent poison from the skin of these frogs and paint it on their blow-darts to give them a deadly effectiveness. Abbott Labs, a major pharmaceutical company, has been studying a synthetic version of one of these compounds that is as powerful as morphine, but non-addictive. Other new drugs being developed from natural products include treatments for high blood pressure, diabetes, paralysis, and new forms of antibiotics. Of the antibiotics presently in use, 80 percent come from nature. There is a vital need to develop others to combat constantly morphing drug-resistant bacteria.

While he delved into the shamans' ancient secrets, Mark became alarmed and enraged about a looming environmental disaster. The Amazon's rainforests, threatened by logging and deforestation, were quickly disappearing, taking their potential medical miracles with them.

In 1995, Plotkin co-founded the Ethnobiology and Conservation Team, later renamed the Amazon Conservation Team (ACT). This group partners with South American tribes to protect both the rainforests and their cultures. A major thrust of their work is to create a cadre of "Shamans' Apprentices," young natives who will learn to be both traditional healers and conservation leaders. "Almost all of us at ACT have been working with these particular tribes for over a decade—in some cases, for 20 years. They often see us as family members," Mark shares. "This creates a different, more effective dynamic."

ACT also works to map and protect the remaining Amazon rainforests. The boundaries of existing tribal reservations are sometimes poorly marked and are often threatened by logging or fires that can sweep in from agricultural fields bordering the reserves. "The Indians seldom have guard posts at their boundaries and need to learn how to control fires that spread from adjacent soybean farms," Plotkin said. ACT and its indigenous partners have now mapped 27.5 million acres in the eastern Amazon.

Once the territory is correctly charted, land can be improved. Mapping represents one of the best means to stop encroaching development and the extinction of one of nature's largest and most resourceful irreplaceable treasures. "There's no question we're making an impact and have helped improve protection of millions of precious acres," Plotkin said. "We dream of helping Indians stop the destruction of all ancestral forests."

The mission of ACT is also to demonstrate to the world that the rainforest is extremely valuable when protected and managed. Herbal medicine has become a booming trend. Pills derived from roots and plants are no longer sold only at off-the-beaten-path health-food stores. According to one recent study, Americans spend six billion dollars a year on medicines derived from tropical plants. One-quarter of all prescription drugs sold in the United States use plant chemicals as their active ingredients.

Mark Plotkin's ACT and the shamans are in a race against time. The rainforest is in danger of dying off, taking with it the ancient secrets of the medicine men and women as well as the plants themselves. Even with the potential of new tropical drugs, the fight to preserve the rainforests and its tribal healers remains a huge challenge. The golden nuggets of both the shamans' wisdom and the medicine gifts planted by God in the rainforests should be argument enough for the protection of this extraordinary resource. For Mark, the call of the jungle and its people continues.

≈≈*Ripples*

INDIANS IN RED BREECHCLOTHS

AN EXTRAORDINARY NEW MAP has been created by rainforest Indians in red breechcloths carrying handheld GPS (global positioning system) devices. It demarcates 10 million acres of the pristine Tumucumaque region of the northeast Amazon rainforest. ACT has worked with four Indian tribes living in the northeast Amazon to help them map their boundaries. These tribes—the Tirios, Kaxuyana, Wayana, and Apalai—are small bands of forest dwellers that have teetered on the edge of extinction. The participants believe this map is the first and most important step in creating a plan for the protection of the region's legendary forests and will serve as a blueprint for similar efforts in rainforests around the world.

The Tumucumaque Indigenous Reservation project involves the Indian tribes in the mapping process, clearly demonstrating the extent to which the Indians there are in fact occupying their ten million acres of reservation. Based on their map, the four tribes of this reservation have been able to better organize and develop their resources that they have prepared it wisely. The location of the widely coveted medicinal plants they know so much about have been illegally taken abroad from the Amazon rainforest in the past; it is not revealed in the map. The Tumucumaque map covers the largest area and is the most detailed indigenous map of the Amazon ever created.

Tackling the daunting task of mapping one of the most famously difficult environments on the planet, Mark Plotkin's ACT and four Indian tribes have taken a bold step to save rainforests. They tread the uncharted territories with modern technology held in the capable hands of Amazon Indians wearing red breechcloths.

►Mark Plotkin co-founded the Amazon Conservation Team (ACT) in 1995. In partnership with both the Brazilian government and Amazon Indian tribes, they have mapped 27.5 million acres in the eastern Amazon and are working to establish a mapping and conservation center to train Indians throughout South America. For more information, read Mark Plotkin's *Medicine Quest* and *Tales of a Shaman's Apprentice*.

ACT NOW: Save the rainforests, its indigenous people, and their healing wisdom.

AMAZON CONSERVATION TEAM
4211 N. Fairfax Drive, Arlington, VA 22203
E-mail: info@amazonteam.org | Web site: www.amazonteam.org

24: Dr. Jack McConnell
Volunteers in Medicine Clinic

Dr. McConnell, greeting VIM Clinic's first patient,
three-year-old Malikah Housey

RETIREMENT GONE AWRY

*"It was as if we had wired the clinic for electricity, and
the little child turned the lights on."*—Dr. Jack McConnell

WHEN DR. JACK MCCONNELL retired to a luxurious home nestled on a golf course in Hilton Head, South Carolina, in 1989, he decided retirement wasn't all it was cracked up to be. "At that time I was 67. My golf handicap was going down, my waistline was going up, and I thought, *Can it be that I worked 35 years for this?*" Little could he have guessed that he was about to embark on the most rewarding phase of his life.

As a child, Jack was influenced by his father, a Methodist minister who never made more than $150 a month. "Daddy never had a car. He said he couldn't put his seven children through college *and* support Mr. Ford at the same time. But six of us graduated from college, four went on to get master's degrees, and three completed doctorates." At dinner, the elder Mr. McConnell would ask each of his children: "What did you do for someone today?" As the years passed into decades, that question stuck with Jack. "What did I do for someone today?"

Every time he left his gated retirement community, Dr. McConnell was confronted with fellow islanders living in relative poverty. "These people were not lazy scallywags. In fact, it was just the opposite. They were at the bottom of a work tier, struggling to rise out of poverty. They didn't earn enough money for medical care, but worked too much to qualify for Medicaid." When he asked where they received their health care, the answer was always the same—in the emergency room or nowhere.

"Why in the world doesn't someone help these people find adequate health care?" the retired doctor murmured as he drove home one day. Then he stopped suddenly. "That's not the right question," he thought. "Why haven't I been helping these people find adequate health care? Okay, God, I got the message. But I have no idea where to begin, and I will need your help."

Perplexing challenges have never daunted Jack McConnell. A nationally recognized scientist and business executive, he is widely acknowledged for his many medical contributions, such as developing the Tine Test used on millions of patients for the diagnosis of tuberculosis, collaborating on the creation and marketing of Tylenol tablets, or conducting a program that led to the first commercially available MRI instrument in the United States. Even in retirement, he remained active in research toward mapping the sequence of the human genome. However, he hadn't yet dreamt of his Volunteers in Medicine Clinic—the project that would become closest to his heart, consume his future, and effect systemic change in medical care throughout the country.

After three years of retirement, Jack prayed for direction and God answered. He described his vision of a free clinic in Hilton Head to friends and strangers alike—retired doctors, nurses, dentists, and other professionals—and volunteers signed up. Armed with the commitment of 16 physicians and research proving that 8,000–10,000 Hilton Head islanders were without medical care, Jack went to work.

Free clinics are not a new concept. Jack's VIM Clinic, however, is conceptually unique, built on the foundation of Christian love and his idea of a "Circle of Caring," where those both giving *and* receiving medical help are healed and nourished together. Plus, the staff professionals in this circle are all medical retirees. "We don't call our visitors 'patients.' We call them 'friends and neighbors.'"

Jack knew that before he did anything else, he had to overcome two gigantic hurdles—acquiring both malpractice insurance and special licensing for retired medical staff. Undeterred, he lobbied politicians and local medical associations. In May 1992, an amendment was passed by the state's General Assembly that waived fees and the special examination (SPEX) required to license volunteers working in free clinics. In February

1993, South Carolina's Governor Campbell signed into law an amendment that created a Special Volunteer License. Jack then approached the Joint Underwriters Association to provide malpractice insurance. The Association confirmed that South Carolina's Good Samaritan Law extended to free care clinics like VIM, and they provided the volunteers with medical insurance. In that same year, the IRS also granted the project nonprofit status. He helped create a federal program providing immunity from suits to those who are properly licensed and practice free of charge in a free health clinic.

Meanwhile, Jack set out on an intense public relations campaign to recruit medical volunteers, assemble active and honorary Boards of Trustees, and inform everyone he knew on the island about his dream clinic. The doctor's persistence paid off when the town agreed to lease a 1.1-acre building site, charging the clinic exactly one dollar per year. Design and building plans were initiated, and a one-million-dollar fund drive for construction and first-year operating costs began in earnest.

Without a dime of federal, state, county, or local government money, VIM volunteers designed and built a 7,000 square foot facility consisting of eight examining rooms, three dental offices, X-ray equipment, a laboratory, and a pharmacy. The doors opened on July 5, 1994 with 60 physicians, 65 nurses, 4 dentists, 3 chiropractors, and 8 social workers. These volunteers offered services in adult medicine, pediatrics, immunizations, ophthalmology (with free frames donated by the Lions Club), cardiology, gynecology, urology, neurology, dermatology, orthopedics, minor surgery, mental health, social services, and dentistry, plus a special ADD clinic for the children—all for free!

"The best thing about the clinic is the culture of caring we've created," beams Jack. "When people come, they're greeted at the door. Kids are shown to a reading room where 'volunteer grandmothers' wait with good books and big hugs. Then escorts lead 'friends' to the reception room. We don't have a waiting room—we don't want people to wait, but to be received! And we don't bother doctors about spending too long with each person. We can't, since we don't pay our staff anything!"

In all, 257 professional medical and 195 lay volunteers staff the free VIM Clinic, most of whom are retirees. Doctors and nurses remain informed of advances in their field. Fridays are always reserved for continuing medical education. "Anyone who helps here is expected to come every Friday," Jack shares. "We will not tolerate poor quality care for the poor."

Dr. McConnell sees his project as a "four-way win" situation for everyone involved. Care recipients win because they receive ongoing care, often for the very first time. Caregivers can finally practice in a compassionate environment free of red tape and bureaucracy, the way they'd always believed it should be. County hospitals benefit because the non-paying primary care patients no longer put a strain on the emergency room, especially when their needs rarely qualify as "emergencies" in the first place. The free clinic saves the small Hilton Head Hospital over seven million dollars a year. "Finally," Dr. McConnell explains excitedly, "the town wins because we are creating a healthy, stable workforce that is no longer tax-dependent, but is still tax-paying. Everybody wins—and it's free."

✦ *"It is only in service that we find and begin to understand ourselves."*

The National Association of Free Clinics estimates that the country's free clinics serve over 3.5 million of the nation's 40–45 million uninsured and underinsured individuals. The United States has about 600 different free clinics across the country staffed by 100,000–150,000 compassionate volunteers with an estimated 37,500 physicians who donate their time—freely. "I hope society will soon recognize the untapped value of the approximately 180,000 retired physicians, the estimated 400,000 retired nurses, the 40,000 retired dentists, and organize them to deliver care to the 40–45 million of our fellow citizens who now have little or no access to health care," shared Jack.

Says the Good Samaritan doctor, "Throughout my life, I have learned that it is only in service to others that we find and begin to understand ourselves. Read Matthew 25:3–40 when Jesus said, 'Take care of the poor, the naked and the hungry, the thirsty, the sick,' etcetera. Those are my marching orders."

≈≈*Ripples*

DR. JACK MCCONNELL AND LANE COUNTY, OREGON'S VIMI

WHEN DR. MCCONNELL'S SUCCESS in Hilton Head picked up some national media coverage, other communities asked him to replicate the VIM Clinic program in their own areas. To that end, Jack founded the Volunteers in Medicine Institute (VIMI) specifically to help other communities create their own clinics. "We now have 45 new clinics and 30 others under development, scattered around the country from the West Coast to the East Coast and all the way to the Gulf Coast. More requests are coming in all the time," shared Jack. "They're all designed for and by locals. You can't impose a clinic on any town; it has to grow out of the soil of that community. Then it will last, and they will own it. We just help."

Just one of 70 examples: In early 1999, a group of inspired citizens explored the idea of establishing a clinic in their Eugene/Springfield area of Lane County, Oregon. With meetings convened by Sister Monica Heeran, former administrator of Sacred Heart Medical Center, the group included physicians, representatives from area hospitals, and retired but active business leaders. They estimated 28,000 of their "friends and neighbors" were without health insurance and, therefore, without adequate medical care.

The group incorporated as a nonprofit and created the Lane County Volunteers in Medicine Clinic. Working out of a vacant medical clinic on West 11th Avenue in Springfield, they opened their doors in February 2001 and started administering doses of medicine and neighborly love. Through 2002, they had treated 5,000 people with 18,000 patient visits. Over 300 people volunteer and more than 250 medical specialists in the Eugene/Springfield area take their referrals pro bono.

That's still just the beginning. As Jack McConnell foresees, "VIMI has three people out in the field and a few others in offices. If I had 20 more, we could do the whole United States in less then 10 years! People want this. They want something meaningful and valuable in their lives. They want to contribute. No one wants to look at poverty and close their eyes, ignoring it."

➤In 1992, retired Dr. Jack McConnell founded Volunteers in Medicine Clinic (VIM Clinic) in Hilton Head, South Carolina. Doors opened in 1994, with a new philosophy in free clinics: the best in quality and personal service for each "neighbor and friend" (no one is referred to as a patient). Their 28,000 annual patient visits are serviced with love by 257 professional medical and 195 lay volunteers, providing a full-range of medical, dental, pediatric, and psychiatric help for the working poor of Hilton Head. Join hands with their Circle of Care.

Over 80 million Americans were without health insurance for all or part of 2002 and 2003. That is approximately 1 in every 3 individuals. In the United States, there are approximately 160,000 retired physicians, 350,000 nurses, and 40,000 dentists. Most are looking for a meaningful way to spend their retirement. Not only do many retired medical professionals still want to practice, but they need to practice. Serving those in need is as therapeutic for the caregiver as it is for the care recipient.

Knowing this potential heart within America, Dr. McConnell went on to found the Volunteers in Medicine Institute (VIMI) to help other communities around the United States start their own clinics, fashioned on his Hilton Head model. Through 2005, 42 VIMI U.S. Clinics have opened their doors.

If your heart pulses, contact:

VOLUNTEERS IN MEDICINE CLINIC
15 Northridge Drive, P. O. Box 23287, Hilton Head Island, SC 29925
Phone: (843) 681-6612 I Web site: www.vim-clinic.org

THE VOLUNTEERS IN MEDICINE INSTITUTE
162 St. Paul Street, Burlington, VT 05401
Phone: (802) 651-0112
E-mail: VIM.Institute@verizon.net I Web site: www.vimi.org

The National Association of Free Clinics (NAFC) was formed in 2001. It estimates that the country's Free Clinics serve over 3.5 million of the nation's 40–45 million uninsured and underinsured individuals. About 100,000–150,000 volunteers serve the uninsured working poor in the more than 600 free clinics located in 47 states across the country with an estimated 37,500 physicians donating their time freely.

To accomplish all of this, tens of thousands of benevolent health-care professionals raise over $300 million annually in private funds and give thousands of hours of their time. In all, the nation's Volunteer Free Clinics contribute over $3 billion in health care value for the uninsured! While that is small compared to the $1.3 trillion health-care spending in America, it is no small feat for non-profit community programs.

NATIONAL ASSOCIATION OF FREE CLINICS
1140 Nineteenth St, NW, Suite 900, Washington, DC 20036
Phone: (202) 223-5130, ext. 132 I Fax: (202) 223-5619
E-mail: info@nafclinics.org I Web site: www.nafclinics.org

25: Betty Bloomer Ford
The Betty Ford Center

A GLAD AWAKENING

*"We're proud of you, Mom. . . . We want you to know that we love you."
My husband told the audience that he was speaking for our kids and our
grandchildren, as well as himself. When he spoke of my recovery, he broke.
He's only done that in public one other time.*
— Betty: A Glad Awakening, by Betty Ford

IT WAS THE AMERICAN DREAM: Elizabeth Bloomer from Michigan
married football hero Gerald Ford, and together they led their family
all the way from the tree-shaded streets of Grand Rapids to 1600 Pennsylvania Avenue—the White House.

Despite her husband's very public career, Betty Ford was a private person and relatively unknown prior to becoming a reluctant first lady. But
eventually with her four children, she faced the spotlight of public life
with intelligence, courage, a strong belief in God, and boundless energy.
What no one knew, including herself, was that she was suffering from two
life-threatening diseases. This reserved and private woman would handle
them both in ways that would have a huge impact on millions in America and abroad. Her courage would arguably make her the most influen-
tial first lady of all time.

After Gerald Ford was sworn in as President in 1974, Betty made a surprising discovery. "As the First Lady, when I spoke, people listened. I could
campaign for women's rights and against child abuse. I had a reputation
for candor and was able to do some good."

Less than two months after her husband took office, Betty underwent
a routine health exam and was told by doctors that she needed immediate surgery for possible breast cancer. During the operation, surgeons
found a malignant tumor and removed her right breast. While still in the

hospital and anticipating chemotherapy, she made a bold decision. Setting aside vanity and social stigma, she went public with her breast cancer. By openly and genuinely sharing her gratitude for the doctors and their diligence, acknowledging them for catching the malignancy and saving her life, Betty Ford inspired women everywhere, and they started talking about breast cancer.

Because of Betty's candor, women all over the world learned for the first time the importance of regular breast exams and mammograms. Amazingly, the first lady wouldn't be the only woman in the White House facing cancer during that short period of time. Less than a month after Betty's operation, her good friend and the Vice President's wife, Margaretta (Happy) Rockefeller, went in for a checkup. She was diagnosed with a malignant breast tumor. Like Betty, she also had a mastectomy. The doctors caught her cancer in time—in no small part thanks to Betty.

That was only the first hurdle in her public life when Betty Bloomer would be honest and candid and change the world in the process. She had become a hero to many women through her cancer experiences. But behind the always smiling and supportive First Lady lurked other shadows. "As a young housewife in Washington, D.C., I had begun taking daily medication for a pinched nerve in my neck. The pills eased my pain as I chased four active little children. As my children grew, so did my pill habit. In all my years in Washington, no doctor ever specifically made a reference to my misuse or abuse of alcohol or prescription pills. And I never made any connection between drinking and health problems," she shared.

Though the White House years were wonderful and full of excitement, Betty still felt she was just a simple girl from Grand Rapids, Michigan, without a college degree, who would never measure up to her public persona. "Feelings of inadequacy are part of the alcoholic personality. I covered these emotions by trying to appear very sure of myself. This worked, unless you remember that I had to spend my sixtieth birthday in a rehabilitation center."

On April 1, 1978, not long after leaving the White House, Betty was finally enjoying a quieter life in the Fords' newly designed and constructed home in California's Rancho Mirage, when she was forced to face a stark reality. Surrounded by her husband, children, two doctors, a nurse, and a couple of close friends, she was finally confronted with the disease she had denied for years.

"I'd never heard of an intervention, and I didn't want to hear *any* of what my family was telling me. As I look back, I realize I had no comprehension of my disease. My denial was at its peak, and denial is a cornerstone of alcoholism." Through the strong love of her family and the guidance of doctors, she tearfully agreed to get professional help.

Betty's treatment began with a medically supervised but painful at-home detoxification. The nurse who collected all the bottles of pills in the house found they filled most of an entire garbage bag. It was to be a tough battle, especially considering Betty suffered from addictions to both drugs *and* alcohol. Over the course of a week, she was slowly weaned from the pills. Then following her chemical withdrawal, she chose to go to the U.S. Naval Hospital in Long Beach where she underwent a month-long treatment for alcoholism side-by-side with Navy wives and personnel.

Alcoholism is a chronic disease; it can be treated but not cured. You'll hear people say, "I was cured," but Betty says they're never really cured. "I know I haven't got this problem licked; to the day I die, I'll be recovering. Looking back, I can see I had a hereditary predisposition to this disease. If I had only known." Alcoholism is also progressive. There is a saying among alcoholics that goes: "You can take a bottle away from a man a thousand times, but he only has to put it down once." At Long Beach, Betty learned to put all her bottles down forever.

Though the treatment process was difficult for the 60-year-old former first lady, Betty's courage to share her experiences took a lot of the public stigma out of having an addiction. It inspired the Fords' good friend and neighbor, Leonard Firestone (president of Firestone Tires), to also seek treatment. As Betty and Leonard found recovery, they decided to give something back. Together with the support of friends, family, Dr. Joe Cruse, and celebrities like Bob and Dolores Hope, Betty and Leonard developed the dream of the Betty Ford Center. With tin cup in hand, they raised the needed three million dollars, bought land in Rancho Mirage, and began to build.

When the Betty Ford Center opened on October 3, 1982, Betty kidded her husband: "Honey, you're just a former president. I am an acting president." The center was an immediate success. Using the Twelve Step program from Alcoholics Anonymous, it gained an international reputation as the leading treatment center for alcohol and drug addiction.

No one ever needed to know about Betty's problem with alcohol and pills, or her intervention. Most people would have gone to great lengths to keep such an ordeal private. Nevertheless, she shared her experiences with a courageous mix of spunk and vulnerability. The world listened and learned, and closet doors began opening. Effective treatment for additiction became available, with the Betty Ford Center leading the way for the millions who were affected.

Previously, great secrecy had kept drug and alcohol addiction from public awareness. Around the country, 90 percent of alcohol and drug treatment beds were located in psychiatric hospitals. Betty Ford's legacy changed these perceptions and, as a consequence, the actual method of treatment for addiction.

With her name on the center, Betty took every detail of the operation personally. Now in her mid-80s, she not only remains the hands-on founding chairman for the Betty Ford Center, but she also continues visiting the patients. She often shares her own personal struggles as well as her belief in God. Sometimes she signs autographs with the encouragement "sobriety is joy." She is keenly aware that through the higher power of God she has been blessed with the rebirth that recovery can bring. Integrated into the program at her center is the Serenity Prayer that is close to her heart: "God grant me the serenity to accept the things I cannot change, courage to change the things I can, and wisdom to know the difference."

Betty Bloomer Ford's openness allowed the world to look at breast cancer *and* addiction with new eyes. She began with the bold step of sharing her own battles with these personal issues and went as far as she could, working tirelessly to create a center that bears her name and continues to save and rejuvenate countless lives. A grateful nation salutes the contributions of this "reserved and private" former first lady.

The "Serenity Prayer," adopted and distributed by the originators of Alcoholics Anonymous, is actually just the first verse of a longer version. It is commonly attributed to Dr. Reinhold Niebuhr and appeared anonymously in an obituary in the *New York Times* in 1932. Years later, an early member of AA brought it to Bill Wilson (AA was co-founded in 1935 by Wilson and Dr. Bob Smith, two alcoholics helping each other toward sobriety). Wilson, known as Bill W., adopted this prayer as an integral part of AA philosophy. Thus the "accidental" noticing of an unattributed prayer, printed alongside a simple obituary of an unknown individual, opened the way toward the prayer's daily use by thousands upon thousands worldwide.

Serenity Prayer

God grant me the serenity to accept the things I cannot change;
courage to change the things I can; and
the wisdom to know the difference.
Living one day at a time;
enjoying one moment at a time;
accepting hardship as the pathway to peace.
Taking, as He did, this sinful world as it is, not as I would have it.
Trusting that He will make all things right, if I surrender
    to His will.
That I may be reasonably happy in this life,
and supremely happy with Him forever in the next. Amen.

—Reinhold Niebuhr

≈≈*Ripples*

Cathey Brown and Rainbow Days

In 1981, when Cathey Brown's mother was hospitalized with internal bleeding, Cathey was confronted with her family's alcohol problem for the first time. One night after surgeons had removed half her mother's stomach, the doctor told Cathey, "If you continue to drink, in 10 years you'll be where your mother is now." With Catherine, her beloved five-year-old daughter waiting at home, Cathey began weighing the hereditary implications of alcoholism.

Soon after, Cathey was watching *Good Morning America* from her Dallas home when Betty Ford came on to discuss her personal struggles with alcoholism and the upcoming opening of the Betty Ford Center. "I began to think for the first time that if a former First Lady could have this problem and be so public about it, that maybe I wasn't so bad, maybe I could do something about my problem. I didn't want my young daughter doomed to repeat the cycle that had been in our family for generations." Cathey quit drinking soon after that morning, April 17, 1981.

Told by a psychologist that there was nothing she could do about her daughter's high risk for alcoholism, Cathey took matters into her own hands. Intensive research led her to develop a curriculum-based support-group program for counseling the children of alcoholics. It took off right away. Cathey remembers, "In October, I had 14 kids, and by the summer, I had 45 to 50."

Within a year, Cathey's program developed into Rainbow Days and rapidly expanded. By 2005, Rainbow Days had expanded to over 6,000 children a year and trained thousands of professionals to implement the program. Cathey, her team of staff, and volunteers provide hope for children of addicted families.

In 2000, Cathey Brown received a Visionary Award personally handed to her by Betty Ford for her work with the children of Rainbow Days. It was Cathey's chance to personally and publicly thank the woman she credits for changing her life and saving her daughter's future. "It was truly momentous for me because Mrs. Ford has had an influence on thousands of women like me who have watched her from afar. Her courage and her vulnerability have made a huge impact. And she didn't have to do it."

➤From its earliest days in 1982, the Betty Ford Center has treated women and men suffering from alcohol and chemical dependency. The Center has always saved 50 percent of its space for women and 50 percent for men, who reside in separate halls. The program lasts 4–12 weeks.

Since its founding in 1935 by Bill W., Alcoholics Anonymous (AA) has grown in just the U.S. and Canada to include almost 1.3 million active members in more than 57,000 groups—all run by volunteers. Worldwide, AA has over 2 million members with 105,000 groups. People who once drank to excess now acknowledge they can not handle alcohol and now live a new way of life without it. AA serves addictions of all kinds. Meetings are professional, free and confidential.

Bill W.'s wife, Lois W., co-founded Al-Anon in 1951 with Annie B. They created a fellowship of friends and family of alcoholics who share their experiences, strength, and hope in order to solve their common problems. Volunteers run over 26,000 Al-Anon/Alateen groups in 115 countries, each with an average size of 13 members. Meetings are also professional, free and confidential.

Battle with Betty on this sobering issue and contact:

THE BETTY FORD CENTER AT EISENHOWER MEDICAL CENTER
39000 Bob Hope Dr., Rancho Mirage, CA 92270
Phone: (800) 854-9211
Web site: www.bettyfordcenter.org

RAINBOW DAYS
4300 MacArthur Ave, Suite 260, Dallas, TX 75249
Phone: (214) 887-0726
Web site: www.rainbowdays.org

ALCHOLICS ANONYMOUS (AA)
Web site: www.alcoholics-anonymous.org

AL-ANON OR ALATEEN
In the U.S.: (757) 563-1600
Worldwide: (888) 4 AL-ANON (425-2666)
Web site: www.al-anon.alateen.org

26: Marie Johnson
American Sewing Guild

SEW MUCH FABRIC, SEW LITTLE TIME

W HEN HER NEIGHBORHOOD SEWING GUILD presented a crucial need for children's clothing by an organization called Aid to Women, Marie Johnson was off and cutting. In a 22-month period, this productive widow from Cedar Rapids, Iowa, sewed over 350 children's items, including T-shirts, shorts, pants, dresses, and pajamas. Her philosophy is as simple as it is sincere: "Wouldn't it make that mother feel good to have one nice outfit to put on her baby?" Love goes into every garment she makes, and love goes out to everyone she meets. Incidentally, Marie is 84 years old.

Marie's talents, combined with those of her fellow guild members, provided 180 blankets for local public hospitals and 250 hats and mittens to an elementary school that was close to her home. She also sews items specific to patients' needs, like walker bags, nursing home lap robes, and mastectomy pillows. It's often difficult to buy a lot of the unusual things Marie and her fellow "sewers" produce, like totes stuffed with toiletries for homeless people, clothes for premature babies, and cancer caps. Most people don't realize, for example, that it's not just a matter of covering a bald head. What is important is to provide a soft and comfortable cap that doesn't have seams rubbing against the scalp. Everything they create is designed to make people feel better.

"I've been sewing since I was nine, and most of my sewing life has been devoted to making things for others," said Marie. "My grandmother worked in a men's pants factory and my mother made up her own patterns from newspapers."

Marie's labors and generosity have touched so many lives that her American Sewing Guild (ASG) friends nominated her for their national ASG Community Service Award in 2002—and she won. Forty women wrote nomination letters, telling stories about how Marie had spent most of her life teaching and sharing her sewing and using her two hands to help others.

"She is our guild's matriarch, mentor, and master tailor," read Marie's nomination for the ASG award. Letters about Marie went on to say that 10 years before, she was instrumental in getting their ASG chapter organized. One friend, Tessie Williams, said of Marie: "She sees 'needs' and does something about it. One way or another, she'll get those needs met."

+ *"She sees 'needs' and does something about it. One way or another, she'll get those needs met."*

Margo Martin, ASG's executive director, added, "In her later years, she worked in a local shop where she conducted sewing classes. Even if women couldn't afford to pay, she would teach them. Since she has retired, Marie has spent much of the last 10 years of her life sewing practically night and day to clothe needy children."

Marie's Cedar Rapids chapter of ASG proudly raised the money to fly the 83-year-old to Philadelphia to collect her national award. Many of her family surprised her by flying in from around the country. Not one for fanfare, Marie didn't understand all the fuss. "I wanted to make clothes for children at Aid to Women, so the ASG said if I wanted to sew, they'd bring me material. Well, I had fabric coming out of my ears. It took me two years to sew it all up," Marie explained.

ASG has about 130 sewing chapters all over the United States involved in various types of community-service projects. There are literally thousands of neighborhood groups creating clothes for the needy. Most of the projects involve sewing for women and children in crisis. One of the most popular projects is sewing teddy bears and dolls for local police and firefighters to use in dealing with children in traumatic situations. These toys are comforting and often useful in building a bridge between a child and the people trying to help them.

Today, millions of women sew. Over 20,000 of them have joined the American Sewing Guild, using their craft and their own two hands to create things that send ripples of love to people in need. There has been a resurgence of women who like to sew and who enjoy using their talents as both a creative and charitable outlet. Marie Johnson is one of those women. Not only does she meet the needs of strangers, but she encourages others just like her—women with warm hearts and busy fingers who want to cover the world in gifts of love.

➤American Sewing Guild, incorporated in 1993, now has 20,000 members volunteering their time to sew items needed in schools, hospitals, and community organizations. By 2005, they had 130 chapters in 39 states.

Sew what? If you want to make a stitch of difference, contact:

ASG NATIONAL HEADQUARTERS
9660 Hillcroft, Suite 510, Houston, TX 77096
Phone: (713) 729-3000 I Fax: (713) 721-9230
E-mail: info@asg.org I Web site: www.asg.org

27: Don Stephens
Mercy Ships International

MERCY ON THE HIGH SEAS

THE WORLD'S LARGEST non-governmental hospital ship grew from the prayer of a teenage girl and its impact on a 19-year-old Colorado farm boy.

In 1964, Don Stephens sat cross-legged in an airplane hangar. His team of Youth with a Mission (YWAM) had sought shelter there against the fierce winds of Hurricane Cleo as it swept across the Bahamas. Together they prayed for the storm to abate and for the safety of every person on the island. By the time the sky cleared, lives and homes had been destroyed and many had died. "Wouldn't it be wonderful," one of the students said, "to have a ship that could come in after this tragedy to bring hope and help for those in need?" As he sat huddled from the storm, Don never imagined that after quietly nurturing his vision for 18 years, it would become a reality, morphing into the world-impacting nonprofit Mercy Ships International.

A few years later, Don and his young wife, Deyon, read about a hospital ship that had served in developing nations after WWII. Don did some research and learned that 95 of the world's 100 largest cities are port cities. He knew a hospital ship would be an effective vehicle to provide medical services.

In 1977, a doctor friend in India arranged for Don to meet Mother Teresa and the Sisters of Charity. "I was deeply and profoundly impacted," he says, "seeing them care for the severely handicapped in one of the world's neediest cities." Mother Teresa's listening and observation skills were keen. Within minutes of their meeting, Mother Teresa learned Don and Deyon had a one-year-old handicapped son. She told Don that his son was a part of God's design and purpose and would help on his journey to becoming the eyes, ears, mouth, and hands for the poor. This was a profound message to the 32-year-old.

Don asked himself again and again: *What was he willing to give his life for?* He found the answer in scripture. When John the Baptist sent his disciples to ask Jesus if he was the one they had been waiting for, Jesus replied, "The blind receive sight, the lame walk, those who have leprosy are cured, the deaf hear, the dead are raised, and the good news is preached to the poor." "Jesus' answer," Don says, "was to allow the good news to be seen, then heard. Mother Teresa followed that same model—she practiced, proclaimed, and lived the Gospel. Because of that, she communicated its message to the entire world of seeing and doing the good news.

At the time, Don and his family lived in Switzerland where he served as YWAM's director for Europe, the Middle East, and Africa. Don and Deyon discovered that some Swiss friends from their Bible study owned a shipping company. A maritime superintendent for Swiss Atlantique helped Don realistically assess his vision for a hospital ship by conducting a feasibility study and business plan. "Without that study, Mercy Ships would likely not exist today. We needed help from professional marine operators at every fork in the road," Don recalls. "We faced a sharp learning curve."

Don's vision was to create a floating hospital out of a retired Italian cruise liner. "If we allow the medical aspect of Mercy Ships to become the heart of the ship," Don thought, "every port in the world will be open to us. If anything else becomes the central focus of the ship, those ports could close and many of the world's needy would miss the opportunity to see and hear of a God who loves."

The plan solidified. Armed with specific data—the ship would need 80,000 liters of water and 20 tons of fuel each day it sailed—Don visited a dozen banks in search of venture capital. Firmly believing that God was leading the project, donations and negotiations came together. Seven months after finding the ship and with almost one million dollars borrowed from a Swiss bank, they owned her. "She was seaworthy, and she was finally ours."

The *Victoria* was towed from Venice to Greece. With her large dining rooms, forward lounge, small hospital unit, and five cargo holds, this was indeed a project bigger than the 175 Mercy Ship volunteers had foreseen. They poured their efforts into scraping, sanding, needle gunning, and painting to prepare the ship for the survey that would launch the next 30 years of service. Don, Deyon, and their volunteers spent three long years in Greece refurbishing the 522-foot vessel.

Ship and crew were almost ready for sail in early 1981. Don believed that a 40-day fast prior to public service, just as Jesus had fasted prior to his public ministry, was the next step. On the thirty-sixth day of the fast, one of the volunteer workers, Becky, was walking along the beach. Suddenly, fish began to jump out of the ocean at her feet. With her own hands, Becky gathered armfuls of fish. The next day, Don and Deyon also witnessed fish jumping out of the ocean. Their Greek friends proclaimed, "God is with these people." That day, they counted hundreds of fish. The crew took it as a promise of provision and harvest ahead for the first Mercy Ship, renamed the *Anastasis*—the Greek word for resurrection. On July 7, 1982, four years after her purchase and a whole lot of volunteer elbow grease later, the ship and her crew were ready to sail on her first mission of mercy.

Funds to pay for shipyard work poured in from groups around the world, such as 100 Huntley Street, the 700 Club, the PTL Club, the Billy Graham Evangelistic Association, and YWAM. Flying a Maltese flag, she headed for California, then on to deliver relief supplies to the Ixil Indians in Guatemala, and then to provide hurricane relief in the South Pacific. Her goal: to help the poorest of the poor. Don, Deyon, and their four children lived onboard this first Mercy Ship for 10 years, along with more than 400 dedicated crewmembers. When the couple moved off the *Anastasis,* it was to better care for their handicapped son. Living on land also allowed Don to organize a larger fleet that included the *Caribbean Mercy* and the *Africa Mercy.*

When God wants something to happen, miracles simply happen. In 1983, businessman Keith Larkin donated a former Canadian coastal passenger ferry, the *Petit Forte,* which took her maiden voyage to Haiti as the *Good Samaritan.* This Mercy Ship eventually sailed to the Amazon where crew and volunteers conducted dental outreach and ministered throughout the Caribbean and Central America. In 1991, she was the first ship in 30 years to sail from the United States to Cuba. In 1994, after a 12,000-mile voyage to New Zealand, she was renamed the *Island Mercy* and worked among the islands of Southeast Asia and the Pacific until she was retired from the fleet in 2001.

Today, Mercy Ships has more than 850 crew and staff from more than

40 nations who serve full-time on board their ships, projects, and offices in 17 countries. More than 1,600 volunteers from all walks of life give of their time and skills each year. Since the maiden voyage of the *Anastasis* in 1982, an estimated 109,000 doctors, nurses, and non-medical crew have shared their talents and hearts with the poor.

The global charity Don founded in 1978 is well on its way to meeting his original goals. To date, the charity has provided 18,000 operations, treated more than 300,000 people in village medical clinics, performed 110,000 dental treatments, taught local health-care workers, provided more than $21 million worth of medical equipment, hospital supplies, and medicines, and completed more than 350 construction and agricultural projects. Mercy Ships has been financially viable, in part, because volunteers pay room and board to help offset some of the expenses.

From vision to reality, God has taken Don Stephens, his wife Deyon, and their four children on the cruise of a lifetime. All the while, Don remains keenly aware of *who* steers his ship. "When I see Mercy Ships bringing hope and healing in the developing world," he says, "I sense his pleasure. This is what God made me for. This is the DNA God put in me."

≈≈*Ripples*

AIAH'S STORY

It was a routine Wednesday. A young boy named Aiah had sold a pair of shoes and jeans at the market in Kono, Sierra Leone, Africa—enough for a couple of decent meals. But the end-of-day routine changed instantly as yelling began. "The rebels are coming!" Aiah joined the stampede, then . . . Rat-a-tat-tat. Ping! A bullet entered behind one ear and exited through his right eye. Three weeks later, he awoke in the hospital—with just one eye.

Civilians had fought off the attack, and Aiah had been found unconscious but alive. For months afterward, he tried to discover what had happened to his family. His father, who had suffered severe burns when rebels lit him on fire in a previous attack, had escaped to Guinea with his brothers and sisters. No one had seen his mother. Local doctors said they could not help Aiah. Foreign doctors left when conflict flared.

With all hope gone and little to live for, a friend told Aiah of a Mercy Ship on its way to Freetown. In line with thousands of others at the ship's screening, Aiah could not dare to hope. Then a nurse gently took his arm and led him to the front. He had an appointment card!

In November 2001, Aiah underwent the first of three surgeries to rebuild his shattered eye socket and prepare it for a prosthetic eye. The procedures continued when the ship returned in 2003. "I think of all the waiting and disappointments. I had no more hope," Aiah says. "But the Mercy Ship came and gave me surgeries free of charge. I am so grateful; there are not enough words to tell. Only God could make this possible."

►Mercy Ships, a global charity, has operated hospital ships in developing nations since 1978. Following the example of Jesus, they bring hope and healing to the forgotten poor, mobilizing people and resources worldwide, and serving all people without regard for race, gender, or religion. Since the maiden voyage of the *Anastasis* in 1982, an estimated 10,000 doctors, nurses, and non-medical crew have shared their talents and hearts with the poor.

Today, Mercy Ships has more than 850 crew and staff from more than 40 nations who serve full-time on board their ships, projects, and offices in 17 countries. More than 1,600 volunteers from all walks of life give of their time and skills each year. To date, the charity has treated more than 300,000 people in village medical clinics, performed 110,000 dental treatments, taught more than 5,500 local health-care workers, and performed more than 18,000 operations such as cleft lip and palate, cataract, orthopedic, and facial reconstruction. Mercy Ships has donated more than $21 million worth of medical equipment, hospital supplies, and medicines, and completed more than 350 construction and agricultural projects in more than 50 nations.

"Climb onboard" by giving or going. Contact:

MERCY SHIPS INTERNATIONAL OPERATIONS
Box 2020 Garden Valley, TX 75771
Phone: (903) 939-7000
E-mail: info@mercyships.org | Web site: www.mercyships.org

Part 4

Passionaries for God and Country

INTRODUCTION BY DR. ROBERT SCHULLER

Dr. Robert Schuller is the best-selling author and pastor of the Crystal Cathedral in Garden Grove, California, which broadcasts The Hour of Power, *shown around the world every Sunday.*

As you read the following profiles of this section, you will find prime examples of "possibility-thinkers"—people with big dreams who have moved mountains, for God and for country. These passionaries all personally exemplify my own belief: *if you can believe it, you can achieve it.* If you are questioning whether God still works through people, you'll stop wondering after reading about these miraculous lives.

Life has handed each of these inspiring individuals challenges that they have faced with courage. Courage isn't a gift, but a decision. Courage is not the absence of fear; it is the presence of a calling—a dream that pulls you beyond yourself. Each of them knows that God never allows a situation to exist for which there is not a corresponding solution. In the Bible (Joshua 1:9), God clearly tells us to "Be strong, be courageous," with the promise that if we follow this call, we will be prosperous and successful.

Some of these passionaries are personal friends of mine and have changed our world with their daring dreams and fearless faith. They direct and focus their teams' purpose-filled volunteers. They each point their compass toward God, their country, and prayer, keeping their life focused on compassionately loving others in his name.

All of these men and women are people with faith who had the courage to step into tomorrow. They trusted the sunshine, not the clouds. Their legacy is that they have invested in eternity and have shown us new possibilities for directing our own lives to make a difference for God. Like them or those who "ripple" in their wake, you, too, can live your dreams, move forward with faith, and know that, with God, all things are possible.

28: Military Salute

O UR MILITARY is a source of pride and security for the United States and the world. Going above and beyond is their norm, serving is their creed, and protecting us is their goal. The profiles of Bob Hope, Gary Sinise and Laura Hillenbrand, Shauna Fleming, and Betty Mohlenbrock reflect the valiant role that servicemen and servicewomen hold in our hearts.

Bob Hope, USO

THERE'S ALWAYS HOPE.

HOPE AND GLORY

A CENTURY OF LIFE and laughter came to a close in 2003, marking the final curtain call of Bob Hope's splendid legacy of entertainment and service that touched the entire world. No one has performed more at benefits or raised more money for charities, especially his beloved United Service Organizations (USO). Asked how much he'd raised over the years, he'd always quip, "Not enough."

Born Leslie Townes Hope to an impoverished English stonemason, the comedian parlayed his humor into his own 1938 radio show. That same year, he was featured in the first of his nearly 70 movies, *The Big Broadcast*, in which he crooned his signature song, "Thanks for the Memories."

Bob Hope will remain an American institution in the entertainment world, a master of one-liners, quick-wit, and genius comic response who regaled his fans in over 500 TV specials. In 1998, he sent the Library of Congress over 85,000 pages of jokes that will remain his legacy of humor.

The comedian's career was intertwined with the history of the USO. In 1940, as America's military was rapidly ramping up preceding World War II, President Roosevelt challenged six private organizations—the YMCA, YWCA, the National Catholic Community Service, the National Jewish Welfare Board, the Traveler's Aid Association, and the Salvation Army—to handle the on-leave recreation needs for the members of the Armed Forces. Those six pooled their resources and created the United Service Organizations (USO) in February 1941. Throughout the war years, patriotic entertainers brought live shows to the GIs, both in this country and to soldiers fighting overseas. By 1944, there were over 3,000 USO locations in the United States staffed mostly by precious volunteers.

Bob Hope made his first USO tour in 1942, and spent much of his life entertaining battle-weary GIs on location in remote areas around the world. He brought a bit of home, "hope," and international focus to our military serving and fighting overseas. He organized and produced their shows, sharing makeshift military stages with Hollywood's best and most glamorous talent. Together, they warmed the hearts and boosted the morale of our soldiers abroad, sometimes under fire. Bob Hope took these road tours personally, and the GI audiences adored him. From 1942 in the midst of World War II, to his 60th and final tour in Saudi Arabia and Bahrain in 1990, his USO tours spanned six decades. Hope estimated he had logged 10 million miles traveling to entertain our GIs.

The USO's commitment to be America's link with her men and women in uniform has withstood the test of time. Hope's baton of USO ambassadorship has been handed to various huge-hearted entertainers including Wayne Newton, Robin Williams, Gary Sinise, and others who continue to love, support, and entertain our troops. With the continued dedication of their legion of volunteers and charitable support from individuals and corporations, the USO will continue to provide its "touch of home" for as long as there are men and women serving our country.

Look in the sky on a clear night, and if a star is twinkling madly, making you smile, chances are Bob Hope is beaming laughter down from the heavens. *Thanks for the memories, Bob!* To salute this USO "Ambassador of Good Will," as well as the world's "ambassador of good humor," here are a few of the master's classic one-liners:

- On presidents: "I have performed for 12 presidents and entertained only 6."
- On receiving the Congressional Gold Medal: "I feel very humble, but I think I have the strength of character to fight it."
- On never winning an Oscar: "Welcome to the Academy Awards, or, as it's called at my home, 'Passover.'"
- On going to heaven: "I've done benefits for ALL religions. I'd hate to blow the hereafter on a technicality."
- On turning 70: "You still chase women, but only downhill."
- On turning 80: "That's the time of your life when even your birthday suit needs pressing."
- On turning 90: "You know you're getting old when the candles cost more than the cake."
- On golf: "Golf is my profession. Show business is just to pay the green fees."

- On his early failures: "I would not have had anything to eat if it wasn't for the stuff the audience threw at me."
- On sailors: "They spend the first six days of each week sowing their wild oats, then they go to church on Sunday and pray for crop failure."

Operation USO Care Package

Until Every One Comes Home.®

Due to the threat of anthrax following 9/11, the Department of Defense suspended forwarding personal care packages from the American public to any service member. The USO stepped in to fill this void and support our active military by creating Operation USO Care Package. This program enables individuals to express their support by sponsoring a care package which includes a personal message to their military recipient. As of May 2006, the USO has distributed more than 850,000 care packages to deploying or deployed service personnel at embarkation points and other sites in the war zone, as well as at locations served by the USO.

Members of the public can donate a care package by making a monetary donation of $25, and this package is valued at over $80. Their Web site at www.usocares.org makes donating easy. This USO program is run by over 5,000 volunteers who put the packages together and send them out. Major corporate sponsors include American Airlines, AT&T, Avon, Bass Pro Shops, Lockheed Martin, and Northrop Grumman. Each USO care package contains, at a minimum, a 100-minute prepaid international calling card, a disposable camera, toiletries, sunscreen, and a generic message of support from the sender.

≈≈*Ripples*

ANN-MARGRET AND RICHARD,
AN ANONYMOUS VIETNAM VETERAN,
BY HIS WIFE

RICHARD (MY HUSBAND) never really talked a lot about his time in Vietnam, other than that he had been shot by a sniper. However, he had a rather grainy, 8 × 10 black-and-white photo he had taken at a USO show of Ann-Margret with Bob Hope in the background that was one of his treasures.

A few years ago, Ann-Margret was doing a book signing at a local bookstore. Richard wanted to see if he could get her to sign the treasured photo, so he arrived at the bookstore at twelve o'clock for the 7:30 p.m. signing. When he got there after work, the line went all the way around the bookstore and circled the parking lot. Before her appearance, bookstore employees announced that she would sign only her book, and no memorabilia would be permitted.

Richard was disappointed, but wanted to show her the photo and let her know how much those shows meant to lonely GIs so far from home. Ann-Margret came out looking as beautiful as ever. When it was Richard's turn, he presented the book for her signature and then took out the photo. When he did, there were shouts from the employees that she would not sign it. Richard said, "I understand. I just wanted her to see it."

She took one look at the photo, tears welled up in her eyes, and she said, "This is one of my gentlemen from Vietnam, and I most certainly will sign his photo. I know what these men did for their country, and I always have time for 'my gentlemen.'"

With that, she pulled Richard across the table and planted a big kiss on him. She then made quite a to-do about the bravery of the young men she met over the years, how much she admired them. There weren't too many dry eyes among those close enough to hear. She then posed for pictures and acted as if he were the only one there.

Later at dinner, Richard was very quiet. When I asked if he'd like to talk about it, my big strong husband broke down in tears. "That's the first time anyone ever thanked me for my time in the Army," he said. That night was a turning point for him. He walked a little straighter and, for the first time in years, was proud to have been a veteran.

I'll never forget Ann-Margret for her graciousness and how much that small act of kindness meant to my husband. I now make it a point to say "thank you" to every person I come across who served in our Armed Forces. Freedom does not come cheap, and I am grateful for all those who have served their country.

(This story has been authenticated by Bruce Thompson, Webmaster of Ann-Margret.com.)

➤The USO is chartered by the Congress as a nonprofit, nongovernmental, charitable organization. Its mission is to increase the morale and provide recreation-type services for active military personnel. Currently operating 122 centers, including 6 mobile canteens around the world, the USO annually serves some 5,000,000 soldiers. These centers often offer free cell phones, Internet use, and warm welcomes for servicemen and their families. More than 33,500 members in the USO international corps of volunteers provide an estimated 375,000 hours of service each year. Soldiers, sailors, airmen, Marines, and Coast Guards value the volunteer contributions that deliver a "touch of home" to our troops.

Since 1941, the USO's commitment to be America's link with her men and women in uniform has withstood the test of time. With the continued dedication of its legion of volunteers and charitable support from individuals and corporations, the USO will serve our soldiers for as long as there are men and women serving their country.

Sign up, salute our troops, enlist, and join today. Contact:

USO World Headquarters
2111 Wilson Blvd, Suite 1200, Arlington, VA 22201
Phone: (703) 908-6400
Web site: www.uso.com

Operation USO Care Package
P. O. BOX 8069, Topeka, Kansas 66608
Phone: (877) USO-GIVE
Web site: www.usocares.org

The USO and its logo are registered trademarks of the United Service Organizations, Inc.

Gary Sinise and Laura Hillenbrand, Operation Iraqi Children

It's for the Children

WHILE SOLDIERS WITNESSED firsthand the disastrous living conditions experienced by Iraqis, well-known actor Gary Sinise (*Forrest Gump, Apollo 13, CSI: NY*) went to Iraq on two different USO tours and personally met with many beautiful children in this war-torn country. Having witnessed them drawing in the dirt and seeing their staggering need for books and school supplies, he was touched and challenged to make a difference. Upon his return to the United States, he turned to the school his own children attended and asked them to get involved by making kits of school supplies. Their first shipment of 25 boxes was gleefully received by the Abu Hassan School.

A few months later in early 2004, Sinise and best-selling author Laura Hillenbrand (*Seabiscuit*) teamed up with a mutual vision: find what could be done for the children in Iraq who our soldiers have fought so valiantly to protect. "When we first got together and began talking about founding a program to support these children, we didn't know what to expect," shared Sinise. "From our research, we knew there was a wellspring of citizens searching for a way to reach out to Iraqi children. However, we had no idea if that wellspring was deep and broad enough to bring the kind of massive support they would need in order to thrive."

Sinise and Hillenbrand started a grassroots program called Operation Iraqi Children (OIC) to give Americans and American soldiers a practical way to assist the Iraqi people. "As hopeful as we were," they admit, "we never could have anticipated the outpouring of generosity that we encountered."

As American soldiers marched through villages in Iraq during Operation Iraqi Freedom, they were horrified to see the immense needs of children and the squalor of their schools left dissipated by Saddam Hussein's ruthless dictatorship. The students lacked all basic school supplies routinely taken for granted by American children. "Imagine sending your child to a school in which there are virtually no books, no pencils, no paper, no blackboards. This is the reality for Iraqi children," says Hillenbrand. "The future of the Iraqi nation is being squandered for lack of basic school supplies." It is one thing to be talking about pencils and papers, yet these children, she says, were also "corralled in sweltering one-room buildings without air conditioning, fans, windows, solid floors, or even toilets."

Many American soldiers took it upon themselves to help resolve the plight of these children. Soldiers got the word out to family members and church groups and started collecting supplies from home and handing them out in the villages. They would occasionally come under fire as they worked to rebuild schools and deliver pencils and notebooks. School teachers have been overwhelmingly appreciative of the personal commitment the military has made on behalf of the children who now have some basic tools for education for the first time in their lives. "I have seen Iraqi kids climbing on our soldiers, hugging them and kissing them," remembers Sinise, who accompanied soldiers to a school they were rebuilding. "The folks I saw had hope in their eyes and gratitude in their hearts for what was being done."

Gary noted this "beautiful interaction between our soldiers and the Iraqi people," saying, "They were so welcoming. It was a great moment when the principal took us into his office, a room that was no bigger than a janitor's closet. On the wall was a plaque that was dedicated to the Coalition Forces for giving his country its freedom. The principal had made the plaque especially to thank the soldiers who had helped to rebuild his school. This was not much of a school, compared to schools here in the U.S., believe me. But it was so much better than what they had before our soldiers got there."

The program, started by Sinise's initial trial shipment of 25 boxes of school supplies, has really taken off. As word of the program spread, the effort was picked up by legions of volunteers through People to People International. Within one year of starting OIC, over 200,000 school kits have been sent to Iraq. Sinise celebrates, "I have seen [the Iraqi children's] smiling faces and their attempts to say 'I love you' in broken English." With every kit, American soldiers and OIC volunteers are changing Iraqi lives.

(Quotes from Sinise and Hillenbrand can be found on their OIC Web site.)

≈≈*Ripples*

You Can Build School Supply Kits

THE MOST EFFICIENT WAY to get the essential school supplies to Iraqi students is to assemble the OIC School Supply Kits exactly as recommended on the Web site listed below. They will be distributed individually in Iraq by military personnel. The simple contents of these standardized kits will help facilitate customs clearance and will guarantee that each child receives the same items. The Iraqi children and their teachers are thrilled when they are personally handed their own kit of school supplies. This is an opportunity for a small case of supplies to give big doses of international good will.

➤In 2004, actor Gary Sinise teamed up with author Laura Hillenbrand and created Operation Iraqi Children (OIC) to give Americans a practical way to reach out and support our soldiers' efforts to assist the Iraqi people. Within one year of starting OIC, over 200,000 school kits have been sent to Iraq, donated, assembled, and shipped by growing numbers of volunteers as word of their effort spreads. OIC's Web site has kit-making directions.

OIC is one of many great programs administered by People to People International (PTPI), private citizens who promote international understanding through direct people-to-people contacts. PTPI is a private sector nonprofit founded in 1956 by President Dwight Eisenhower.

Reach out to Iraqi children. It's as easy as A-B-C. Contact:

OPERATION IRAQI CHILDREN
6200 E. St. John, Kansas City, MO 64123
E-mail: OICInfo@ptpi.org I Web site: www.operationiraqichildren.org

PEOPLE TO PEOPLE INTERNATIONAL
Web site: www.ptpi.org

Shauna Fleming,
A Million Thanks

Eric Draper

THE POWER OF A GRATEFUL HEART

ON NOVEMBER 22, 2004, 15-year-old Shauna Fleming hand-delivered a special thank-you note to President Bush in the White House. What made it even more special was that it was the "one-millionth letter of thanks" that she had collected and delivered to the military. With tears in her eyes and pride in her heart, she delivered it to the Commander-in-Chief.

The year before, the intrepid Shauna was challenged by her father, Michael, to get her school to do something positive for the military men and women serving our country. When she was in seventh grade, her dad had founded an annual campaign called Valentines for Troops, which distributed over a million and a half valentines to U.S. troops within two years.

After praying about her dad's challenge, this freshman from Lutheran High School in Orange, California, started a national campaign to collect and distribute one million letters, e-mails of thanks, and appreciation to our current and past military service members. She called it A Million Thanks. "I just decided to 'go for it.' It never occurred to me that I wouldn't succeed. I had an invincible mental image and knew no one would stop me. My friends loved the idea and wanted to help."

Shauna approached her school principal, Gregg Pinick, with the idea of using the letter campaign as a school service project. Pinick responded with enthusiasm saying, "I can't think of a better way for students to express themselves for the sacrifices made by the men and women in our military. Lutheran High had never taken on such an audacious dream. The whole school was excited."

Shauna's father helped with public relations, and word spread far and wide. Letters started pouring into the school. To handle the amount of mail they received, the school organized the students into opening, sorting, and packaging teams. The mail was collected and then distributed to a variety of military bases, USOs, and VA hospitals. "I was really proud of my school," says Shauna. "Without their support, A Million Thanks would have been no more than a dream."

Shauna's grandmother has created five "memory books" of places her granddaughter has traveled and e-mails received. Within these pages are e-mails from one particular American soldier in Iraq, Chris Surdyk. "Chris and I shared an incredibly strong passion to do whatever we could to make sure our country stayed free," said Shauna. "He told stories of many ways American soldiers helped the Iraqi people." Chris shared how his dysfunctional family had left him longing for love and support. He told Shauna, "I felt so alone over here. Through A Million Thanks, I now have 30 pen pals. While I didn't receive one note from my family last Thanksgiving, I got a card and a letter from every one of those 30 pen pals." Chris experienced "family" love from new friends half a world away.

Shauna prays for direction and keeps one special verse from Romans in her heart: "God works for the good of those who love him, who have been called unto his purpose." As small miracles and answered prayers occur, she smiles and calls them "God Winks," named after a book series by Squire Rushnell. When things don't go according to plan, she tells herself that he has a purpose. His purpose seems to be far larger than she'd originally dreamed, as doors continue opening. This high school student now has her own radio show and her book, *A Million Thanks*.

Within a year and a half after launching her vision, 1.5 million people have written letters touching hearts stationed abroad. Just as Shauna's "thank-you" program rippled out from her dad's Valentine's program, A Million Thanks is spreading. New high school and college groups around America are catching the excitement of banding together as a community to salute the military. If Shauna is an example of teenage power unleashed, our future is secure.

➤In 2003, the dream of Shauna Fleming's A Million Thanks was to have people send out a million letters of love to servicepeople serving abroad. Within 18 months, her school and program had touched the hearts of 1.5 million military, simply through people who took the time to write.

Write today! Join the ranks and care for our troops through letters. Contact:

A MILLION THANKS
Mr. Gregg Pinick, Principal
Lutheran High School, Orange, CA
Phone: (714) 998-5151, Ext. 602 I E-mail: GPinick@amillionthanks.org

Shauna Fleming
E-mail: SFleming@AMillionThanks.org I Web site: www.amillionthanks.org

Betty Mohlenbrock,
Family Literacy Foundation
and United Through Reading

UNITING MILITARY ABROAD
AND THEIR CHILDREN

I N 1989, San Diego reading specialist, teacher, and mother Betty Mohlenbrock was deeply concerned about the illiteracy rate being so high in this country. One of the greatest contributing factors was that parents weren't reading aloud with their children. Studies showed that this simple activity was the single best way to secure a child's future academic success. Reading together also dramatically strengthens the bond between adult and child by providing a bridge for communication and sharing. Challenged to take action, Betty created the not-for-profit Family Literacy Foundation (FLF) with a lofty goal: to ensure that children from all backgrounds are audibly read to regularly.

The original, simple concept grew beyond the family advocacy into a school literacy program. In 1991, Betty branched out even further with United Through Reading, a seed that would later grow into a larger-than-

literacy opportunity. Getting underway, the idea was simply to enable our overseas, enlisted servicepeople to be videotaped reading a children's book and have that video sent to their children who missed them back at home. Their initial trials proved that children at home loved cuddling up and hearing the sound of their mom or dad reading them a story over and over again. From there it grew into a full-fledged quality-of-life program for military families, keeping parents and children connected while separated during long deployments.

The positive impact of the trials was so overwhelming that United Through Reading was soon adopted by the whole Navy. Family Literacy Foundation trained deployed personnel to manage the program while the ship is at sea. These volunteers promote the program, schedule videotaping sessions, and provide coaching tips to participants. Homefront supporters initially assisted with creating shipboard libraries of children's books. Families who received the videotapes were encouraged to respond to the deployed loved one through letters, e-mail, or even photographs of the child watching the parent's tape. They called this the "Full Circle Method of Communication."

The Navy raved and this program soon spread to the Marines and beyond to other branches of the armed forces. The military recognized a huge dilemma: the most commonly cited reasons for leaving the service were the frequency of deployments and the subsequent effect on time away from family. General Peter Pace, Chairman of the Joint Chiefs of Staff, recently wrote to Betty: "With characteristic heroism and spirit, our military families support these efforts while enduring extended deployments and separations. United Through Reading is an absolutely fantastic way to help Service members and their loved ones stay connected in the face of such challenges."

Thousands of children and parents are feeling much closer than they have in the past and kids have less fear about Mom or Dad's absence. Reunions are easier, morale is higher for all involved, and the spouse at home enjoys the support of the deployed parent. One spouse coordinator on the homefront who was promoting the program to other families on the USS *Anchorage* shared, "It was incredible to watch my children's eyes light up. They start smiling and before I knew it, my son was talking back to the video as if his Daddy was in the room with him. It was great!"

By 2005, Betty's United Through Reading has benefited over 175,000 children and their parents by sending home "read aloud" videotapes. One story that especially touched Betty's heart was reported to her by one of the homefront coordinators aboard the USS *Mobile Bay* who shared: "I personally have taken pictures and videotaped our children's responses to the tape they received from their sailor dad. Because it has been played over and over again, our son has much of the book memorized and recites it as he holds on to the books. Friends who have come over and witnessed this 'reading' of the book are amazed, not because he's only four years old, but because he's autistic and they can see that he's enjoying each and every time he sees his dad on video.

"I will be sending a tape to their dad so that he can see the effect that he has on them, even while he's so far away. Recently, our son was watching the tape and moved a chair up to the TV so he could reach it since it was high on the dresser. He first touched the screen, touching his dad's cheeks and then he hugged the TV. He didn't say a word, but he didn't have to…his actions were enough. I e-mailed my husband and told him 'Keep them coming!! He hears you and he sees you and he knows you love him!' For a child with autism, it's harder to break through with a connection of love. . . For this family, it was a miracle."

Betty's strategy for reaching all deployed military took great strides when she was recently notified by the White House that Mrs. Laura Bush had agreed to be the honorary chairperson of United Through Reading. Also, Target stores and its employees have taken up the bandwagon, committing to the expansion of these "read aloud" videotapes. Diligence, determination, and a great idea has paid dividends for Betty's plans.

Imagine from a child's eyes hearing the words and seeing your parent reading a book every day. Betty won't be satisfied until all the deployed military have access to this dream—and to their families. A little bit of home brings a lot of hope and love to servicemen separated continents away from their families. Betty and her dream of affecting literacy and family communication have taken flight, gliding with precision accuracy toward accomplishing its "golden books" mission.

➤In 1989, Betty Mohlenbrock created Family Literacy Foundation in San Diego to help end illiteracy, focusing on reading aloud to children. Family Literacy branched out in 1991 to include United Through Reading, which allows our overseas enlisted servicepeople to be videotaped reading a children's book and have that video sent to their children who miss them back at home. United Through Reading has benefited over 175,000 children and their deployed military parents by sending home "read aloud" videotapes.

Shape up or ship out: Support our military families. Contact:

FAMILY LITERACY FOUNDATION
3525 Del Mar Heights Road, #348, San Diego, CA 92130
Phone: (858) 481-7323
E-mail: info@read2kids.org I Web site: www.read2kids.org

29: Chuck Colson
Prison Fellowship

PRISONER #23226

WHEN CHARLES "CHUCK" COLSON stepped through the gate of the Fort Holabird stockade to freedom on January 31, 1975, he vowed never to set foot in a prison again. It was a promise he would happily break thousands of times.

With his signature black horn-rimmed glasses and close-cropped haircut, Chuck Colson was once known as the White House "hatchet man." Feared by even the most powerful politicos during his four years of service to President Nixon, he had a reputation for being power-hungry and hard-hearted. This fiercely patriotic man believed that helping his president was helping his country. But many smiled when this deeply reviled attorney was sent to jail for his minor role in the Watergate scandal.

Born to working-class parents, Colson grew up in Massachusetts. Both in high school and among his fraternity brothers, he was known as a practical joker. After a stint in the Marines, he dabbled in politics while earning his law degree at night. After winning the presidential election in 1968, long-time friend Richard Nixon appointed Colson as Special Counsel to the President of the United States.

In the legal world, that is about the highest position attainable. After Nixon won re-election in 1972, Colson returned to a lucrative private law practice with his wife Patty at his side.

Despite a highly successful life, something was missing in Chuck's life. Through a business friend's guidance, he became a Christian and developed a personal relationship with Jesus. His newfound faith was almost immediately tested as he went from the pinnacle of legal success to the depths of degradation. Not long after being "born again" came Watergate, prison, and a hard dose of humility. For seven months, this once powerful aide and confidant to the President washed laundry for other inmates.

In the dreary penitentiary camp, Colson began scribbling notes, describing the drama and disgrace of going from the White House to prison. Scratched out on a yellow pad, his story later became the best-selling book, *Born Again*. When Colson was released early by a judge, Christian friends suggested he start a prison ministry. "The thought of going back into prison chilled me; the stench was still pungent in my nostrils." And yet he couldn't forget the face of one tattooed prison veteran, Archie, whom Colson had promised while saying goodbye, "I'll help in some way," Colson insisted. "I'll never forget this stinking place or you guys." Archie shouted back, "Bull!"

In the months following Colson's release, the faces of his former inmates haunted him. "The sensation of helplessness, of time standing still, walls closing in, and fears of assault were memories that stubbornly refused to be erased as the weeks passed," Colson shared. Somehow, he had to keep his promise to Archie and the others.

During a Bible study with his one-time-enemy-turned-friend, former Senator Harold Hughes, Colson made a reference to "the lousy prison system." Without missing a beat, Hughes challenged him, "If you think it's so bad, then it's time you got busy and did something." Colson replied, "I'm thinking about it."

Starting this lofty challenge with a small idea, Colson arranged two-week discipleship classes for up to a dozen federal prisoners at the Fellowship House, just across the Potomac River in Virginia. Norm Carlson, the no-nonsense director of the Federal Bureau of Prisons, took a chance and allowed prisoners selected by Chuck and his team to be furloughed in order to attend the programs.

Although there weren't any incidents, it became obvious to Colson that his ministry could only really get off the ground if he gave it his full-time attention and effort. He went from his vow to never enter another jail to visiting regularly on behalf of prisoners.

During his own imprisonment, Colson had seen and experienced first-hand the difference that faith in Jesus Christ makes in people's lives. He became convinced that the real solution to crime is ultimately not found in therapeutic interventions, institutional regimes, or legislative reform, but through spiritual renewal. With the constant support of his wife,

Patty, Chuck and his friends incorporated Prison Fellowship (PF) in 1976. The purpose was to bring together men and women from various Christian churches to share their faith and the love of God with prisoners, ex-prisoners, and families.

Word of PF's mission and success rippled across vast oceans as representatives from groups that had developed in Australia, Canada, England, New Zealand, and the Bahamas met to form Prison Fellowship International (PFI) in 1979. PFI would meet the same needs of prisoners and families in other countries. Since then, Colson's brainchild has become the world's largest prison ministry.

Colson studied a Christian prison program that had originated in South America. Emulating that very successful program, PF created the InnerChange Freedom Initiative (IFI). It is a biblically-based, Christ-centered, 24-hour-a-day prison model where incarcerated participants volunteer to be immersed in a values-based environment, supported daily in academics, life-skills, spiritual development, and job preparation. The prisoners are mentored by a local Christian volunteer both in jail and following their release. This prison program was immediately effective.

In 1997, their first U.S. program opened in the Carol S. Vance Prison in Texas with the cooperation of the Texas Department of Criminal Justice. IFI/PF was wildly successful, and has now been replicated in correctional facilities in Iowa, Minnesota, and Kansas as well as internationally in Australia, Bulgaria, Chile, Ecuador, England, Germany, Latvia, New Zealand, and Taiwan. While the national U.S. recidivism (return to prison) rate is nearly 70 percent, in prisons with IFI/PF programs it is less than 10 percent. When you consider that the cost of housing each inmate averages $41,000 per year and therefore the total cost of housing more than 2 million incarcerated people exceeds $40 billion a year, the savings in both dollars and souls is enormous!

In recognition of his work on behalf of prisoners and their families, Colson received the prestigious 1993 Templeton Prize for Progress in Religion. He has written more than 20 books that collectively have sold more than 5 million copies. Royalties from these books and speaking engagements are donated to Prison Fellowship.

Now in his 70s, Colson shows no sign of slowing down. Though former Attorney General for Virginia Mark Earley now serves as PF president, Colson continues to dedicate his time as founder and chairman. Breaking that long-ago vow to never again enter prison has become routine as he returns time and time again to visit and speak with inmates. When he speaks he imparts a sense of hope and God's love that didn't exist before in the hearts of those shut away and forgotten.

Colson has visited prisons throughout the United States and the world and has built a movement working with more than 100,000 prison ministry volunteers in 117 countries. But ask Chuck Colson what keeps him going back into the bleak prisons that he remembers all too well and he motions to the plaque on his desk inscribed with a quote by Mother Teresa, one of Chuck's heroes. It reads: "Faithfulness; not Success."

≈≈*Ripples*

RON HUMPHREY

"I'D WALK THROUGH FIRE for Chuck Colson," affirms Prison Fellowship senior writer Ron Humphrey. "Through PF, I've been able to give back to others as others gave to me and to my family when we were in need."

During his two-year service as a civilian advisor in Vietnam, Ron fell in love with Kim—a Vietnamese war widow and mother of eight. When the Communists conquered South Vietnam in 1975, Kim and her children waited in the American Embassy compound in Saigon for evacuation helicopters that never came. She was captured and spent nearly a year in a Communist prison, accused of working for the Americans.

As details of her situation leaked out, Ron used diplomatic sources to first arrange her release from prison and then for Kim and the four youngest of the children to be taken out of Vietnam in 1977—the others would follow years later. Once he was reunited with Kim in the States, their fairytale dreams of building a new life together would quickly dissolve. On January 31, 1978, two months after Kim's arrival, Ron was arrested for espionage. Because of his fervent quest to rescue Kim from the Communists, he was accused of violating security restrictions. Although it was later acknowledged that Ron's involvement posed little risk and that the real culprit had escaped, he was sentenced to 15 years in prison.

While enraged at being unjustly incarcerated, Ron read *Born Again*, Chuck Colson's autobiography, and decided to write to the author. Subsequently, Colson visited Ron in jail and offered real hope and encouragement. Ron liked what he heard and started attending the PF programs and chapel services.

Throughout Ron's eight years of imprisonment, he and Chuck Colson regularly corresponded. When he was released in early 1990, he joined the PF staff where he's served enthusiastically for 17 years. Ron Humphrey knows he's come full circle—from an incarcerated parent having Christmas gifts donated to his children through Angel Tree, to directing that very same program, to becoming senior writer for PF's *Inside Journal* and *Jubilee*. With a wink Ron adds, "Who says God doesn't have a sense of humor?"

➤Founded in 1976 by Chuck Colson, Prison Fellowship (PF) offers love, hope, and direction to more than two million men and women incarcerated in America's prisons and jails. Across the nation and in 117 countries, 100,000 volunteers reach out to give hope to the hopeless. Colson has visited more than 600 prisons throughout the United States and the world. Some of these PF ministries include:

- The InnerChange Freedom Initiative (IFI): A revolutionary, Christ-centered, Bible-based prison program that supports inmates and ex-cons through their spiritual and moral transformation. IFI conducts programs in Texas, Minnesota, Iowa, Kansas, and Arkansas. While the national recidivism (return to prison) rate is nearly 70 percent, in prisons with IFI/PFprograms, it less than 10 percent.

- Wilberforce Forum: Named for one of Colson's heroes, William Wilberforce (an 18th-century British parliamentarian who stood against his party in a campaign to abolish the slave trade), their call is to teach clear biblical views of Christian principles on current events and controversial issues affecting everyday life. It produces Colson's five-times a week radio broadcast, Break-

Point, which is aired on 1,000 stations with an estimated nationwide audi-ence of more than a million. It also prints magazines and web information and works to shape public policy on criminal justice reform, freedom of religion, and human rights.

- Angel Tree: Founded in 1982 by Mary Kay Beard, a former prisoner and PF staff member, this ministry has given more than seven million children of pris-oners Christmas gifts in their incarcerated parent's names. Youth summer camping programs and mentoring opportunities are also offered.
- *Inside Journal:* A newspaper circulated exclusively to inmates, It offers Bible studies and guidance on getting through a prison sentence. It also advises prisoners on living after release, as well as advice on parenting and maintain-ing a marriage from behind bars.

    Break out, reach out, and get involved by contacting:

PRISON FELLOWSHIP
44180 Riverside Parkway, Lansdowne, VA 20176
Phone: (703) 478-0100 I Fax: (703) 554-8667
Web site: www.pfm.org

30: Fern Nichols
Moms In Touch International

THE POWER OF PRAYER

IT ALL BEGAN with one mom and her kids. In the early 1980s, as Fern Nichols prepared to send her two oldest boys to junior high school in British Columbia, Canada, she found herself growing apprehensive as the start of the school year approached. She and her husband had done all they could to prepare their children—given them warnings about drugs and alcohol, discussed increased homework loads, and did all they could to encourage healthy self-esteem. As parents, they had always emphasized the importance of choosing the right peer group and raised both boys to withstand unhealthy peer pressure. Still, the thought of what they might face in junior high made Fern shudder. What mom hasn't had similar misgivings?

Above all things, Fern knew that her greatest weapon, and the one in which she felt most confident, was prayer. Even as she prayed, the weight of what her boys were apt to confront in the pressure-cooker of junior high overwhelmed her. Not wanting to bear her fears alone, she asked God for another mother who felt the same burden to pray with her for their kids and the school. Her prayer was answered when one mom came to pray. Then another was at her door, and another. Before long, mothers from other schools were asking Fern to come teach them how to pray.

Most great movements begin small with just a ripple—one person, one dilemma, one solution. Moms In Touch began just that way—one mom, one challenge, one prayer. "I didn't have a dream about anything [coming of this]," Fern says of what is now an international organization. "I just had a passion for the Lord, a passion for prayer, and a passion for my kids."

Meeting week after week, Fern worked out an efficient format for the hour they spent together that guaranteed no time wasted. It consisted of no coffee or snacks, no lengthy visiting, and it began and ended on time.

She also adopted a "plan for prayer" that kept them all talking to God instead of to each other. Her agenda included a focus on a particular characteristic of God found in the Bible (i.e., his mercy). This was followed by silent introspection and confession, thanking God for what he'd done the week before in answer to their prayers. They would then ask him specifically to help work out situations in their kids' lives and in the school during the coming week.

It wasn't long before these praying moms began to see changes in their children. A new sense of courage, an unseen kindness between siblings, and even a better understanding of algebra came about. Moms prayed for healthy friendships, diligence in homework, and for things as large as bullies and as small as finding a misplaced retainer. They prayed for safety on field trips, for their kids to get caught if they were involved in unsafe or illegal activity, for curriculum concerns, and for student-teacher rapport.

"One teacher proclaimed to be a Christian and yet was the grumpiest teacher in the whole school," Fern recalls. "He was known as 'the grump.' His attitude was, 'I've taught my math class. Don't bug me.' He wouldn't even stay afterwards to help kids with their work. We began to pray that this man would start seeing those kids through Jesus' eyes. By the end of the school year, his attitude had changed so much that he had his room opened at the end of every school day for any of the kids who wanted help. This was huge!"

Though their primary focus was their own children and their schools, the moms began to notice other benefits emerging. "They were so excited that they were learning how to pray! Even women who had been brought up in the church had never prayed like this before. As time went on, various women have said to me, 'This is just revolutionary! It's changing my life.' That first year we saw God was changing *us* as we prayed for him to change our children!"

In 1985, the Nichols family moved to Southern California where Fern started over and she again found just one mother to pray with her. By word of mouth, her group had grown to 20 mothers by the end of the second year. Together they compiled a list of every school in their district and prayed each week for one school, asking God to raise up moms to pray there. One by one, the moms saw it happen. The fall of 1987 brought the first published Moms In Touch booklet, and in the following January, the first Moms In Touch retreat was held with 35 women. They prayed for national exposure and God answered their prayers. Fern got a call that spring from a producer at *Focus on the Family*. By May, she and 12 other moms were on the air talking to Dr. James Dobson! That first radio program brought more than 20,000 responses.

During the retreat the following year, these mothers prayed that every school in San Diego County would have a Moms In Touch group. "Then the Lord touched our hearts and we said, why would we just want San Diego? So we prayed for all of California, and then the West Coast, and then we prayed all the way across the United States. Later we asked: What about Russian moms? They need this ministry. So we asked God for the whole world."

Within its first 15 years, Moms In Touch International (MITI) had spread across the nation and across the world to over 110 countries on six continents. This simple vision mushroomed into 18,500 groups, each of which is entirely volunteer-led. MITI booklets, which explain the "Four Steps of Prayer" and how to start a group, have been printed in 21 different languages as well as in braille.

Moving stories of encouraged children, major changes in schools, and stronger moms still pour into the San Diego headquarters on a daily basis. Columbine High School, the tragic site of a student shooting spree, has a MITI group. "One mom who lost her son on that horrific day told me she could not have handled what happened were it not for her faith, which was solidified through her Moms' group. When she felt herself falling into despair, it was like the Lord would catch her in the safety net of his omniscience."

Fern Nichols is convinced that "we must spend time with our heavenly Father daily. It's a choice every day for me. Am I going to spend time with God or not? You never know what he's prepared to accomplish when we do. Can you imagine what we might be missing out on when we don't? And there is something about a peace that surpasses understanding when you have been in the prayer room."

Over 100,000 mothers around the world know that same peace.

≋*Ripples*

The Praying MOPS

In 1973, a decade and a half before there was Moms In Touch, eight women gathered in Wheat Ridge, Colorado, to address the same great need—specifically for mothers of preschoolers. Knowing that "mothering matters," they founded MOPS (Mothers of Preschoolers), a support group that helped moms meet the challenges of raising preschoolers. They met, talked, laughed, and had a small devotional as their preschoolers played. Individuals from this core group took their concept of MOPS with them as they moved on, developing their leadership skills and forming new groups. Word spread in churches, conventions, and through magazine articles fueling requests for their materials.

In 1981, this group of dedicated women elected a Board of Directors and became incorporated. The following year, as interest mushroomed, 150 women from 5 states gathered for the first all-day MOPS leadership seminar. In 1988 they went international and hired their first staff. In 1989 they also hired Elisa Morgan as the first president and CEO of the organization. Five years later, they developed the *MOMSense* radio program and later reached out to moms through *MOMSense* magazine to help nurture every mother of preschoolers, whether or not she attended a MOPS group.

Currently, more than 3,860 local MOPS groups, each comprised of 10–200 women, meet across the United States and in 33 other countries. MOPS International exists to encourage, equip, and develop every mother of a preschooler to reach her potential as a woman, mother, and leader. They incorporate many parenting resources such as MOPS groups, events, books, and leadership training.

One mother's sentiment on the Web site captures their spirit: "MOPS opens doors and lets women know that mothering and mothers matter. MOPS means I am able to share joys, frustrations, and insecurities of being a mom. It is important to feel normal and not alone. Burdens are lifted when the woman next to me says: 'I know exactly how you feel!'"

➤Founded in 1988 by Fern Nichols, Moms In Touch International has inspired groups of two or more moms who meet for one hour each week to pray for their children and their children's schools, teachers, and administrators. There are currently almost 18,500 registered MITI groups led by volunteers in all 50 of the United States and many more in 110 countries on 6 continents throughout the world. MITI booklets, including "The Four Steps of Prayer," have been translated into 21 languages, including Braille.

Pray for your kids and school them in the spiritual basics. Contact:

MOMS IN TOUCH INTERNATIONAL
P.O. Box 1120, Poway, CA 92074-1120
Phone: (800) 949-MOMS
E-mail: info@momsintouch.org I Web site: www.momsintouch.org

More than 2,700 local MOPS groups, each comprised of 20–200 women, meet across the United States and in 19 other countries to pray for their preschoolers.

MOTHERS OF PRESCHOOLERS (MOPS)
2370 South Trenton Way, Denver, CO 80231-3822
Phone: (303) 733-5353
E-mail: info@mops.org I Web site: www.mops.org

31: Bill Hunter
Presidential Prayer Team

ONE NATION UNDER GOD

*"My faith sustains me because I pray daily. I pray for guidance
and wisdom and strength. There are thousands of people who pray
for me who I'll never see or be able to thank. But it's a humbling
experience to think that people I will never meet have lifted me
and my family up in prayer. And for that I'm grateful."*
—President George W. Bush, March 6, 2003

AFTER THE PRESIDENTIAL ELECTION of 2000, news of hanging
chads, recounting votes, and negative rhetoric in the news threatened to divide our country. Bill Hunter wanted to know what an ordinary
American living in Scottsdale, Arizona, could do to help change the dis-
course and get America back on track. So he prayed.

As a bronze sculptor, Bill had created a patriotic silver-dollar-sized coin.
Bill and his wife, Sue, proposed to his church's Sunday school class that if
anyone would commit to pray daily for our president and our nation, he
would give them this patriotic coin as a reminder to pray. People carried
them in their pockets, placed them on night stands and desks, attached
them to refrigerators, and sent coins to friends and relatives. The concept
was the right thing at the right time. When a friend learned of the project, he supplied the funds to mint the first 5,000 coins.

The "heads" side of the coin shows General George Washington kneel-
ing in prayer during the winter of 1777. The story is true. A local farmer
was out and about just before dawn on a cold morning walking through
the snow when he heard a voice. It was General Washington praying for
his starving and dying troops at Valley Forge and praying for our
nation. At the top of the coin are the words, "The Presidential Prayer
Team," the name Bill chose for this new-found effort. The coin also reads,

"In God We Trust," and Psalm 33:12, which says, "Blessed is the nation whose God is the Lord."

It was during this time that Bill, a rocket scientist and businessman turned artist, met Dr. Cornel Haan, and together they started the Presidential Prayer Team, a ministry to pray for the president and nation. Hunter completed the business plan and raised money, and they both obtained endorsements from leaders of national spiritual groups. Their ministry was set to launch in early December 2001.

Then the unexpected occurred. On September 11, 2001, the plans for the ministry were were dramatically transformed as Bill watched the most devastating terrorist attacks in American history unfold on television. He knew there was a desperate need for everyone to pray every day for our president, our country, and our leaders. Bill wanted to encourage this unceasing prayer using the image of the coin he had sculpted as an inspiring reminder. The decision was made to launch the prayer project immediately!

Utilizing the Internet as the vehicle to launch this idea, Bill and friends put together an effective Web site and had it operational in just a few days, along with a toll-free telephone number. The e-mail "forward" button was used over and over as word spread like a virus on the Internet. People took the Presidential Prayer Team (PPT) prayer requests to churches, schools, Bible studies, their friends, and the work place. Membership in the PPT was offered free. In the first week more than 100,000 people joined. Every hour 2,000 people were joining in a commitment to pray.

Bill Hunter: One Step at a Time

Nothing in his careers as a businessman or engineer could have prepared Bill for what God had in mind. Growing up as an Eagle Scout in a small New Mexico town instilled in his young heart the deep traditional values of God and country. As a boy he learned how to work hard and had dreams of doing something for his country.

Bill attended the University of Colorado on a full Navy scholarship and there met the love of his life, Sue. He was a Command Duty Officer and the Chief Engineer of a destroyer. Upon completing his active duty commitment, he elected to enter the space race, first as a rocket engineer followed by directing manned maneuverable spacecraft planning for the Air Force. Early in the rocket business, Bill was involved in developing a new method to steer rockets. Bill recalls, "In early aerospace work there was no such thing as assurance of success. There were few experts. We learned that a fingerprint or a human hair in a propellant line could blow up a whole rocket. The space program advanced because we believed solutions and technology not yet available would be there when we needed them."

At 31, Bill earned his master's in engineering from UCLA and left spacecraft work to direct systems engineering for the first Navy combatant ship designed by private industry. The corporate push was to bring aerospace technology into ship building. He left the ship building industry to run one more space program before leaving aerospace altogether for a new career in corporate business start-ups.

✦ "I never really started any project knowing how to do it. With each new thing, I just took one step at a time and dreamed and then took the next step."

After starting more than 10 businesses, in 1988 Bill and Sue moved to Arizona, where he pursued a long-time desire to sculpt in bronze. His favorite sculpting subject was no surprise—American patriots and heroes. His work is sought by collectors and is currently in a presidential museum with several pieces in the White House, the Pentagon, various museums, and the Rotunda of the Arizona State Capitol. This became a business that later transitioned into manufacturing an extensive line of bronze door hardware and decorative door handles.

Surprisingly, given his wide range of skill and successes, Bill thinks of himself as just a run-of-the-mill person and never had a vision of how large any of his ventures could become. He said, "I never really started any project knowing how to do it. With each new thing, I just took one step at a time and dreamed and then took the next step. My motto is: Just get started and follow through, work hard, surround yourself with the best people you can afford, and take good care of them." He also shares that the Navy and space business provided opportunity and taught responsibility that were invaluable. Bill is a quick study, enjoys challenges, and is bold enough to take giant leaps of faith enabling him to achieve so much.

Presidential Prayer Team

Since September 11, millions have joined the Team's commitment to pray daily for the president. There is no fee or obligation for joining. Members receive weekly updates by e-mail. Bill's unique prayer coins are available through PPT.

The initial goal of his PPT was to involve a million people in daily prayer for our president, leaders, and nation. Immediately after the launch, that goal seemed to be too small for a God-sized dream and the goal was increased to 1 percent of the U.S. population—2.8 million. Prior to the second anniversary, 600 days after launch, the 2.8 million goal was reached. The PPT continues to mature with quality and content heralding a call to America to pray for our president, leaders, and nation.

As Bill shared, "We've seen with 9/11 that nothing lasts forever. In the twinkling of an eye, everything that man can create can be destroyed. It is best if we align with the God of the Universe through his son, Jesus Christ, and step forward when we hear the little voice that says…take a step of faith."

≈≈*Ripples*

FROM THE PRESIDENTIAL PRAYER TEAM

EARLY IN 2003 as the war against terrorism progressed, the PPT launched an "Adopt Our Troops" campaign to pray for men and women serving around the world defending our freedom. In the first week alone, 100,000 individuals had signed up to "adopt" a military serviceperson, encouraging each one of them directly through prayer.

There was so much activity on the Web site that on March 19, 2003—the first day of Operation Iraqi Freedom—the server crashed when it hosted more than 9.8 million hits. This virtual army pledged to pray daily for our troops. On the first anniversary of Adopt Our Troops, PPT responded to the requests to know more about the status of the troops for whom members had been praying and the effects of those prayers. They now provide updates on the registered troops that can be viewed online by intercessors.

"Prayer makes a difference," says General John Wickham, former U.S. Army Chief of Staff and a member of the PPT Honorary Committee. General Wickham further says, "Your prayers for the troops, and the knowledge that you are praying for their families, will encourage and strengthen the brave men and women who serve our country."

≈≈*Another Ripple*

American Defenders of Freedom (ADF) is the term Bill Hunter uses for our military. In 2005, he created a ministry separate from PPT, whose mission is to take prayer directly to our troops. With the dream that no one should face injury or possible death for the sake of others and not know their prayers are heard by God, Bill designed four new coins to represent each of the four branches of the military—Army, Navy, Air Force, and Marine Corps. When a soldier reaches into his or her pocket, this coin will be a reminder to pray and a symbol of God's promises to be with us, hear our prayers, and uphold us. All ministry tracts and materials for ADF will be used along with these coins to support existing chaplaincy organizations. The mission is simple and straightforward: Take prayer to all American Defenders of Freedom. The ministry is self-supporting and Internet-driven and can be accessed at www.americandefendersoffreedom.com.

➤Since September 11, 2001, more than 2.8 million people have joined the Presidential Prayer Team's commitment to pray daily for the president, our leaders, our country, our children, and our troops. An "Adopt our Troops" campaign was launched to pray for the men and women serving around the world to defend our freedom. Over one million people have "adopted" a military serviceperson, encouraging each one of them directly through prayer. Joni Eareckson Tada and Michael Smith, the honorary co-chairs of PPT, now also emphasize the importance of kids, who have their own interactive Web site, Presidential Prayer

Team for Kids, at www.pptkids.org. They make it fun for kids to get involved and pray. This site teaches kids about their own very important roles in shaping the future of our country.

When you join the Presidential Prayer Team, you will receive the official blue and gold static cling window decal to proudly display in your window or on your car. You'll also receive weekly e-mail prayer updates. All member information will forever remain confidential.

To join their heavenly team, contact:

PRESIDENTIAL PRAYER TEAM
P. O. Box 89130, Tuscon, AZ 85752
Phone: 1-800-295-1235
E-mail: info@PresidentialPrayerTeam.org
Web site: www.presidentialprayerteam.org

32: President
George H. W. Bush
Points of Light Foundation

LIGHTING UP OUR FUTURE

"The response [to Points of Light] has been overwhelming. Since the President issued his call to service, more than 45,000 people have called the United States Peace Corps to request applications for only 6,300 open slots. You don't have to score a touchdown to win points with someone. You don't have to go to medical school to help a person feel better. You don't have to walk on the moon to change the Earth, and you don't have to sign a bill to change your state or country. Kindness and heroism can't always be drawn in a picture. Many acts of kindness never make the evening news or the morning paper."
—former First Lady Barbara Bush, June 2004

PRESIDENT GEORGE H. W. BUSH had a vision: to acknowledge, encourage, and empower unrecognized volunteers across America. In 1990, Bush directed the creation of the Points of Light Foundation. It was named after the phrase that had become inseparably linked with him following his 1989 Inaugural Address when he said, "I have spoken of a thousand points of light, of all the community organizations that are spread like stars throughout the Nation, doing good. . . . The old ideas are new again because they are not old, they are timeless: duty, sacrifice, commitment, and a patriotism that finds its expression in taking part and pitching in."

The brilliance and importance of passionate people doing the extraordinary was recognized and researched by the Points of Light Foundation. They help coordinate and acknowledge the more than 100 million volunteers in this country giving their time, talent, and energy to help others solve social problems and build strong communities. Sharing the common goal of working to make a difference, these volunteers represent all backgrounds and beliefs—children, seniors, corporations, small groups, families, and individuals ranging in age from 5 to 95—an unpaid army of millions.

Points of Light has volunteer centers in over 350 communities and has gained a national reputation as "America's Address for Volunteering." It partners and coordinates with various volunteer organizations.

President George H. W. Bush, who wisely commended volunteers and congratulated them for their magnificent efforts, shared, "Points of Light are the soul of America. They are ordinary people who reach beyond themselves to the lives of those in need, bringing hope and opportunity, friendship and care." The awards and recognition programs of the Points of Light Foundation celebrate the success of these "ordinary" volunteers and highlight the impact that various individuals, groups, businesses, and families have made in their communities.

Unlike any other national acknowledgment or honor, the Points of Light Awards have been given on a *daily* basis since the program's inception in 1991. While the rest of this book is dedicated to giving fuller profiles of individuals, the following short acknowledgments are just a sample of a few of the daily Points of Light Award winners. The numbers reflect the order in which they were given. These highlights capture just a bit of the magnitude and magnificence of the accomplishments of these individuals. Just imagine the ripples.

#2376. *Fashionably Frankford, Philadelphia, PA,* a project operated by students at Frankford High School that provides business clothing to needy men and women who have completed a job-training program.

#2377. *Virginia Proctor, Decatur, GA,* who co-founded the International Nursing Services Association, now known as Global Health Action (GHA), to train health professionals worldwide in leadership and management skills. Ms. Proctor has also raised money for GHA's Give a Goat Project that provides Haitian families with goats that they can use for milk, meat, or income.

#2187. *Allen Baca, Round Rock, TX,* who in his career as a corrections supervisor, found illiteracy to be a major problem for many people on probation. To help remedy the problem, Mr. Baca volunteered for 16 years with the Bell County Jail's GED Program and also began a literacy program for senior citizens.

#2369. Nancy Simmons, Kansas City, MO, who serves as a police athletic league volunteer by coaching a youth basketball team and providing access to a court she built for neighborhood youths in her backyard.

#2371. Palm Coast Lions Club, FL, whose members volunteer at the Suncoast Tape Library for the Blind, in St. Petersburg, helping to augment and maintain a collection of over two million Braille books and cassettes.

#2320. Anthony Leanna, Suamico, WI, who started the Heavenly Hats program when he was 11. Through this program, he collects new hats from businesses and individual donors and distributes them to children and adults who have lost their hair following chemotherapy.

#2389. John Betterton and John Berryhill, Roxboro, NC, who purchased a recently closed local school building where they worked and converted it into a charter school that they now direct.

#2072. Interplast, Mountain View, CA, a nonprofit group that sends medical volunteers to underdeveloped countries to provide needy children with free reconstructive surgery to correct such problems as cleft palates and disfigurement from severe burns.

#2064. Z. Salty Leatherwood, Daytona Beach, FL, founder of Project Care, a nonprofit group that provides mentally ill adults with Christmas and birthday gifts, social activities such as parties and bingo games, and other services.

#2086. Debbie Parnham and Loretta Winn, Phoenix, AZ, who founded the charity Life Sentence three years ago after each woman lost a son to gun violence. Sharing their stories with more than 6,700 adults and teenagers at schools, churches, detention centers, and prisons, the two discuss the rippling effects that crime has on families and the need for people to make responsible choices.

#2088. Vivian Hanson Meehan, Riverwoods, IL, president of the National Association of Anorexia Nervosa and Associated Disorders, who since founding the group in 1976, has instituted various community-based and national programs including support groups, hotlines, referral lists, and public education activities.

#2267. Volunteers at the Pasadena Senior Center, Pasadena, CA, who teach computer skills and English as a second language, take grocery orders for homebound individuals, and provide other services to the elderly. Many of the volunteers are themselves in their 90s.

#2232. Curtis Sliwa, New York, NY, who founded the group that later became the Guardian Angels Safety Patrol, which has expanded its activities—originally designed to reduce crime on the city's subway trains—to include after-school programs for at-risk youths.

#2239. Brian Orloff, Clearwater, FL, a high school senior who has volunteered at a local hospice since he was 13. In addition to working with patients, he serves as a mentor for the hospice's support groups for siblings.

#2142. Charlene Clark, Concord, NH, a pet therapist who has volunteered at a local psychiatric hospital since 1994. Ms. Clark and her dog, Buster Brown, visit with mentally ill patients, some of whom are unresponsive to human and drug therapies alone but respond positively to interaction with animals.

The list goes on: one person or group every day since 1990 has been recognized for the brilliant light that each has cast, providing for and loving their fellow man.

───────────────────────────────

►In 1990, President George H. W. Bush directed the formation of the Points of Light Foundation to encourage and recognize the spirit of volunteerism. The foundation helps coordinate and acknowledge the more than 100 million volunteers who work through a host of inspirational programs under its umbrella, which include: 1-800-VOLUNTEER.org, 50+ Volunteering Initiative, AmeriCorps Promise Fellows Program, Disaster Preparedness and Volunteers, THE EXTRA MILE, FamilyCares, Seasons of Service, and Kids Care Clubs.

Light a candle, send a flicker of hope, shine bright in the darkness. Call:

POINTS OF LIGHT FOUNDATION
1400 I Street NW, Suite 800, Washington, D.C. 20005
Phone: (202) 729-8000
E-mail: Info@PointsofLight.org | Web site: www.pointsoflight.org

33: Millard and Linda Fuller
Habitat for Humanity

GIVING AWAY A FORTUNE CREATES A DREAM

STANDING BEFORE A THRONG of television cameras and onlookers, Colin and Mercedes Baynes trembled with joy as they finally took possession of their new home in Harlem, New York, in September 2000. This was no ordinary house. It marked the 100,000th home built by the international nonprofit organization Habitat for Humanity. It was also a major milestone in the lives of Millard and Linda Fuller, who gave up a fortune 25 years earlier in order to save their marriage and build a dream. Their dream has grown into the fifteenth-largest homebuilder and the twelfth-largest charitable organization in the United States. Millard Fuller proudly handed the Bayneses the keys to their special new home that blessed day in Harlem.

Raised from humble beginnings in Alabama, Millard Fuller was determined to become a self-made man. While still in school, he and a college buddy created a direct mail order and a publishing business. Their enterprise prospered, but Fuller's workaholic habits took a toll on his health and integrity, and eventually threatened his young marriage to Linda. "I found myself a millionaire before I was 30 years old, however it had negative consequences on my marriage. In 1965, Linda left me," Millard confesses. "She had a Lincoln and a big house, a maid, a cabin on a lake with 2 speedboats, and 2,000 acres of land with horses and cattle and the whole nine yards—but no husband because I worked all the time."

Millard pursued her. In a New York taxi, the Fullers decided to try to save their marriage and asked God to guide them. And they were guided —all the way to a small, rural, Christian community near Americus, Georgia, called Koinonia Farm (*koinonia* comes from the Greek word for "community"). Intending to visit for two hours, they stayed for a month after meeting with a captivating man of faith, Clarence Jordan. It was there the Fullers realized their lives had gotten off track, and they both needed to come back to their Christian roots.

✦ *"I see life as both a gift and a responsibility. My mission is to use what God has given me to help His people in need."*

In a remarkable act of faith and love, the Fullers took a drastic step and decided to sell all their possessions. The proceeds went to the poor. Removed from the material distractions that had once sapped the life out of their marriage, they sought an entirely new focus. "It was actually with Clarence that we brainstormed the concept of starting a housing ministry in Georgia to give low-income families a decent place to live."

A few years later, Millard returned to Koinonia Farm with his wife and four children, where they initiated several partnership enterprises, including a ministry in housing. Together with their friends, the Fullers were able to make modest, affordable homes available to low-income families on a no-profit, no-interest basis. Their bold idea was inspired by Exodus 22:25, which counsels those lending money to the poor not to act as creditors by charging interest. "From the beginning, we saw it as a new frontier in Christian missions, a way to share God's love in a practical way by building houses—selling them on what we call God's finance plan."

In 1973, after five years of constructing homes in Georgia, Millard and Linda moved to Zaire, bringing their concept to central Africa. As success took hold in Zaire, Millard believed their model could be expanded and applied around the world. Returning to the United States in 1976, the Fullers teamed up with a group of close associates and formed a nonprofit they named Habitat for Humanity International. The first house under the Habitat banner was built in San Antonio, Texas, in 1978.

Millard wanted Habitat to be "a hand up, not a handout"—the new homes are affordable, but not free. Homeowners are also expected to invest their own labor as "sweat equity." This lowers the cost of the house and increases the pride and dignity of ownership. As the new owners make payments, the money is used to build even more homes.

The Fullers devoted all of their energy to expanding their vision throughout the world. One measure of their success is in the numbers: from 1973 through 2005, Habitat built more than 200,000 affordable homes for more than 1 million individuals, utilizing more than 2,100 local affiliates in 100 countries. Somewhere in the world, a new Habitat home is completed every 26 minutes—that's more than 20,000 houses a year.

Many people assume former President Jimmy Carter is the founder of Habitat, based on his well-known and visible support, including hands-on hammering of houses. Actually, Carter is simply one of Habitat's most famous volunteers, an avid carpenter who first picked up a hammer alongside Fuller in response to a bold and unique invitation. In 1984, eight years after the organization got off the ground, Millard walked up to the former president's home in Plains, Georgia, knocked on the door, and recruited his help. To this day, Carter and his wife, Rosalynn, participate each year in a weeklong Jimmy Carter Work Project at a Habitat site somewhere in the world. "Millard Fuller is an inspiration to all of us who have joined him as volunteers," says Carter. "His faith and perseverance have made continual progress possible."

More presidential praise came when Millard Fuller was awarded the Medal of Freedom in 1996. In that speech, former President Bill Clinton noted, "Habitat is the most successful continuous community service project in the history of the United States. It has revolutionized the lives of thousands. Millard Fuller has done more to make the dream of home-ownership a reality in our country and throughout the world than any living person."

Millard has lofty goals, and yet enormous challenges remain. In the United States alone, more than 20 million people live in inadequate housing or are completely homeless. Habitat set a target ratio of building at least one house overseas for each one built in the United States. Because they are smaller and often made from different materials, homes built in third-world countries are affordable even though incomes are desperately low. In the United States, the average cost of a new home is $200,000 while the average cost of a Habitat home is $46,600. Habitat international homes can cost as little as $800 to build.

Every year students pour in from around the country and abroad to help build these special houses. "Our first official campus chapter opened in 1987 at Baylor University in Texas. Now, more than 750 student groups work in 25 countries worldwide. On many college campuses, Habitat for Humanity is the largest student volunteer group. The future of this movement lies with the young people," shared Millard. Business, church, and community groups all over the country provide thousands of people from all walks of life—all with big hearts and handy hammers.

✦ *"Go for your dreams in life. Find out what it is that melts your butter and then put your energies into it."*

Each time a home is finished, a dedication service is held and the homeowner is given a Bible. It has been Millard's experience that so much more happens through Habitat than just putting up drywall and hammering in nails to get a few houses built. The lives of those who move in are changed: Children do better in school, parents increase their income, family health is renewed, and family relationships are generally strengthened and improved. They also keep up their home and neighborhoods, rejuvenating their communities. The gift goes on: New homeowners often turn around and volunteer to work on other houses so that more will be blessed just as they were.

In 2005, Millard left Habitat for Humanity International. Again with Linda in his corner and God in his heart, they started the Fuller Center for Housing to do what they do best—eliminate "poverty housing" in this country and around the world. The Fullers gathered a board together at Koinonia Farm to chart the course of their new organization, starting on the same grounds where they had launched their Habitat ministry so many years ago. "It is fitting," said Linda Fuller, "that we returned to Koinonia Farm to organize this new ministry, which will witness to the Gospel of Jesus Christ by helping like-minded organizations build simple, decent homes." The Fuller Center broke ground in 2005 on new houses for Katrina victims and a project in Nepal, with blueprints for a development in Bucharest and wherever else God may lead them.

"I see life as both a gift and a responsibility," says Millard Fuller. "My mission is to use what God has given me to help his people in need. Go for your dreams in life. Find out what is it that melts your butter and then put your energies into it." In 1968, Millard poured his energies into changing himself and changing the world—one house at a time. The explosive growth of homes has never stopped.

≈≈Ripples

MILLARD'S MIRACLE

Millard Fuller shared one of his favorite memories—a wonderful story from Durban, South Africa. "We had a woman working out there with us who was a chaplain. She'd been a chaplain at Ground Zero in New York and had helped bury many people who lost their lives in that tragedy. The week before she left New York to go to South Africa to build Habitat houses, the firemen gave her a party to express their gratitude for all she had done for them and their families in NYC. At the party they gave her a piece of melted glass from the Twin Towers that she brought with her to South Africa.

"A Habitat house among the last of 100 constructed in Durban happened to be numbered 9-1-1. It went to a family who had never had a house before. At the end of the week we held a ceremony with hundreds of people to turn over the key and a Bible. The chaplain affixed her special piece of melted glass into the wall right by the front door. It was and will remain a symbol of building up from the wreckage of the Twin Towers—in contrast to the tearing down that occurred on September 11th."

➤In 1976, Millard and Linda Fuller founded Habitat for Humanity International as a nondenominational, ecumenical, Christian housing outreach. By 2005, they had built their 200,000th home, providing shelter for more than 1 million people worldwide. Now at work in 100 countries, somewhere in the world every 26 minutes, a new Habitat home is completed—that's more than 20,000 new houses a year. Habitat for Humanity International has become the 15th largest homebuilder and the 12th largest nonprofit in the United States.

According to Millard Fuller, more than two million volunteers participate in Habitat. Student volunteers are crucial to Habitat: 750 campus volunteer groups now operate throughout 25 countries to provide more than 3,000 communities with safe shelter.

Help build a better world and raise the roof by contacting:

HABITAT FOR HUMANITY INTERNATIONAL
121 Habitat St., Americus, GA 31709
Phone: (229) 924-6935, ext. 2551 or 2552
E-mail: publicinfo@hfhi.org I Web site: www.habitat.org

THE FULLER CENTER FOR HOUSING
701 S. Martin Luther King Blvd, Americus, GA 31709
Phone: (229) 924-2900
E-mail: info@fullercenter.org I Web site: www.fullercenter.org

34: David Leonard
Salvation Army and ARC

FROM COCAINE ADDICT TO SALVATION ARMY CADET

"MY NAME IS DAVID, and I'm an addict." David Leonard is no longer a half-drunk drug addict buying crack cocaine in an Atlanta flophouse. He is a uniformed Salvation Army officer cadet, training to become a full-fledged Salvation Army officer and pastor. Yet he still introduces himself with those significant eight words: "My name is David, and I'm an addict."

"I could so easily be dead," he recalls. "I was married, with two beautiful children, but I lost my way through selfishness and a desire to please myself. I lost my happiness and very nearly lost my life."

He describes his journey into despair following a divorce that led to a dark period of rage and anger. "I dove headlong into a life of drugs and alcohol. My goal was to numb myself to life's pains."

One night, leaving a hotel room where he had just bought a small amount of crack cocaine, David found himself staring into the barrel of a handgun. "Empty your pockets!" he was told. He tried to comply without losing his precious purchase, but watched in alarm as the small bag slipped to the floor. When ordered by his assailant to lie down, David did as he was told, keeping focused on protecting his stash. With a gun pressed to the back of his head, he wasn't so much fearful of being shot as relieved that the attacker hadn't seen his cocaine. In that moment, he was more anxious about losing the drugs than losing his life. Protect his dope; that was the only thing that mattered to David. That was the experience that finally opened David's eyes. "Afterwards, I took an honest look at my life, and I knew I was going to die unless I changed."

David Leonard turned to his sister—the only family member still talking to him. She helped him research the best drug-addiction program in the country and lent him money for a one-way plane ticket from Atlanta to San Diego. "It was my sincere desire to get clean and sober and to try to make something of myself," David said.

Two days later, David stood in line at the Salvation Army Adult Rehabilitation Center (ARC) with four other men for the single bed that had become available. Somehow, he was chosen. David believes this was not an accident. "There is a waiting list. They normally have more people applying for the program than there are beds. There is no real reason why I should have gotten in over the other four guys; it was just God's will."

The six-month San Diego ARC program was one of the toughest around. "We had 12-Step study classes, anger management, relapse prevention, and chemical dependency courses. We were assigned homework, and we had to go to a minimum number of AA meetings a week." Alcoholics Anonymous is just one of the organizations with which the Salvation Army works in cooperation to help people turn their lives around. The Army believes in the fellowship that comes from those meetings as well as good old-fashioned hard work.

"We had to work 40 hours a week in our work therapy assignment. When you get into serious addiction, the things normal people take for granted we didn't do—like bathing, shaving every day, making your bed, washing your clothes, showing up for work, eating meals regularly. You have to learn to discipline yourself, basically relearning how to live as a normal person. It was really, really painful and hard," David recalls.

The San Diego Salvation Army Adult Rehabilitation Center (ARC) has a long and successful history. In the past 25 years, more than 18,500 individuals have completed the six-month program for either drugs or alcohol. The percentage of participants who are clean and sober a year later is 38 percent. This soars to 86 percent for those who continue an additional 6 months in the aftercare program called "Bridge House." Staying for at least one year really makes a difference.

The final door for David Leonard opened in March 2002. He received a letter notifying him of his acceptance as a cadet at the Salvation Army School for Officer's Training. "I never dreamed I would serve others as a

Salvation Army officer, just as my mom and dad have done. I'm so grateful that I had a second chance and that people believed in me and gave me the opportunities that they did. I have been called to serve the alcoholic and addict that I once was."

In his two-year training program, he discovered his calling and life's challenge—to grow saints and to serve a suffering humanity. "From near death in a flophouse, I have rediscovered what my life was meant to be. My life and future lie in giving away what was so generously given to me: hope, sobriety, and service to others. This is really what I want to do."

≈≈*Ripples*

CHANTELL AND THE SALVATION ARMY

Chantell and her six children fled to a safe house in another city to get away from her violent husband, only to have him follow them there. "I filed for a divorce and went to the shelter," says Chantell. "While we were there, I found out about the Salvation Army and its services. The Army called the safe house every week to see if anyone wanted to go to church," said Chantell. "I did not want to go because I was scared to go anywhere, but after a while I decided it would be good for me and my kids."

Although Chantell was worried, she remembers well a visit from a corps officer who assured her that in the church she would be safe and everything would be okay. The small family returned to church with a sense of security and confidence. "My kids are always doing something at the Army," says Chantell, "whether they are studying in Bible class or joining other groups of kids from around our area in a youth council meeting."

Chantell began working—first at a senior citizens center, then as a school bus driver—and saved enough money to move her family into their own apartment. "It was a big step for us."

When, unbelievably, their apartment building burned down, "The Salvation Army officers were there within 10 minutes of the fire," said Chantell. "We were devastated and needed support, which they gave." A letter of recommendation from the Army helped her get a Habitat for

Humanity house. The new house was more than a home; it was exactly what the Salvation Army had been to them: a haven.

►For more than a century, the Salvation Army has brought hope to the downtrodden. More than 3.5 million volunteers ring bells at Christmas kettles, operate Salvation Army thrift centers, or work with young people.

With 9,222 centers and 60,000 employees nationwide, the Salvation Army touches and helps an average of some 33 million people annually. It is best known for its work with the homeless, the poor, and the addicted. And the Army marches on to do much more. It serves as the probationary arm for county judges where each year up to 50,000 people on probation report to Army staff. It reaches the younger community with 156,000 children attending summer camps and about 100,000 kids dropping by its community centers every year. The Army serves up 62 million meals annually.

Five million people are touched by Army visits to nursing homes, hospitals, and prisons. The Salvation Army is there in emergencies, dispensing meals, and offering shelter to the displaced. Within a half-hour of the September 11 terrorist attacks, Army officers were on the scene in New York, soon assisted by more than 5,000 volunteers. Similarly, their response to the Hurricane Katrina catastrophe was immediate. Within one month, they had raised $145 million to provide food, water, shelter, cleaning equipment, and financial aid to hurricane victims.

The Salvation Army is an international Christian organization operating in 109 countries. It was founded in 1865 by William Booth to offer "soup, soap, and salvation" to London slum dwellers. Peter Drucker, founder of the Drucker School of Management, calls the Salvation Army "the most effective in the U.S., putting money to maximum use." *The Chronicle of Philanthropy* agrees, calling the Salvation Army "the #1 charity in the United States."

Salute hope, sobriety, and service: ring a bell! Contact:

THE SALVATION ARMY NATIONAL HEADQUARTERS
615 Slaters Lane, P. O. Box 269, Alexandria, VA 22313
Phone: (703) 684-5500 I Fax: (703) 684-3478
Web site: www.salvationarmy.org

ARMY'S ADULT REHABILITATION CENTER (SAN DIEGO)
1335 Broadway, San Diego, CA 92101
Phone: (619) 239-4037
Or for the nearest ARC in your location, contact:
E-mail: SArmyMaj@aol.com I Web site: www.salarmy.net/dir/Bus2x.html

35: Denny and Leesa Bellesi
Kingdom Assignment

GO AND DO GOOD FOR GOD

"Invest this while I'm gone," the master told them. "When I come back, I'll expect an accounting of what I gave you." —Matthew 25:14–30

"I HAVE AN ASSIGNMENT for you that will change your life—a Kingdom assignment," Pastor Denny Bellesi challenged 100 unsuspecting volunteers during a typical service in November 2002. These simple words launched a "movement" of Bible-sized activity and resulting miracles that ricocheted around the world and have never stopped.

It had been a dream in the hearts of Bellesi and his wife, Leesa, for ages: find a way to light a fire that would affect the world for God. They never guessed the answer would come to them in a movie theater, but that's where their flame was lit with a "how" and "Go now!" The movie was the 2000 hit *Pay It Forward*, based on Catherine Ryan Hyde's book of the same title. The movie's tagline, "Sometimes the Simplest Idea Can Make the Biggest Difference," captured the spirit of a vision they had been incubating. What that vision would actually become was beyond their imagination and bigger than their dream. They simply looked at one another and said, "It's time."

As only God could design, Bellesi's upcoming series of sermons were on the parable of the talents from the Bible in which Jesus explains the stewardship of wealth, challenging us to multiply God's gifts of money and talent. Pastor Bellesi approached his church's Missions Outreach Team with an unusual request. He wanted to use $10,000, which they had set aside for local outreach, for an experimental and risky investment. The team took some convincing. "Dream with me here," said Bellesi, catching their attention. "We're not talking about a means to an end; we're talking about an explosion of Kingdom participants acting on behalf of the

King. It's the kind of project that could change the world." They prayed and threw the dice in his direction.

With "knocking knees," as he recalls, Bellesi stood before his congregation and asked for volunteers. When he'd drawn enough members to the front—100 random people who still had no idea what they were being called to do—he pulled a fistful of cash from his pocket and started handing out one-hundred-dollar bills, one to every volunteer standing. "Each of them held the money away from their bodies as though it might bite them," Bellesi admits, "as I began to give them their assignment."

> ✦ *"The dreaming and praying begins today. Your assignment is just around the corner. Let the spark ignite and watch the wildfire begin."*

"First, they must recognize that the money did not belong to them; rather, it belonged to the Master. It was God's money. Second, they were being trusted to invest the money in a way that would extend God's Kingdom. They could buy a homeless man dinner and a Bible or start a mission that might live on for 100 years. I told them, 'Whatever you do is between you and God.' Lastly, they must return in 90 days and share the results of their investment with the congregation."

Bellesi closed his sermon by saying, "The point is this: All we have and all we are, is a gift from God. We've been entrusted with gifts of time, energy, money, and passion—each of these talents should be treated like a literal $100, handed to us straight from God. It's up to us to invest those resources in the Kingdom and watch the Master bless us in the process." By the end of four services, he had given away the entire $10,000—in trust.

What had started that Sunday as fear and doubt among people soon changed to a buzz that grew with each passing hour as many people began to pray in ways they never had before. Bellesi emphasizes, "These were not the standard do-gooders—those who typically volunteered, gave large sums, or were recognized pillars of the church. These were the people with scars and skinned hearts, deadlines and demands. Some participants, unbeknownst to us, were homeless!"

Yet these were the meager resources God was about to multiply infinitely. Three months after God's challenge through the voice of Pastor Bellesi, 99 of the 100 random volunteers returned on the church's "Report Night." Nearly 2,000 Coast Hills Community Church congregants were there to witness, along with crews from *Dateline* and *People* magazine, who were there to report the results of God's handiwork.

The congregation was shocked to find that in just three months, one of the $100 bills alone had become $13,000. Another $100 had started up a whole new church. Stories and miracles poured out of these volunteers. The overall investment of $10,000 had become more than $150,000 and laid the groundwork to directly impact nearly 250,000 people locally, nationally, and internationally. Bellesi told his church that evening, "Well done, good and faithful servants," as tears and emotions flooded the congregation of friends and neighbors who had come to hear the stories of faithfulness—and the assignment was just gaining steam.

Denny's wife, Leesa, began to collect and document the stories, which were growing exponentially. Within one year, the original $10,000 of "talents" had multiplied into an amazing $750,000, spinning off a variety of nonprofits. One woman watched her money grow from $100 to over $350,000 in a year, starting a ministry for women and children in need. As word of these Kingdom Assignment miracles took wind through the press, sparks ignited. People and churches emulated the Bellesis' idea of "paying forward" God's riches.

When you flip through even a few of these stories and imagine the real people within them—how a life can be utterly changed by the simplest gestures—it makes you eager to get up and do something. It inspires you to look around with a hungry curiosity and a prayer: Where is God working, and what can be done?

Denny Bellesi celebrates this contagious phenomenon, explaining, "It was about becoming part of the Kingdom. The Kingdom that Jesus was referring to in the Gospels is not some faraway place. It's right here, right now."

Bellesi ties one of the important lessons learned from this "Kingdom experience" back to the simple wisdom of his grandmother's advice: "Do it and it's done." He discovered firsthand, "Most people who are making things happen are not superheroes. They're just putting one foot in front of the other. It's not that they're taking the easiest path, either; it's that when you take the path that's right, it always seems easy."

Denny and Leesa Bellesi close their book, *Kingdom Assignment,* recognizing that obstacles and fears exist, and that prayer can cancel those things out: "God can do anything. If you want a changed heart, a changed life—if you want to make a lasting difference in the Kingdom while there's still time—nothing will stop you. Absolutely nothing. Do you realize what would happen if every believer would take on such a Kingdom Assignment? The dreaming and praying begins today. Your assignment is just around the corner. Let the spark ignite and watch the wildfire begin."

≈≈*Ripples*

STORIES FROM DENNY AND LEESA'S CHALLENGE

As WE BEGAN to hear stories of how people handled the Kingdom Assignment, a common theme appeared: Everyone who participated wanted to do their very best for Jesus. This was not only true for the hundred who accepted the challenge, but it became contagious among the congregation. What started out in our minds as being a kind of creative, outside-the-box way to teach a spiritual lesson was quickly becoming a 'quest' of sorts. And it began to take on a life of its own—a God-driven, God-powered life. It was clear that the Kingdom Assignment was not only changing the lives of the people involved, but the very core of who we were as a community.

Terry Zwick . . . As an attractive woman, long-time church member, housewife, and mother of four great children, Terry Zwick was successful at everything she attempted. Most people had no idea of the personal trials she faced, like having escaped an abusive relationship years earlier, or her struggles to support her adored husband who was losing his eyesight to a terrible disease.

Surprising even herself, Terry volunteered that fateful day in November to take Bellesi's Kingdom challenge. With a prayer for God's guidance, she put the money in her pocket. That same night she went to a party with friends at a restaurant. Bubbling over with excitement, she described her new assignment as she boldly held up her $100 bill. The silent room erupted with offers of involvement and support. She left that night stunned, clutching $1,800 she'd unexpectedly gathered, along with a basketful of supporting ideas.

One friend at the party that night steered her to Lisa, an abused woman holding down two jobs and in desperate need. This woman had two children living at home and a third child staying in a live-in recovery facility. When Terry met Lisa, she was filled with emotion and knew that God had brought them together to be friends, united by the common understanding of having been abused. Most of the $1,800 was given to Lisa for rent and Christmas gift certificates for her children.

A few days later, Lisa gratefully called Terry and asked if she could use some of her leftover money to buy gifts for other children they knew who had far less. Touched deeply, Terry quickly agreed, realizing that God was using the $100 to keep the giving going forward. Subsequently, Terry's husband, who was a lawyer, was able to help Lisa with a legal problem she was having concerning her middle child. Lisa's family began attending Coast Hills Church with Terry. But God wasn't finished quite yet. Members of the church also helped Lisa and her children with babysitting, dental work, and buying a computer for her star-student son.

As Terry continued to pray, her heart was filled with passion to multiply God's assets even further by creating a home for families who had financially lost everything and had no place to go. She bought a completely dilapidated duplex, which she bought with a leap of faith and a very small down payment.

Terry recalls sitting amid depressing squalor in one of her duplex's apartments with a phone and an open telephone book on her lap, tears in her eyes, and hope in her heart. She needed help. With eyes uplifted to God, she started pointing to random tradespeople in the book, dialing, and asking for help. Strangers from a phone book responded to Terry's pleas. One furniture store gave $20,000 worth of furniture; a construction company donated $150,000 worth of labor and products to rebuild the structure. As the donations came in, Terry was shocked that, when the duplex she called "Hope's House" was finished and furnished, the décor was coordinated and decorated despite being pieced together from random individual gifts. When people who saw it for the first time said, "Great job decorating," Terri would just smile.

Within one year, two families in desperate need had short-term shelter for up to six months, giving these families a second chance to get back on their feet, go to church, and be coached to make it on their own. The value of that $100 bill had multiplied to a staggering $350,000 by that time. After two years, her investment was worth $750,000 and growing.

When asked how this experience has affected her, she said: "God has given me some tough situations in my life and I'm glad he did, because I'm able to relate with people. I truly, truly try to seek ways to have an impact on someone's life, and now I can say, 'Oh my gosh, with God's help, it really can happen.' I see people catching the spirit of giving. I can spend the day with someone, and because of what I've done for them they may turn around and do something for somebody else. I'm so excited to see this spirit, which keeps on growing."

Steve and Alex . . . There was a time when Steve wouldn't have set foot in a church. But just two weeks after losing his precious six-year-old daughter, Alex, to unknown causes, he broke down, his spirit entirely crushed, and told God he couldn't go on. They were the first words he'd spoken to God in years, and the answer came in a soothing inner whisper, "Go to church." No one knew his story or what brought him there as he stood facing an unfamiliar congregation with $100 in his hand and "a mission from God."

Joining with his wife and their neighbors, they decided on creating a neighborhood "Wishing Tree" to fulfill the Christmas wishes of needy families, and dedicated the project to Alex's memory. In less than 72 hours, 80 wishes had been "adopted" and the $100 grew into $8,000 by Christmas. Further, this grieving father discovered he was a blessed man. Steve illustrated that greater return in a letter he wrote to the Coast Hills pastor and congregation, saying: "Perhaps the most profound impact from this project was that a man, after spending most of his adult life living in darkness, stepped a bit further into the light."

Brooks . . . wanted to use his $100 "to help children grow up with the Boy Scouts' discipline and love for God, family, and country." Brooks found out about a group of kids less than 30 minutes away who longed to be a troop yet couldn't afford even the five dollars for handbooks, much less uniforms or activities. Explaining the Kingdom concept to his son's troop, Brooks tossed his "bequeathed" $100 bill in a bowl saying, "That's a special bowl because, when God's Kingdom is at stake, it has a way of multiplying the money inside." In two weeks, they'd raised enough to start and equip a troop for the neighboring boys, one of whom was a boy named Anthony, whose dream was to be a Cub Scout. The second he received his uniform, Anthony ran into a bathroom and immediately tried it on. He came out with his fist raised above his head exclaiming, "I just want you to know, this is the best day of my life!"

Michael . . . A "quiet believer," Michael regretted volunteering at first. His $100 burned a hole in his wallet and his conscience until his wife, who worked for the Red Cross, told him about a family with more than their share of trials. That family had lost two children in the same year to two different diseases. Their remaining child, Mateo, was facing another debilitating disease that caused him to lose his teeth. To this high-school sophomore, this further embarrassment was the last straw.

Michael, no longer quiet about what God was doing, campaigned feverishly to raise money to help Mateo and, in the process, even led a co-worker to Christ. After Michael reached his financial goals, a dentist in the congregation tied a bow on the effort by deciding Mateo was also his assignment. Mateo would have his smile back and many new reasons to use it. Michael, the "quiet believer," now proclaims to those who will hear, "I'm a child of the King. Everything I am is part of being in the Kingdom of God, on Assignment for him."

Unforeseen Ripples . . . The actual printed story of Bellesi's challenge multiplied through the media soon after Coast Hills' three-month Report Night—from the local *Orange County Register*, to the Associated Press, to 10,000 newspapers across the United States. NBC's *Dateline* and *People* magazine also featured reports of these heavenly activities.

Rippling across the country with pinpoint precision, the Kingdom Assignment found a retired Southern California dad. He had read the *Orange County Register*'s article on the Kingdom Assignment phenomenon. Curious, he laid down $100 of his own money at a casino (not recommended for all, but apparently God's tool for this story). He promised to safely pocket any winnings, betting only $100 each time, and to stop the first time he lost. In three minutes, he had $500 and left.

This man sent the new hundred-dollar bills "anonymously" to each of his five children, wrapped in copies of the Bellesi article. His daughter Stephanie—a 29-year-old single mom, full-time college student, and waitress raising three kids—could have used the $100 herself. But the day the envelope arrived, she'd headed home early after a canceled class and happened upon a family in a horrible accident in rural Mississippi. She gave them her love and comfort first at the crash site, later at the hospital, and all the way home. When they showered her with thanks and praise, she handed them her father's envelope, saying, "Just read this." The $100 was still inside. The struggling family used the money to buy dinner and medication for their injuries. The greater worth, the family later told her, was the gift of believing someone loves you.

Soon after, when a friend of hers passed away, Stephanie sent her own $100 to her friend's widow, wrapped in another copy of the article—a new bundle of miracle-potential, headed for its own story.

➤In November 2002, Pastor Denny Bellesi challenged 100 random volunteers to each invest $100 of "God's money" into projects that would extend God's kingdom. Within a year, that $10,000 investment was worth over $750,000. More than just money, lives were changed, and miracles exploded around the country.

To find the power of being on God's investment team, check out:

KINGDOM ASSIGNMENT
Web site: www.kingdomassignment.com

Postscript

T HE IMPACT OF THIS BOOK will be measured by those who read these profiles and are inspired to act. I hope that you know that each of us can make a difference—large or small—to change our world for the better and will want to get involved.

Just as I've enjoyed chronicling the passionate adventures of others, I have been inspired by each one of these courageous heroes and I hope that you are inspired as well. While *Passionaries* is not a "how-to" book, I trust that at least one profile will inspire you to find a cause that you are passionate about. I can offer three ways that you can act: start it, build it, or join it.

- You can start an organization like the passionaries profiled.
- You can work with others who share your passion to build momentum for a cause.
- You can join one of the organizations in this book or any of the thousands of nonprofits in existence. Use the contact information provided at the back of each chapter.

Throughout the years of putting this book together, the "how in the world did something like this ever get started and grow?" aspect of each nonprofit has fascinated me. I have observed that there are two common threads that can be found in all of these profiles of passionaries.

First, someone is challenged by adversity or acutely aware of the sufferings of others. Then there is a moment in time, a "click," when an idea or solution connects with passion and the "I can do that" is felt. When the momentum builds, others come alongside, miracles happen, and lives are enhanced.

Second, when these individuals take action, they do it with all their might and soul. They are focused, energetic, and faithful. Passion breeds enthusiasm, which is one of the most powerful engines of success.

So use this book as your inspirational guide to make a difference in our society. We are surrounded by inspiring individuals and their stories of courage and change. You, too, can create your own story.

This is just the first volume of what I hope to be a *Passionaries* series. My goal in chronicling these stories is to highlight and celebrate high-impact, financially efficient, volunteer-friendly, eclectic, and interesting nonprofit organizations started within the past 35 years. If you would like to nominate individuals or organizations to be profiled in future editions, please use the contact information that can be found on the Web site: www.passionaries.org. I have already earmarked several individuals for the next *Passionaries* book:

- John Van Hengel (Second Harvest)
- Eunice Kennedy Shriver (Special Olympics, Inc.)
- Adam Walsh (National Center for Missing & Exploited Children)
- Bob McElroy (Alpha Project)
- Tom Houston (SeaKeapers)
- Lance Armstrong (LiveStrong)
- Chris Crane (Opportunity International)
- Nancy Rivard (Airline Ambassadors)
- Debbie Spaide (Kids Care)
- Gary Haugen (International Justice Mission)
- Norma Hotaling (Sage)
- Suzie Zeegan (Elizabeth Glazer Pediatric Aids Foundation)

A large percentage of the profits from *Passionaries* will be given to the foundation, Passionaries, Inc. This foundation will help to support the nonprofit organizations within these pages and will help to foster the dreams of emerging passionaries. We will continue to publish books, to share information, to promote the message of giving, and to provide materials that would be helpful for others embarking on this adventure. If you would like to learn more about the activities of this foundation, go to the Web site www.passionaries.org.

What you do and how your life is changed after reading this book is important to me. Discover the world of passionaries and keep in touch with me through my Web site at www.passionaries.org. I care.

Vounteer Statistics

PROFILE	PROGRAM	NUMBER OF VOLUNTEERS
Stan Curtis	USA Harvest	125,000+
Dr. Mimi Silbert	Delancey Street Foundation	Not tracked
Susan Corrigan	Gifts In Kind International	20 to 1,000s
Paul Newman	Newman's Own/Hole in the Wall Gang Make A Difference Day	Not tracked 3 million
Millie Webb	MADD	2 million+
Michael Spencer	American Red Cross	1.2 million
SENIOR CORPS		
John McConnell	RSVP	480,000
Louise Jackson	Foster Grandparents	30,000+
Trevor Ferrell	Trevor's Campaign	2,000
Tom Harken	ProLiteracy Worldwide	113,000
Mary Kay Beard	Angel Tree	534,000
Chris and Friends	Make-A-Wish Foundation	25,000
Nann Gonzalez	ROCK Ministries	200
Brandon Keefe	BookEnds	20,000
Wendy Kopp	Teach For America	14,000+
Hugh O'Brian	HOBY	5,200
Dr. Laura Schlessinger	My Stuff Bags/Operation Family Fund	Not tracked
Domingo Guyton	YMCA	600,500
Joani Wafer and Dawn Bodo	Kids Korps USA	6,000
Jimmy Murray	Ronald McDonald House Charities	30,000
Nancy G. Brinker	Susan G. Komen Breast Cancer Foundation	75,000
James Jackson	Project C.U.R.E.	5,500
Roxanne Black-Weisheit	Friends' Health Connection	50
Mark Plotkin	Amazon Conservation Team	10
Dr. Jack McConnell	Volunteers in Medicine Clinic	465
Betty Bloomer Ford	Betty Ford Center	100
Marie Johnson	American Sewing Guild	20,000
Don Stephens	Mercy Ships International	1,600/year

MILITARY SALUTE

Bob Hope	USO	33,000
Gary Sinise and Laura Hillenbrand	Operation Iraqi Children	1,300
Shauna Fleming	A Million Thanks	2 million+
Betty Mohlenbrock	Family Literacy Foundation/ United Through Reading	800
Chuck Colson	Prison Fellowship	50,000/year
Fern Nichols	Moms In Touch International	100,000
Bill Hunter	Presidential Prayer Team	3 million
George H. W. Bush	Points of Light Foundation	Not tracked
Millard and Linda Fuller	Habitat for Humanity	2 million
David Leonard	Salvation Army	3.5 million
Denny and Leesa Bellesi	Kingdom Assignment	100+++

Selected Readings ⁓

Books

Bellesi, Denny and Leesa. *The Kingdom Assignment: What Will You Do With the Talents God Has Given You?* Grand Rapids, MI: Zondervan, 2001.

Bright, Bill. *The Journey Home: Finishing with Joy.* Nashville: Nelson Books, 2004.

Brinker, Nancy, and Catherine McEvily Harris. *Race Is Run One Step at a Time: My Personal Struggle and Everywoman's Guide to Taking Charge of Breast Cancer.* Irving, TX: Summit Publishing Group, 1995.

Buford, Bob. *Half-Time: Changing Your Game Plan From Success To Significance.* Grand Rapids, MI: Zondervan, 1994.

Elliott, Barbara J. *Street Saints: Renewing America's Cities.* Philadelphia: Templeton Foundation Press, 2004.

Fleming, Shauna. *A Million Thanks.* New York: Doubleday, 2005.

Ford, Betty, and Chris Chase. *Betty: A Glad Awakening.* Garden City, NY: Doubleday & Co., Inc., 1987.

Fuller, Millard and Linda. *More Than Houses: How Habitat for Humanity Is Transforming Lives and Neighborhoods.* Nashville: Nelson Books, 2001.

Harken, Tom, and Walter Anderson. *The Millionaire's Secret.* Nashville: Nelson Books, 1998.

Kopp, Wendy. *One Day, All Children: The Unlikely Triumph of Teach for America and What I Learned Along the Way.* New York: Public Affairs, 2003.

McConnell, Jack B. *The Story of the Volunteers in Medicine Clinic.* Englewood, CO: Estes Park Institute, 1998 and 2003.

Nichols, Fern. *Every Child Needs a Praying Mom.* Grand Rapids, MI: Zondervan, 2003.

Plotkin, Mark J. *Medicine Quest: In Search of Nature's Healing Secrets.* New

York: Penguin, 2000.

Stephens, Don. *Ships of Mercy: The Remarkable Fleet Bringing Hope to the World's Forgotten Poor.* Nashville: Nelson Books, 2005.

Warren, Rick. *The Purpose-Driven Life: What on Earth Am I Here For.* Grand Rapids, MI: Zondervan, 2002.

Williams, Roy and Vic Preisser. *Philanthropy: Heirs and Values, How Successful Families Use Philanthropy to Prepare Their Heirs for Post-transition Responsibilities.* Brandon, OR: Robert D. Reed Publishers, 2005.

Web Sites for Rating Financial Efficiency of Nonprofits

Better Business Bureau's Wise Giving Alliance: www.give.org

Charity Navigator: www.charitynavigator.org

Oprah (recommends some terrific Oprah-rated nonprofits): www.oprah.com

Peter Drucker Foundation, Leader to Leader Institute: www.pfdf.org

Notes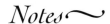

INTRODUCTION

1. Giving USA Foundation, *Giving USA 2005* (Glenview, IL: AAFRC Trust for Philanthropy, 2005), 18, 20, 26.
2. Ibid., 59.
3. *Chronicle of Philanthropy*, (March 23, 2006), 14, 34.
4. Carol C. Adelman, Hudson Institute, "Index of Global Philanthropy 2006", 4, http://gpr.hudson.org/files/publications/GlobalPhilanthropy.pdf.
5. Points of Light Foundation, "10 Year Review of Accomplishments: 1991–2001," 7, http://www.pointsoflight.org/nvw2000/nvw_volunteerstats.html. See also *Chronicle of Philanthropy* (February 17, 2005), 13.
6. Ibid., 22.
7. Adapted from Loren Eiseley, *The Star Thrower* (New York: Harvest Books, 1979) 169–185.

Index

So Others Might Eat (SOME), 51
Southern, Casey, 61–62
Spaide, Debbie, 220
Special Olympics, 107, 220
Spencer, Michael, 40–44, 221
Stahl, Scott, 74
Stephens, Deyon, 156
Stephens, Don, 156–60, 221, 224
Steve (Wishing Tree), 215
Sullivan, Thomas, 105
Sullivan, Tom, 7–8
Suncoast Tape Library for the Blind, 197
Surdyk, Chris, 173
Susan G. Komen Breast Cancer
    Foundation, 118–22, 221

Tada, Joni Eareckson, 193
Tampa Bay Harvest, 12, 14
Target Corporation, 176
Teach For America, 88–92, 221
Teen Korps, 107, 109–10
Teens Against Gang Violence (TAGV),
    103, 105
Templeton Prize for Progress in Religion,
    180
Teresa, Mother, 56, 156–58
Texas Department of Criminal Justice,
    180
THE EXTRA MILE, 198
Thompson, Bruce, 167
3M Corporation, 22
Tirios tribe, 137
Tocqueville, Alexis de, 3
Tose, Leonard, 113
Toys "R" Us, 25
Traveler's Aid Association, 164
Trevor's Campaign, 54–57, 221
Trevor's Youth Farm School, 56
Tuckerman, Don, 114
Tumucumaque Indigenous Reservation,
    138

Ulene, Art, 111–12
Underground Railroad, 49
United Through Reading, 174–77, 222
United Way of America, 22
University of California, Irvine,
    Volunteer Center, 86
USA Freedom Corps, 45
USA Harvest, 9–15, 221
USA Weekend magazine, 32, 34

USO (United Service Organizations),
    163–68, 221

Valentines for Troops, 172
Van Hengel, John, 220
Van Ness, Paula, 78
Vance, Carol S., Prison (TX), 180
Verizon Communications, 57
Victor Gomoiu Hospital, 80
Victory Junction Gang Camp, 30
Village Hope, 33
Visionary Award, Betty Ford Center, 151
Volunteers in Medicine Institute (VIMI),
    143, 144
Volunteers in Medicine (VIM) Clinic,
    139–45, 221

Wafer, Joani, 106–10, 221
Walsh, Adam, 220
The Walt Disney Company, 76
Warren, Rick, 224
Wayana tribe, 137
Webb, Millie, 35–39, 221
Western Colorado Math and Science
    Center, 46
Westinghouse Electric Company, 22
Wickham, John, 193
Wilberforce Forum, 182–83
Williams, George, 105
Williams, Jennifer, 116–17
Williams, Roy, 224
Williams, Tessie, 154
Wilson, Bill, 150, 152
Wilson, Lois, 152
Winfrey, Oprah, 224
Winn, Loretta, 197
Wise Giving Alliance, 224
Wishing Tree, 215
Woodrow Wilson Exemplary Youth
    Services Award, 41
Woodward, Joanne, 27, 30
Woolverton family, 43–44
World Bank, 125
World Leadership Congress, 95, 97

Xerox Corporation, 22

YMCA (Young Men's Christian
    Association), 102–05, 164, 221
YMCA camps, 104
Youngs, Bettie B., 65–66